# THE AUTHORS

John Silvester has been a crime reporter in
Melbourne since 1978. He worked for The
Sunday Times 'Insight' team in London in
1990, and has co-authored several crime
books, including the best-seller
*Underbelly*. He is currently Law and
Crime Editor for The Age.

Andrew Rule has been a journalist since
1975 and has worked in newspapers,
television and radio. He wrote *Cuckoo*,
the true story of the notorious 'Mr Stinky'
case, and has edited and published several
other books, including the original
*Underbelly*. He is a feature writer for
The Age.

# UNDERBELLY 2
## MORE TRUE CRIME STORIES

Published in Australia by
Floradale Productions Pty Ltd and Sly Ink Pty Ltd
November 1998
Reprinted June 2000, March 2002

Gary Allen Pty Ltd,
9 Cooper Street,
Smithfield, NSW
Telephone 02-9725 2933

Underbelly 2
More True Crime Stories

ISBN – 0958 6071 1 7

Cover design by Chris Rule
Typesetting and layout by Write Impression Publishing

**ŭ'nderbĕllŷ** *n.* Under surface of animal thing, esp. as area vulnerable to attack. UNDER- 4 + BELLY[1]]

# CONTENTS

# CONTENTS

# THE HOMICIDE INVESTIGATOR

No greater honour will ever
be bestowed on an officer or
a more profound duty
imposed on him when he is
entrusted with the
investigation of the death of a
human being.

It is his duty to find the
facts regardless of colour or
creed, without prejudice, and
to let no power on earth deter
him from presenting these
facts to the court without
regard to personality.

# CHAPTER 1

# Dead man talking

## New opening was a shallow grave

*The job sounded perfect ... almost
too good to be true.*

FOR Ron Williams, it was the beginning of a new beginning. Warmed by summer's setting sun and a rare inner glow of satisfaction, he stood on an isolated beach in Western Australia, indulging his passion for surf fishing. He was – if not a world – then at least a continent away from decades of disappointment.

For the first time in years the battler from Melbourne could see a future that gave him hope for a better life.

No longer would he struggle in low-paid jobs, a potential casualty in every economic downturn. He felt he was going to crack the big time and become, finally, master of his own destiny.

Standing next to Williams on the deserted beach near Albany, was his new boss and confidant, a man who called himself Paul Jacobs, a successful company director and the driving force behind a national geological firm.

Although the two were the same age and physically similar, Ron Williams looked up to the man he'd known only a few weeks for having the qualities he lacked – drive, ambition and a sense of purpose.

Until they met, Williams had been convinced he was going nowhere. He had worked hard in Melbourne in a variety of dead-end jobs, but had nothing to show for it but a hard-won reputation for dedication. Pats on the back don't pay the mortgage.

In his last job, he'd worked six days a week for a second-hand car parts firm in a southern bayside suburb. Yet he still lived with his elderly mother, lacking the money for a deposit on his own unit. His redundancy payment from Dulux, an earlier job, had long gone. Like many a lonely bachelor, he liked a drink, and found it hard to save money.

Now, aged forty-five, it seemed he finally had a break. In his kit was a signed, legally-binding, two-year contract to work in the mining industry at $60,000 a year, more than twice his wreckers' yard wage back in Melbourne.

Even weeks afterwards, he must have marvelled at the good luck that had changed his life, when he'd spotted a small classified advertisement in the *Herald Sun* newspaper on 26 January, 1996.

It read: 'GENERAL HAND GEO. SURVEY. Duties include camp maint. D/L essential. Suit single person 35-45 able to handle long periods in remote areas. Wage neg. Contract basis. Call 9423-8006 between 6-9 pm.'

He rang the number and found himself speaking to a Mr Jacobs, the man who would be handling the interviews. The nervous applicant slurred his words slightly but the prospective employer didn't seem to notice – or didn't care that the man on the end of the phone sounded a little drunk.

The prospective employer could afford to be selective. After all, fifty people had responded to the advertisement, but he was looking for a particular type, someone with special qualities. Ron Williams sounded most promising.

The first interview was held in modest surroundings – a small unit in the north-eastern Melbourne suburb of Greensborough, rather than a flash city office. That was easy to explain, and Jacobs explained it: he invested in WA exploration, not useless business status symbols.

For Williams the job sounded perfect – adventure, coupled with two years security and the chance to have another go at life, three thousand kilometres from past failures. Much better money, the possibility of being a key player in a small team, and the chance to work with an understanding boss who acted like an old mate. It sounded almost too good to be true.

Jacobs had sifted through the job applications looking for a man who was around his own age, had few ties and would not be missed if he disappeared. He short-listed fifteen names. Not a bad return from an ad that cost him $103.60 to run over three days.

Over the next few weeks Williams returned to the unit for follow-up interviews, each one bringing him closer to the job of a lifetime.

Slowly the form of the interviews changed and the questions became more personal. Williams found himself confiding in the man who could be his boss, telling him of his broken marriage, of childhood difficulties and of changing his name by deed poll fifteen years earlier.

This was new ground for Williams, who tended to be a loner and who tended not to speak freely of his personal life, even to workmates he had known for years.

But Jacobs was a good listener, and a sympathetic one, so the story of Ron Williams's life came out, piece by piece. Finally, Jacobs told him he had passed muster. He had the job.

It was to cost him his life.

THE problem with Paul Jacobs was that he wasn't. His real name was Alexander Robert MacDonald, a Vietnam veteran, bomber, prolific armed robber and escapee. He had escaped from the Borallon Correctional Centre, near Ipswich in Queensland, in September 1995. He had been serving twenty-three years for armed robbery and escape.

In the next two years MacDonald robbed seven banks in three states and got away with a total of $320,800. He was possibly Australia's last bushranger. He robbed country banks, taking hostages to try to prevent bank staff from activating security alarms, and then he used his bush skills to camp out until police road blocks were removed days later.

MacDonald would hike hundreds of kilometres and drive thousands to rob banks in NSW, Queensland and Western Australia. While most modern bandits used high-powered stolen cars to get away from crime scenes, MacDonald used push bikes, small motorbikes or his hiking boots. He'd been out of jail only two months when he first developed a plan to take on a new identity. But, as the plan grew more sophisticated – and cold-blooded – he decided he needed a patsy. Someone whose life he could take over.

Which is how Ron Williams came by the worst lucky break of his life. MacDonald was only three months older than Williams and they had uncannily similar faces and builds, although the escaper was slightly taller.

Williams provided documentation such as driver's licence, deed poll papers and birth certificate for his prospective boss.

MacDonald used them to set up two accounts, one in a bank and the second in a credit union, so he could channel his armed robbery funds. He went to the Registry of Births, Deaths and Marriages to get a copy of the birth certificate he would later claim was his. He was to end up with a passport, driver's licence, five credit cards, a Myer card, ambulance subscription and private health insurance under Ron Williams's name.

But the trouble with taking someone's identity is that there is a living, breathing witness who can expose the fraud at any time.

MacDonald believed he had that base covered. His credo was as old as crime: Dead men tell no tales.

It was brutally simple – and breathtakingly callous. So much so that Senior Detective Allan Birch, an armed robbery squad investigator, later had trouble grasping the ruthlessness of the quiet middle-aged man he was interviewing.

Puzzled about the identity swap, the detective said to MacDonald during an interview in on 26 July, 1997: 'Can you explain to me how you would assume the identity of a person who responds to an advert for employment?'

MacDonald responded quietly: 'You kill them.'

Birch: 'Did you kill Mr Williams?'

MacDonald: 'I did.'

## THE VICTIM

RON Williams was a loner who spent most of his spare time fishing in Port Phillip Bay. He had married in July, 1981, and fathered a daughter but the marriage failed quickly. He legally changed his name from Runa Chomszczak to Ron Williams the same year he was married. He was a handyman who could make a fist of most trades.

He had plenty of workmates but few, if any, who ranked as true mates. He dreamed of adventure, but couldn't see a way out of the rut his life had become.

He lived with his mother and spent as much time as he could at work, not because he was well paid or loved his job, but because it gave him company.

His former boss, the owner of Comeback Auto Wreckers, Kevin Brett, was to say of him: 'He was a great little bloke. He was an all rounder. You name it, he could do it. He was a human dynamo.'

Brett said Williams was a gardener, handyman, storeman, painter and delivery man. He was a statewide reliever for Brett's three car spare parts businesses.

'He would have worked seven days a week if you let him. He lived for his work.'

He was later to die for it.

While Williams didn't speak freely about his private life, his former employer sensed a sadness in his eager worker. 'He was a little timid and easily let down. He'd had some knocks in his life.'

His only outside interest appeared to be fishing and restoring his car. Workmates said he would often head straight to the bay after knocking off work. He worked until the week before he was to go to Western Australia, but also kept a promise to paint the ceiling of a sandwich shop near his old job. That's the sort of bloke he was.

Brett was happy to see his trusted handyman kick on to a new job, but he couldn't help having a twinge of doubt – particularly when he found Williams had to sign a contract with secrecy provisions, and was being paid a retainer for weeks before he was to take up the new position.

His generous new benefactor was paying Williams around $500 a week not to work, which was more than he had been paid to work in Melbourne. It didn't make sense to Kevin Brett, but he kept his doubts to himself, not wanting to dampen the enthusiasm of a man who, he felt, deserved a break.

Brett was to recall: 'He was very secretive about his new job. I asked him about it and he said I had paid him peanuts and we had a laugh. He said the main reason he got the job was that he had no ties.

'He said he took on the job because he wanted to get enough money to buy a unit. I told him there would always be a job here for him.'

His former boss said Williams would never have suspected he was being set up. 'He just wanted to believe in people.'

## THE MURDER

THE new hand asked surprisingly few questions about the work he would be expected to do in the outback. 'Mr Jacobs' told him the business was 'a family concern doing geological survey on order from mining companies in Western Australia.'

He asked Williams to sign an employment contract saying he would not seek, or take any other type of work before they travelled west.

When Senior Detective Birch asked him later, 'Why did you do that?' MacDonald was to answer: 'That was purely and simply because the guy was a little unstable and really didn't seem fully committed to the new employment, and I wanted to have him locked in to the program.'

They left for Western Australia in MacDonald's Toyota Land Cruiser utility in late February, a month after the job was advertised. Williams packed light. The boss already had any provisions they would need. Like any seasoned camper, he had a shovel in the back.

They drove across the country for four days, staying at motels, and drinking and eating together. Both men were excited. Both were looking forward to starting a new life.

Williams wrote postcards to his old workmates, relatives and his few friends. His new boss and mate was his usual helpful self and said not to worry about mailing them. He promised he would do that later.

But one postcard was sent straight after it was written, when the two men arrived in Albany, about four hundred kilometres from Perth. Williams couldn't resist a little good-natured gloating to his former workmates at the car wreckers in Melbourne. He sat down and wrote a card in a pub. It read: 'Hello boss. I'm sitting with the new boss eating oysters kilpatrick. Got to go, new boss is bringing the beer over.'

The condemned man ate a hearty meal. His last.

Shortly after they left Albany, MacDonald turned the dusty four wheel drive on to a dirt track leading to Cheyne Beach. He suggested they go fishing, knowing Williams was certain to be keen.

He had selected the beach by looking at a map because it was isolated. He remembered the district from his last visit, twenty years earlier.

They walked down to the beach from the utility, Williams carrying his fishing rod, MacDonald a khaki knapsack he'd bought in an army disposal store in Mebourne.

Williams fished and the two men chatted for about an hour. Both were waiting for sunset. Williams because he hoped it would make the fish easier to catch. MacDonald because he wanted to catch his prey unawares in the twilight.

As they chatted, MacDonald bent over slowly, undid the knapsack and slipped his hand in. Inside was the ten-shot, sawn-off, semi-automatic .22 that he had tested months earlier by firing into the Mary River, near Gympie in Queensland. He lifted the gun out and, as he was to describe it later, brought it to his shoulder in one smooth motion and fired. He was about a metre away. The last thing Ron Williams saw was the flash leaping from the barrel as the bullet hit him between the eyes.

'He was just standing there ... I shot him once in the forehead and again in the back of the head when he fell to the ground,' MacDonald was to tell police, as dispassionately as if he was talking about slaughtering a sheep.

Senior Detective Birch asked him: 'With what intention, if any, did you take Mr Williams to that location?'

MacDonald: 'Of killing him ... I stopped the motor vehicle, we took some fishing tackle from the rear of the vehicle, proceeded along the beach, fished for perhaps an hour and then I shot him.'

MacDonald said he checked Williams' pulse to make sure he was dead, carried him thirty metres up a sand dune and buried him. 'I dug a hole, placed the body in it, covered it with sand, smoothed out the area (and) put branches and shrubbery over it.'

Senior Detective Michael Grainger: 'You say your intention was to kill him – were you apprehensive or were you just – you – you had a job at hand and you were doing that job?'

MacDonald: 'It was a job at hand.'

He said that as he prepared to shoot he 'just switched off, I guess.'

Birch: 'What do you mean by that?'

MacDonald: 'When you cut off your emotions … I guess it's part of military training that sometimes you need to switch off your emotions … To be able to perform anything that needs to be done.'

It took him two hours to murder his travelling mate, bury his body and clean the area of clues. He left Cheyne Beach at 10pm.

Grainger: 'Why – why did you kill him – what's your reason for murdering Mr Williams?'

MacDonald: 'To assume his identity.'

He was asked by police if he had any mental illnesses and he said he had been diagnosed with a personality disorder.

MacDonald: 'Perhaps I don't share the same emotions that other people do.'

Grainger: 'Do you know that killing someone's wrong?'

MacDonald: 'I know that many people consider it to be, yes.'

Grainger: 'Did you consider the killing of Ron Williams wrong?'

MacDonald: 'No.'

Grainger: 'Why?'

MacDonald: 'To me, it seemed appropriate.'

Birch: 'Have you found yourself in other circumstances where you've found it necessary to kill someone?'

MacDonald: 'Yes.'

Birch: 'When?'

MacDonald: 'In Vietnam.'

But that interview came later. What he did when he left Cheyne Beach was dump his car, throw the number plates into a river, hitchhike back to Melbourne. He'd also discarded two identities, Paul Jacobs and Alexander MacDonald. But he kept the postcards Williams had trusted him to post. And post them he did, gradually, over several months. No-one who got the postcards could know that the return address scrawled on the back didn't exist, any more than the man who'd written them. But his name did. The Vietnam veteran, bank robber and killer had become Ron Williams.

## THE CROOK

ALEXANDER Robert MacDonald was a Queenslander. The first time he saw the inside of a police cell was when he appeared at the Brisbane Magistrates' Court on 1 December, 1967, charged with theft. He was fined $100 and given a two-year suspended sentence.

Perhaps it was suggested that military discipline might help him from returning before the courts because a month later he joined the army, entering the Recruit Training Battalion. In April, 1968, he transferred to the Artillery School in Manly, NSW, to train as a gunner. He had two tours of duty in Vietnam, the second at his own request.

Much later, he was described as having been a commando in the Special Air Services. This was untrue. But police believe he may have learnt about explosives in Vietnam when he was involved in jungle clearances, and he would have become familiar with firearms.

In 1972 he was charged with 'unlawfully killing cattle', fined $50 and ordered to pay $80 restitution at the Caboolture Magistrates' Court in Queensland.

In October that year he literally walked away from the army, going absent without leave from his base. He never returned, and was discharged a year later under a rule for long-term absentees.

Ten years later he would write to the army and ask for his service medals for his two tours of duty. He was told he was not entitled to the medals as he had gone absent without leave.

In March, 1978, the licensee of the Crown Hotel in Collie, Western Australia, found a plastic lunch box at the rear of the hotel with a note addressed to him. It said the box contained a gelignite bomb that had not been primed. It was a warning.

MacDonald demanded $5000 from each hotelier in the district and threatened to bomb their pubs if they didn't pay. He kept his word. Three months later a bomb exploded at the Crown, badly damaging the hotel, and it was only luck that stopped MacDonald being a cop-killer. A local policeman handled and examined the gelignite package only two minutes before it exploded.

MacDonald was arrested after he made an extortion demand for $60,000 from the hotels. He had built a bomb with four sticks of gelignite and had another sixteen sticks hidden in the bush. Police had no doubt he would have continued blowing up pubs until he was paid his extortion money.

He was sentenced to seven years over the bombings and extortion but served far less. He was released in September, 1981, and headed to Queensland.

Thirteen months later MacDonald was again a wanted man. Police said that between November 1982 and March 1983 he robbed several banks and service stations in central and northern Queensland.

It was during this time that MacDonald began to take hostages during robberies. In three bank robberies he took a staff member with him to ensure the police were not immediately called.

On 11 February, 1983, he robbed the National Australia bank at Mossman of almost $10,000. He took a staff member to the edge of a cane fields nearly five hundred metres from the bank and then vanished into the cane on foot.

Police believe he used a CB radio to contact his partner to pick him up.

In July, 1983, MacDonald was arrested in the Northern Territory as he was about to return to Perth. Again, the former soldier showed his extraordinary single mindness. On 28 July he escaped from the Berrimah Jail while awaiting extradition. In the escape he broke his ankle but still managed to travel four painful kilometres. He was forced to surrender after twelve hours on the hop.

He was sentenced to seventeen years jail. In 1984 he was given another six months for attempting to escape from Townsville's Stuart Prison. Not to be deterred he tried to escape again, this time bashing a prison officer and trying to take a female nurse hostage.

He was given another five years for his efforts.

He had served twelve of his twenty-three year sentence for eight armed robberies, two charges of conspiracy to commit armed robbery, four counts of unlawful imprisonment and the attempted escapes, when he decided he'd been in jail long enough. This time his escape was successful.

Despite the fact he was serving a long sentence for crimes of violence and had tried to escape repeatedly he was given a position of trust. At the Borallon Correctional Centre, near Ipswich, he was allowed outside on gardening duty. On 12 September, 1995, he simply walked off. 'I guess I couldn't see the end of it,' he later told police. He had three years to serve until he would have been eligible for parole.

He said he walked away and 'skirted the general Brisbane area.'

Birch: 'So how far would you have walked on foot?'

MacDonald: 'Over a period of a week, a couple of hundred k's I guess.'

He said he camped in the bush near Gympie for about three weeks after the escape.

On 20 October, 1995, he robbed the Westpac Bank in the Queensland town of Cooroy, near Noosa Heads. Then he escaped on a pushbike.

He went into the bank carrying his ten-shot .22 semi-automatic rifle. He said he selected the bank because it was near scrub where he could disappear.

He rang the manager earlier that day to make an appointment. Six staff members were in the bank. He was politely ushered into the manager's office, where he produced the gun and demanded money. He was given $15,000, stuffed it into a travel bag and walked out. 'I got on the pushbike and rode off along some back roads into the scrub.'

He camped out for two nights to beat the police road blocks. He used the money to set himself up with camping gear that he planned to use for more robberies.

He then robbed the Westpac bank at Airlie Beach on 15 December, 1995. 'While I was in prison in Stuart Creek, a chap there had told me how he robbed the bank in Airlie Beach.'

He got there by walking and hitchhiking and then camped in the scrub. He needed only to glance at the bank the day before to know his prison mate had been right. It was an easy target.

Next day he went into the bank and said he had a complaint about an account. Then he produced the gun and demanded money. He walked out with $83,000 and a female teller as hostage. After they'd walked about 80 metres he let the frightened woman go, then walked into the bush.

After murdering Ron Williams he was to use the same method to commit five more bank robberies in Yepoon, in Queensland, Airlie

Beach (again), Laurieton and Coonbarabran in NSW and Busselton in Western Australia.

Unlike most bandits he made little effort to hide his identity. He didn't use the usual armed robber's disguise of a balaclava or rubber mask. He wore a white Panama hat, almost as an identifiable trade mark, until he lost it during one robbery when he was chased into the bush.

He was a disciplined, cool, loner who went to great pains to cover his tracks. He lived quietly in Victoria as Ron Williams and would never pull a robbery there, instead travelling big distances interstate to pull bank jobs. He wanted police to believe that one of Australia's most wanted men was half-hermit, living in a tropical rain forest, coming out only to rob banks. No-one, he believed, would look near Melbourne for the Queensland bushranger.

He even had a fresh tattoo, a parrot with the name Megan, put on his left arm, covering an older tattoo that was recorded on his police record.

He was asked by Senior Detective Allan Birch why he travelled out of Victoria to rob banks. 'You could drive to Tocumwal or to Geelong. Why is it that you went north?' the policeman said.

MacDonald answered matter-of-factly: 'Well, to hopefully convince the police in Queensland that I was still in that area.'

Bizarrely, MacDonald was to come within metres of creating a huge international incident during an attempt to rob a bank at a tropical beach resort.

He took four days to drive from Melbourne to Cairns in his four wheel drive, and then took a bus along the winding coast road, past crocodile farms, caravan parks and five-star resorts to Port Douglas, later to become a popular holiday destination for American presidents, publishers and journalists. He took with him a second-hand black mountain bike he'd bought for $100 at the Cairns Cash Converters, and his dismantled double-barrel shotgun in his knapsack.

For a week he camped near the beach and walked around town. Like any other tourist, he wandered down the main street, past pubs, cafes and the prestigious Nautilus open air restaurant favoured by Bill and Hillary Clinton in happier times. But, unlike most tourists, he kept his eye on the Commonwealth Bank branch in the centre of the town.

He noted staff movements and saw that one man always arrived at the same time and parked his white Falcon in an underground car park, before walking a few metres to the bank.

He decided to abduct the staff member and demand that cash be delivered to him.

On Friday, 30 May, as the young staff member walked out of the carpark, MacDonald strolled over and grabbed him. He walked quietly with the man to the bank and then slipped a note to a female teller. It demanded that all the money in the bank be delivered to a spot on the banks of a river, about eight kilometres from Port Douglas, in exchange for the staff member's life.

The gunman and the hostage drove to the river to wait near a disused bridge next to the highway. It was a popular fishing spot but MacDonald knew it was low tide and the area should be empty. But a fisherman, who obviously could not read a tide chart, wandered up to the robber and his nervous hostage as they waited.

'A chap who had been fishing in the river came along and I had to take him in tow, so to speak,' MacDonald was to tell police.

The three waited about near the road. MacDonald knew there was only a few police at Port Douglas and he could slip into the cane fields or rainforest if they began a search.

But his plan unravelled when he spotted a huge contingent of police on the main road. When he saw four marked police cars, motor bikes and unmarked units he believed he was in big trouble. 'It didn't pan out the way I figured it would.'

What he didn't know until much later was that it was Murphy's Law at work. MacDonald had done his homework on the bank – but he hadn't read the local papers. The Chinese Vice Premier, Zhu Rongji, was in town after a tour around Australia.

Mr Zhu was heading for the Cairns airport with his massive police escort when he passed over the bridge near where MacDonald was hiding.

No-one knew that a killer with a loaded gun got within metres of one of the leaders of the biggest country in the world. But the killer didn't know either. He thought that half the Queensland police force was about to descend on him, so he let the two men go and pedalled his second-hand bike about three kilometres, in one of the slowest getaways on record, then disappeared into the bush once more. He then walked more than forty kilometres back to Cairns, collected his car and drove to Airlie beach to rob the Westpac branch a second time. It was a long way to come from Victoria, and he wasn't going to go home empty handed.

On 2 June, 1996, he turned up at a Somerville boat yard, Yaringa Boat Sales, saying he wanted to buy an old timber cabin cruiser that had been advertised in a boat magazine for $23,000. He didn't seem too worried about the price. He would have been churlish to quibble. Three weeks earlier, on 10 May, he'd robbed the Yepoon Commonwealth Bank of $107,000.

He produced a $500 deposit to settle the deal on the cabin cruiser.

He returned ten days later with a briefcase. He opened it and took out $10,000 in cash. Three days later he was back with the same briefcase and another $12,500.

He was going through a messy divorce, he explained, and didn't want his ex-wife to know about the money. So he carried it in the briefcase. It seemed reasonable to the salesmen.

He was to spend $80,000 on the boat, Sea Venture, fitting satellite navigation gear and reconditioned motors.

He paid $1200 cash to moor the boat at Yaringa and began to live on board. He told locals he was a builder and renovator who dabbled in prospecting.

He began to drink at the Somerville Hotel and developed a group of mates. At least six times he disappeared for up to eight weeks at a time. He told his new friends he was prospecting in Queensland. Which, in a way, he was. But not with a pick and shovel.

Just before Christmas, 1996, he threw a huge party for his friends, supplying all the food and liquor to celebrate completing the main work on the boat. During the refit a worker opened a waterproof case in the boat. Inside he found a sawn-off shotgun. He decided, perhaps wisely, not to ask questions.

In June, 1997, MacDonald told his friends he was short of cash and needed $10,000 before he could finish the boat and sail to the Solomon Islands where, he said, he was going to hook up with a friend.

He said he would head north on 27 June. Police believe he was going back to Queensland for one more armed robbery before sailing out of Australia to freedom.

He loaded up his Toyota with camping gear and provisions, then drove to the Hume Motor Inn in Fawkner and booked in to room eight.

While he was preparing to head north the television program, *Australia's Most Wanted*, screened a segment on the escapee-bandit. Police received a call to look for a Toyota Four wheel drive in Melbourne's north. Within hours they found the car, registered to Ron Williams. A police check confirmed that a Mr Ron Williams was a reported missing person.

A detective walked into the restaurant where MacDonald was sitting and immediately knew he was the wanted man. He was arrested by members of the Melbourne armed robbery squad outside the motel at 5.15pm on Thursday, 26 June, with his brother. He was extradited to Perth, pleaded guilty of murder and sentenced to life in prison.

When police went through his papers they found documents from the Christian Children's Fund. Here was an armed robber who could kill a harmless stranger and steal his identity without a moment's guilt, and yet sponsor a poverty-stricken child in South America.

## THE INTERVIEW

RECORD of interview between Senior Detective Allan Birch and Ronald Joseph Williams, of Ford Road, Shepparton, conducted in the offices of the armed robbery squad on Thursday, 26 June, 1997. There is a long discussion where the suspect refuses to agree to be finger-printed until it is explained that the prints can be taken by force.

BIRCH: 'I suspect you of armed robbery and escape. In simple terms, Mr Williams – I believe you are actually Alexander MacDonald. I have information that Alexander MacDonald is responsible for the commission of a number of armed robberies and has escaped a prison in the state of Queensland.'

Birch then informs the suspect that police have the legal authority to take fingerprints forcibly.

BIRCH: 'If you don't comply or you don't want to comply with that request, then I'll seek authorisation from my superior to take them forcefully from you. All right?'

MacDONALD: 'And who would that superior be? The man who assaulted me earlier?'

BIRCH: 'Well, I don't know what you are talking about.'

MacDONALD: 'The gentleman who was here earlier on with you.'

SENIOR DETECTIVE MICHAEL GRAINGER: 'What I suggest we do at this stage, Mr Williams, is that we suspend the interview.'

(After long discussions, MacDonald agrees to be fingerprinted.)

MacDONALD: 'Well, it would seem that I have no option.'

(After the fingerprints are taken MacDonald knows it is useless to continue the charade of pretending to be Ronald Williams.)

BIRCH: 'Can you please state to me your full name and address?'

MacDONALD: 'Alexander Robert MacDonald, no fixed place of abode.'

BIRCH: 'Right. Mr MacDonald, how did you come to be here in the office of the armed robbery squad?

MacDONALD: 'I was apprehended, shall we say, on Sydney Road at Fawkner.'

BIRCH: 'Where have you been residing for the last, say – six months?'

MacDONALD: 'I live on and off in the Millewa State Forest.'

BIRCH: 'And whereabouts is that situated?'

MacDONALD: 'It's near Tocumwal in New South Wales.'

BIRCH: 'Right, and you live in the forest?'

MacDONALD: 'I use tents and tarpaulins.'

Police asked MacDonald why how he came to be known as Williams.

MacDONALD: 'Well, it's an identity I've assumed since being an escapee.'

BIRCH: 'Right. Now how did you assume that identity?'

MacDONALD: 'By taking identity from the actual person.'

BIRCH: 'Right. Who is Ron Williams?'

MacDONALD: 'He's a guy from Melbourne.'

BIRCH: 'Right, do you know Ron Williams?'

MacDONALD: 'Yes.'

BIRCH: 'How do you know Ron Williams?'

MacDONALD: 'I met him on the pretext of employing him.'

BIRCH: 'Under what circumstances did you meet him?'

MacDONALD: 'I needed an identity. I ran an advertisement in a newspaper ... the Herald Sun ... For someone to take up a position with a geological survey.'

BIRCH: 'And what was the intention at the time of placing the advert?'

MacDONALD: 'My intention was to find a person of suitable age, background. No – no close relatives, and assume his identity.'

BIRCH: 'Right. How many persons responded to that, to that advert?'

MacDONALD: 'Fifty, I guess.'

BIRCH: 'Over what period of time did those fifty people respond?'

MacDONALD: 'Within the space of – yes – a week.'

BIRCH: 'Can you explain to me how you would assume the identity of a person who responds to an advert for employment?'

MacDONALD: 'You kill them.'

BIRCH: 'Did you kill Mr Williams?'

MacDONALD: 'I did.'

BIRCH: 'Can you approximate for me when that occurred?'

MacDONALD: 'Early March, 1996.'

BIRCH: 'Right, and how did you kill Mr Williams?'

MacDONALD: 'I shot him.'

BIRCH: 'And what were the circumstances ... ?'

MacDONALD: 'I required his identity. I transported him to Western Australia. Took him to a beach, and shot him there.'

MacDonald then explained how he put an advertisement

in the paper, under the name Paul Jacobs, for a field hand for 'geological survey work,' and how he had formed a short list of men 'with no dependents, no close relatives.'

MacDONALD: 'He (Williams) was quite drunk at the time (when he rang) which was one of the factors that decided me to interview him further. A few days later Mr Williams turned up at the flat for the interview and looked even more promising.'

MacDONALD: '(He was) a guy of my build, roughly – maybe a little shorter. Obviously of the same age group.' The prospective employee and employer had chatted for about an hour in the flat.

BIRCH: 'When did you form the opinion that he was a person of whom you wanted to assume his identity.'

MacDONALD: 'At that time I was about eighty per cent certain that he was suitable, so I asked him back for a second interview ... at which he could supply more personal details ... educational background, family background, employment.'

BIRCH: 'Was that – in what way was that necessary to you?'

MacDONALD: 'To give me the background story of that person.'

About six other men had telephoned for interviews but MacDonald put them off. At his second interview Williams said he had been brought up in orphanages, had no close family ties and had changed his name from Chomszczak. MacDonald had diligently written down all these personal details.

MacDONALD: 'Yes, he was married to Margaret Joy Manning in 1981, July 1981.'

BIRCH: 'And where is Mrs Manning now?'

MacDONALD: 'He didn't know ... they divorced in 1982.'

BIRCH: 'At the times you were writing down (the personal details) what was your intention with Mr Williams?'

MacDONALD: 'To kill him.' MacDonald then described how he had congratulated Williams, telling him he was the successful candidate, that he would be employed in WA for two years, and would be paid $60,000 a year if he signed a contract that he would not take up alternative employment. Until then, he had promised him a retainer of $500 a week 'to lock him into the program.' He then spoke freely to police about the murder.

MacDONALD: 'It took place on Cheyne Beach in Western Australia at approximately 8pm. I shot him once in the forehead and again in the back of the head when he fell to the ground.'

BIRCH: 'With what intention, if any, did you take Mr Williams to that location?'

MacDONALD: 'Of killing him ... I stopped the motor vehicle, we took some fishing tackle from the rear of the vehicle, proceeded along the beach, fished for perhaps and hour and then I shot him.'

BIRCH: 'Right, where was the firearm?'

MacDONALD: 'It was in a fishing bag that I had with me.' (a khaki knapsack from a Greensborough army surplus store).

Senior Detective GRAINGER: 'You say your intention was to kill him – were you apprehensive or were you just – you – you had a job at hand and you were doing that job?'

MacDONALD: 'I had a job at hand.'

He explained he had previously tested the gun at a bush camp on the Mary River, near Gympie in Queensland.

He said he and Williams arrived at the spot and fished several areas along the beach before he committed the murder.

BIRCH: 'What was he doing?'

MacDONALD: 'I believe he was just standing there. We were talking about something or other.'

GRAINGER: 'So how was it that you were able to distinguish him and kill him in the dark?'

MacDonald: 'I have reasonably good night vision.'

He said that he had been a gunner in the regular army, serving for five years from 1968, and trained to use machine guns, rifles and grenade launchers.

MacDONALD: 'I dug a hole, placed the body in it, covered it with sand, smoothed out the area put branches and shrubbery over it.'

BIRCH: 'What were your duties to perform, or that you performed, in Vietnam?

MacDONALD: 'I'd rather not go into that.'

BIRCH: 'Did you cause a death of any persons in Vietnam, by way of shooting them with a rifle?'

MacDONALD: 'I'd rather not discuss that.'

GRAINGER: 'Prior to the actual killing of Mr Williams, when was it that you decided, right – this is the spot – this is where it's gonna happen?'

MacDONALD: 'When I first saw the area.'

GRAINGER: 'And how long was that before you actually killed him?'

MacDONALD: 'An hour and a half.'

He said that as he prepared to shoot Mr Williams he 'just switched off, I guess.'

BIRCH: 'What do you mean by that?'

MacDONALD: 'When you cut off your emotions ... I guess it's part of military training that sometimes you need to switch off your emotions ... To be able to perform anything that needs to be done.'

GRAINGER: 'Why is it that you – you're telling us all this? Do you have any reason for that?'

MacDONALD: 'Well. It's a foregone conclusion that you would've found this all out anyway.'

GRAINGER: 'Why – why did you kill him – what's your reason for murdering Mr Williams?'

MacDONALD: 'To assume his identity.' He was asked by police if he had any mental illnesses and he said he had been diagnosed with a personality disorder.

MacDONALD: 'Perhaps I don't share the same emotions that other people do.'

GRAINGER: 'Do you know that killing someone's wrong?'

MacDONALD: 'I know that many people consider it to be, yes.'

GRAINGER: 'Did you consider the killing of Ron Williams wrong?'

MacDONALD: 'No.'

GRAINGER: 'Why?'

MacDONALD: 'To me, it seemed appropriate.'

BIRCH: 'Have you found yourself in other circumstances where you've found it necessary to kill someone?'

MacDONALD: 'Yes.'

BIRCH: 'When?'

MacDONALD: 'In Vietnam.'

MacDONALD: (Coughs) 'Pardon me.'

BIRCH: 'You okay. Got a bit of a dry throat?'

MacDONALD: 'I think it's the blasted cigarettes, actually.'

BIRCH: 'They'll kill you, they say.'

MacDONALD: 'So they say.'

He then explained buying the boat to sail to the Solomon Islands.

GRAINGER: 'Would that be in an endeavour to flee Australia?'

MacDONALD: 'I don't know quite how to phrase this. A terminal effort, shall we say.'

GRAINGER: 'You intended to kill yourself in the Solomon Islands?'

MacDONALD: 'That's correct.'

GRAINGER: 'Why is that?'

MacDONALD: 'Because I didn't see any future.'

GRAINGER: 'Why would it be necessary to kill yourself in the Solomon Islands?'

MacDONALD: 'More pleasant surroundings.'

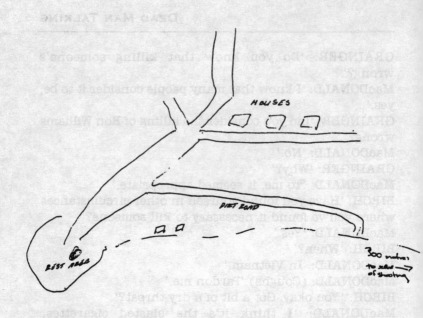

The map that Alexander MacDonald drew to show police where he had buried Ron Williams' body.

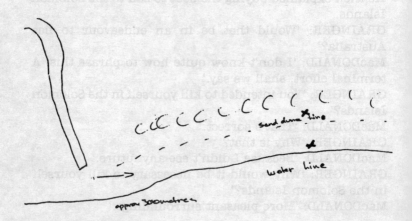

# CHAPTER 2

# Till death do us part

## The night daddy didn't come home

*'He was lying almost as if he was asleep.*
*That he might be dead was the last thing*
*that entered my head'*

*LONG after midnight she hears the familiar rattle of a vehicle crossing the cattlepit at the front gate, the drumming of tyres on gravel, the hum of a motor. She sees a man in the moonlight and, for a second, her heart leaps. Then she realises it's not her husband. It's the local policeman. She goes to the door, sick with fear. She knows it's bad. When he puts his arms around her, she knows it's the worst. 'Rob's not coming home,' he says gently.*

NOT all love stories end in tragedy, but many a tragedy begins with a love story.

Darina Pasco's begins when she's seventeen, the week she arrives from New Zealand to train at the Sydney Adventist hospital. On her first Saturday night in Australia she meets Rob Foots.

That was in 1971. 'We've been together ever since,' says Darina. She corrects herself. 'I mean, we had twenty-four years together ... ' The generous face clouds and hardens. 'We should have had another twenty-four.'

She often switches tenses – and moods – when talking about the love of her life, the father of her four children. She is kind and open, but something else lurks close to the surface, now, a weariness and a wariness that at any moment can wipe away the happiness of remembering the good times. Before 8 August, 1995.

The boy she meets in the early 1970s is big and strong, but so baby faced it's hard to believe he's already on the way to owning his own electrical business. Pictures taken of them show a pair of awkward big kids gazing into each other's eyes.

They're teenagers in love, but they take a more traditional route than many through the permissive society eddying around them. They marry at Wahroonga, in Sydney, in 1974.

Rob Foots is a goer, and always was. Youngest child and only boy in a big family, at eight years old he sells eggs from his own hens, and has a milk run. At fourteen he leaves school and starts work in the family electrical business.

As he grows up, he manages a difficult balancing act between living life to the full and observing the principles of his family's Seventh Day Adventist faith.

Like the business, young Foots thrives. He becomes the sort of man of whom people say he never preaches his religion, but lives it. He is generous. He does nothing by half measures. He believes right is might, that God helps those who help themselves.

And so, in a sense, Rob and Darina are pioneers without a frontier to go to. They do the next best thing. In 1981, after their two daughters are born, they move to the country.

THE first stop in the Foots family adventure is a five-hectare block at Tabletop, near Albury. There they set up their business – and have their third child, Justin.

They prosper, and buy a bigger place, sixty-five hilly hectares on the Victorian side of the border, on the banks of Lake Hume in a district called Talgarno. The view of the drowned valley is sensational. But you can't live on a view.

They call the place 'The Foothills'. Their commitment to it is almost biblical. They plant trees down the drive, and build a huge shed, where they live for nine months while building the first stage of the magnificent sprawling house they had dreamed up for the point overlooking the lake. It becomes a 'granny flat', where they rig up four tiny 'temporary' bedrooms – and live in it for six years.

As Rob Foots expands the business over the Riverina he spends every spare moment building the dream house. Typically, he thinks big. It's all solid brick and soaring ceilings and tall chimneys, deep windows, a spa and ensuites.

Along the way, a fourth child is born: another boy, Carl. 'He's the image of his father,' Darina says. She says he's 'a Godsend', and means it literally.

They move in two days before Christmas, 1993. They've been married twenty years, and this is their present to each other.

So here they are, a happy family in a new house. The children go to the Border Christian College, where Rob is on the school board. He's also taken up singing, practising as he drives his ute to distant jobs, and wins medals at local eisteddfods. They have a canoe and a ski boat and a labrador dog.

Every morning at dawn, he takes the dog, Jake, for a jog. Every evening, after a family dinner, he goes to the shed to prepare for the next day's work, then shares a spa bath with Darina to talk over the day's doings. They are content; true believers in their promised land.

It lasts one year and eight months.


BEFORE church on Saturday, 5 August, 1995, Rob Foots goes for a morning walk along the Talgarno road, which lets him check his cattle and fences. He has rigged a temporary fence along the roadside so his cattle can graze down grass that would otherwise be a fire hazard.

The fence is basic: a few wires strung on star pickets, known by farmers as steel posts. The posts are light and strong, and can be driven into the ground with a sledge hammer or post driver. And, at about $3 each, they're cheap.

But few things are so cheap that a thief won't steal them. Several times in the previous five years, someone has cut the wire and stolen Rob Foots's posts. It always happens on moonlit nights in winter, when the ground is soft, out of sight of the house.

Each theft, though not a big financial loss, leaves Rob more angry. Which is why, when he returns from his walk, he says 'the buggers have knocked off more posts'. After church they drive down the road to have a look. They find some loose steel posts leaning against a tree, as if the thief has forgotten them. 'They'll be back to get the rest,' Rob predicts. But he doesn't mention it again.

Tuesday, three days later, is the same as any other in the family's well-ordered lives. Joanne has just started at Avondale College at Coorambong, north of Sydney, leaving the three younger children at home. They have their evening meal together, as usual, then watch *Funniest Home Videos* and *Just Kidding* on television.

At 8.30 pm Rob goes to the shed, about a hundred metres from the house, to do his accounts and pack his utility ready for the next day's work.

At 9pm the telephone rings. Corrine answers it. Using the Commander system, she puts the call through to the shed and tells him it's 'Uncle Ray', a family friend also on the school board.

Darina realises there is a school board meeting that night, and that Rob has missed it. At 10 pm, she fills the spa, ready for the nightly ritual of a bath and a talk before bed. But, this time, with Rob working later than usual, she has it alone.

By the time she finishes, the time is creeping towards 10.30 pm. She rings the shed telephone extension. She tries her husband's mobile telephone, then the two-way radio fitted to the ute. No answers. She feels the first pang of fear.

It's a freezing August night. She puts on her dressing gown and walks towards the shed, thinking he might be stuck underneath a vehicle. But the shed is empty. No Rob. No ute.

Darina decides he might have suddenly gone to the school board meeting after all. She tries to ignore the fact he never leaves the property without telling her. Stomach knotting, she rings the school, to see if the meeting is still going. No answer.

She recalls, later, each action and each thought. 'I looked at my watch,' she is to say. 'It was 12.30. I thought, if he's not home by 1am, I'll go and look for him myself.'

That doesn't happen. Ten minutes later, someone comes looking for her instead.

IT HAS been a bad time for the de Hennin family, and about to get worse. This Tuesday night, Jim and Julie de Hennin, who live on a property past the Foots's, have been to Albury to see one of their daughters, whose husband was accidentally electrocuted two weeks earlier. They drive home in separate cars, Jim ten minutes behind his wife. It's some time after 9.30 pm.

As he takes the bend past Foots's gate, de Hennin sees a vehicle on his left, skewed on a steep angle to the road, headlights shining into the paddock. He thinks his neighbor might need help with stray cattle, and stops.

He recognises the vehicle as Rob Foots's Holden Rodeo. Its motor is running and the driver's door wide open. Inside is an open briefcase, with a jacket lying across it, a mobile telephone, and, barely visible, a notebook.

De Hennin calls out. No answer. He walks to the front of the ute and peers outside the wedge of light. Then he sees his neighbor, face down on the ground just to the left of the beam.

'He was lying almost as if he was asleep,' de Hennin is to recall. 'That he might be dead was the last thing that entered my head.' But as soon as he picks up Foots's hand he realises it's all wrong. There's no pulse, and the hand is cold.

He calls the emergency number on his mobile telephone. The ambulance people say to keep the patient warm. He calls home. His wife knows first aid and his daughter, Kirsten, is a trainee nurse. They come quickly and work furiously at resuscitation.

Not until they roll the body over to get at his mouth does de Hennin suspect foul play. There are spots of fresh blood on the green grass. And, under the shirt, a neat hole in his chest.

Pat Garrett, the local policeman, arrives. 'Keep working on him,' he says. 'Don't give up.' He and de Hennin see the grass and the soft ground is torn up where a vehicle has reversed past the ute. A perfect set of tyremarks, etched in red mud, leads onto the bitumen, towards Albury.

Much later, after a detective arrives from Wodonga, Garrett goes off to face the toughest job a cop has to do.

AFTERWARDS, Darina sits in the silent house with the policeman for a long time. She forces herself to ask the question. 'How did it happen?'

He finds a gentle way to speak the unspeakable. 'He had a small hole just here,' he says, brushing his chest with his hand. He didn't use the words 'died' or 'dead' or 'shot'. Darina knows what he means, but is grateful.

She often ponders, later, the coping mechanism that gets her through that night and ones that follow. When Garrett offers to call her closest friends she says firmly, 'No, you won't. I will.' She doesn't want a stranger breaking the news.

She calls John and Julienne Bullock. It's after 1am. John answers, sleepy and apprehensive. She says: 'Rob's been shot and he didn't make it.' After a second's pause, it sinks in. 'We'll be there.' They live twenty minutes away, by normal reckoning, on the other side of the lake. They make it in ten.

The policeman goes home after they arrive. The three sit for hours, talking. They veer from tears to laughter. They don't wake the children – there will be enough sleepless nights for them in the weeks and months ahead. But, after daybreak, they can't put it off any longer. They wake them and break their hearts.

Darina calls her sister and brother-in-law in Sydney, and they agree to drive to Coorambong to tell the oldest daughter, Joanne, then bring her the 650km south to Albury.

Recalling that first day of the rest of her life, Darina says: 'Rob did everything in a big way – big wife, big house, big family. Even departing it was in a big way. That morning there were planes and helicopters flying overhead and I thought "Goodness me, darl, you really know how to do it".'

THE homicide squad knows about Rob Foots's death before his widow does. Three detectives on the on-call crew are paged in the first hour. By midnight they're driving north.

Detective Senior Sergeant Jeff Maher is in charge, with senior detectives Graeme Arthur and Phil Shepherd. When they get to Talgarno it's after 4am and minus-six degrees. A local detective and two crime scene experts from Wangaratta shiver in the frost.

At first light, traffic starts to trickle by. The detectives block the road and speak to drivers to see if, being locals, they had seen anything useful the night before. Some did. This narrows the time of the shooting to less than an hour, after 9.30 but before 10.30. At breakfast time they speak to Darina, and ask to see any firearms in the house. It's painful, but their job is to eliminate potential suspects, and the first people to eliminate are family members. Then they doorknock neighbors. No-one knows anything, except that Rob Foots isn't the sort of bloke who gets shot.

Shepherd, who is to see the case through to the end, has a long talk to the dead man's friend, John Bullock, who is close enough to know if he had any enemies in business. Meanwhile, the body is moved and sent to Melbourne for a post mortem, and a metal detector turns up a freshly-fired .22 calibre bullet case.

The only obvious motive seems to be that Foots interrupted a thief. But the detectives are cautious about this, because steel posts are used by farmers – and, as Shepherd says later, 'cockies don't tend to pinch stuff from other cockies.'

So who would want to steal the posts, apart from legitimate farmers? It can only be someone who wants to build a fence. The police wonder if it could be marijuana growers stealing posts rather than arousing suspicion by buying new ones.

Next day, there's more to work with. The bullet the pathologist removes from Rob Foots's body matches the .22 shell from the scene. It went through the heart, then downwards through the liver and lodged in the tenth rib.

The muddy tyre tracks are identified as being made by near-new Kuhmo KH-832 Powerguards, a tread pattern available for only eighteen months. The axle width indicates the vehicle is a light Japanese four-wheel drive. The fact the tracks turned towards Albury-Wodonga, and that the shooting happened on a weeknight, means it's probably someone local.

It isn't a flying start, but it's something. The detectives ask every tyre dealer in the border area for records showing who has bought Kuhmo Powerguard tyres in the previous six months.

As this information trickles in, they start cross-checking registrations of four-wheel-drive owners against licensed shooters, looking to draw up a short list of locals who own guns and four-wheel-drives. Such methods can get results eventually – providing the process of elimination is strict enough not to let a suspect slip through the net with a plausible manner and ready alibi. By the time Rob Foots's funeral is held six days after his death, many routine inquiries have been made, but there's little to show for them. The funeral is at the Seventh Day Adventist church in Albury. There have been thirty death notices in the *Border Morning Mail*, and more than 500 mourners crowd the church. When a video tape of Rob singing a hymn is played on a big screen, people weep.

Two days later, the police retrace their steps. They go back to Foots's farm to check the dead man's possessions. When a detective goes to fetch Foots's diary, he's given the notebook that had been lying on the briefcase in the utility. He notices, he says later, what could be a car registration number scrawled faintly on the plastic cover.

The number is that of a Nissan four-wheel-drive twin cab utility … registered to an address in Firebrace Track, Granya Gap, about twenty minutes away up the road running past Foots's property.

Shepherd and fellow detective Steve Tragardh drive to Granya Gap. They find the property. There is no house, only a locked shed. But there are tyre tracks. And the tread pattern matches the muddy ones found at the crime scene.

It seems, then, that Rob Foots has not just sung at his own funeral, but solved his own murder. But it proves a little more complicated.

Back at Albury police station, the detectives soon find out that the Nissan's owner lives in the town. He is David Cox, a sixty-year-old grandfather who has worked forty years for the railways before being made redundant the year before.

On appearances, Cox doesn't seem a likely killer. But someone who knows more about him than they do thinks otherwise. An anonymous tip which arrives, by coincidence, while the detectives are at Granya fingers Cox as a suspect because he has a four-wheel-drive, likes guns – and has an old conviction in NSW for stealing farm fencing materials.

Shepherd doesn't want to show his hand – yet. He and Tragardh sit off Cox's place, a bungalow behind his aged mother's house in South Albury, a down-at-heels area near the Murray. They sneak a look at the Nissan's tyres – and get a surprise. They are Kuhmos – but worn out, and a different tread pattern from the ones at the crime scene.

This is the first move of a chess game. Shepherd traces the car's previous owner. He says he sold it to Cox just nine months before – but not with Kuhmos on it. Question: why would Cox replace one set of tyres with another set of old tyres? Answer: to cover his tracks. But how to prove it?

A few days later, Cox buys new tyres at the local K-mart – and leaves the old ones there. The police seize them, and take them to a tyre expert, who points out that the soapy lubricant used to fit tyres is on them, meaning they have been fitted some time in the previous month.

By this time, forensic tests prove the tyremarks at Cox's Granya property are identical to those at the crime scene. But where are the new tyres that made them?

The police move. On 30 August they take out a warrant, go to Cox's house, inspect the Nissan and search the house. They find fourteen firearms. They take Cox to the police station. He denies everything, convincingly. His wife, meanwhile, backs up his alibi that he was home all night on 8 August.

The last question Shepherd puts to him that day is if he has any idea how Rob Foots died. 'Cox looked at me with the most earnest expression and said he was sorry he hasn't, because he wanted to help.'

They take him home. But not for long. Early next morning, 31 August, they arrest him. This time they point out the damning inconsistencies in his story. He changes it.

COX admits stealing steel posts from Foots's property more than once, and to being there on the night of the killing. But he claims that he and his adult son Phillip (who is slightly handicapped as a result of cerebral palsy) were shooting rabbits when confronted by the angry owner.

Cox's story is that Foots assaulted him and his son, and that he, Cox, grabbed the rifle to scare him when he tripped over a piece of wood, accidentally firing a shot.

He can't explain why the bullet hit Foots's heart, then travelled downwards at an angle of thirty degrees. Or why there is no sign of a struggle. Why Foots's hands weren't grazed from throwing punches. Why neither father nor son suffered any visible cuts or bruises. Nor does he explain why steel posts were found already pulled from the ground, ready to load.

What he does explain is the mystery of the missing tyres.

Aware that the new Kuhmos – bought only days before the shooting – would be an obvious lead, he removed them himself, replacing them with the old tyres, which he had kept as spares. He then drilled holes in the new tyres and threw them in the Murray.

Cox takes the police to the river, and they retrieve one of the new Kuhmos. They are not so lucky with the murder weapon, which Cox claims he threw into Lake Hume. Several searches fail to find the rifle.

Cox's son Phillip is no help. In the interview room he says he cannot even tell the time, let alone remember the events of the night. Sceptical detectives note he is competent enough to hold a driver's licence, and is married with several children.

Darina is at the funeral parlor trying to choose a plaque when her mobile telephone chirps. It's Shepherd, keeping his promise to tell her first about the arrest. 'I laughed, cried, and clapped. I had tears streaming down my face. I drove straight around to the school to tell the kids.'

Later, Shepherd drives to Granya to check Cox's property. He unlocks the shed. Inside it are bundles of brand new steel posts, bought and paid for.

*DAVID Cox was found not guilty of murder at Wangaratta on 7 November, 1996. He was found guilty of manslaughter and sentenced to seven years imprisonment with a minimum of five, and three months for stealing seventy star pickets valued at $245. His wife, Irene Mary Cox, distressed by the trial, died suddenly three months later. She is buried in Albury cemetery ten metres from Rob Foots. David Cox made an official complaint to the Victoria Police, demanding the return of a pair of pliers and a rifle magazine. Darina Foots put the family property on the market a year later.*

# CHAPTER 3

# Thursday

## The day Al ran out of friends

*'If we kill him, will it start a war?'*

APPEARANCES can be deceptive. So can crooks. As Alphonse John Gangitano strutted along Bourke Street, central Melbourne, in the warmth of an early January evening in 1998 he looked nothing like a heavy crime figure whose power base was spinning into terminal decline.

Strolling along in the twilight with his loyal friend, bail justice Ms Rowena Allsop, his driver, 'Santo', and a solicitor who was part of his expensive defence team, Gangitano showed no sign of being nervous about fronting court next morning.

He was, after twenty years in and around the underworld, no stranger to the criminal justice system. He did not have to ask where the accused was expected to sit when he entered a Magistrates', County or Supreme Court.

Gangitano was 'quite jovial" Ms Allsop was to recall of that evening on 15 January. 'We went past a bookshop and he bought me a book on Oscar Wilde,' she was to remember of the criminal she described as 'a very special friend.'

'We both had an interest in Wilde. We laughed at the quote, "There is only one thing in the world worse than being talked about, and that is not being talked about".'

According to Ms Allsop, Gangitano was widely read and, for a Melbourne gangster of Italian origins, had picked three unlikely role models: John F. Kennedy, Napoleon and Wilde. It seemed he was attracted to – and secretly craved – fame and recognition.

The group met at a trendy eatery, Barfly's restaurant, near Spring Street, and then Ms Allsop and Gangitano, dressed in fashionable jeans and a crisp white Versace overshirt, went for a wander, window-shopping in two bookshops.

Ms Allsop, well known in political circles, seemed not to be worried about being spotted with a suspected killer less than a hundred metres from Parliament House. After all, her relationship with Gangitano had been the subject of scrutiny – and disapproval – all the way to the office of the Attorney-General.

The two stopped when urged to come in for a drink at one of the bastions of conservative Melbourne, Florentino restaurant. Gangitano ordered a scotch and Ms Allsop, a teetotaller, had a coffee.

Gangitano, who was on a court-ordered 9pm curfew, lingered over his drink until around 8.45. Ms Allsop reminded him that he should head home. Gangitano smiled and said there wouldn't be a problem if he bent the bail conditions by a few minutes. It wouldn't be the first time. The bail justice was seemingly unconcerned about the minor breach of the rules. There was no need to nit-pick.

'He kissed me on both cheeks and I wished him well for court the next day and then he left,' she said later. 'He didn't seem worried.' Santo met him at Barfly's to take him home to Templestowe in a late-model blue Holden. Ms Allsop never saw him again.

The relationship between the bail justice and the gangster had long been the subject of interest in legal, political and criminal circles. Rowena Allsop had been popular with many detectives because of her enthusiasm and energy as a bail justice. She was always prepared to come out late at night for a court hearing when called by the serious crime squads. She was fond of publicity, and other bail justices grumbled about her high profile, but no-one doubted her availability and sincerity.

The former athlete and football umpire moved easily with the champagne set. Why then would a respected Order of Australia recipient and confidante of many police be seen in public on the arm of a notorious criminal? When she appeared with Gangitano at a kickboxing show in Melbourne and jumped into the ring to present a trophy, many old friends shook their heads. Of course, tastes in friends and entertainment can be peculiar: sitting not far away from the gangster and the bail justice was a well-known lawyer and merchant banker, once mooted as a future Liberal Prime Minister.

Ms Allsop had to endure criticism that, as a bail justice, she should not have befriended a man reputed to be one of the state's biggest crime figures.

If she thought her friendship with Gangitano would not reflect on her legal role, the illusion was shattered when she glanced at a police notice-board at an inner city police station while on duty.

On it was a typed list of eleven independent people to be called to observe interviews with minors and disadvantaged suspects to ensure their rights were protected. Next to Ms Allsop's name, scrawled in pen, was: 'Do not use ... roots Gangitano.'

Ms Allsop gave character evidence for Gangitano in 1996 that brought out into the open a relationship that some police had been questioning privately for nearly two years.

She told the Magistrates Court she had met Gangitano for coffee and late-night meals. 'He sees me as a role model in the community,' she told the court. 'He asked if I would be a professional person he could call on from time to time.'

Rowena Allsop became an unpaid bail justice in 1989 and was used by the homicide and armed robbery squads more than any other. She had a reputation of being able to be trusted with confidential information. But when she began being seen with a police target many detectives had second thoughts. After Ms Allsop gave evidence for Gangitano, a senior CIB officer instructed squad chiefs that she was effectively banned.

According to Ms Allsop, she became the victim of a vicious rumour simply because she was an attractive, single woman who tried to help a man who asked for assistance.

She knows that when police questioned her 'friendship' with Gangitano, it was shorthand for alleging that she was sexually involved with him. 'It was totally malicious, outrageous and without basis. I wonder if there would have been all the fuss if I was married with two children or I was a man,' Ms Allsop, a divorcee, asked. 'I know how the police rumour mill works. A lot of females, including some police-women I know, have been victims of it over a number of years.'

Police first started to turn on Ms Allsop when she walked in one door at the Carlton police station as Gangitano arrived through the other. 'We were having coffee in Lygon Street when my phone went ,asking me to attend at the Carlton station. He had to go there to report on bail and I was going there so I drove him the one block to the police station.'

Amid the controversy, the Attorney-General, Mrs Jan Wade, confirmed she would review the relationship, the police association claimed the issue was of 'grave concern' and the Victorian Law Institute said those involved in the criminal justice system should have no outside association with police, lawyers or their clients. The institute failed to mention several celebrated cases of affairs between police and lawyers, including one consummated in the interview room of a crime squad.

'I know I have done nothing wrong. But in the end people will believe what they want to believe,' Ms Allsop said in her own defence. Many believed the worst. Whether her relationship with Gangitano was brave or stupid is a matter of conjecture – and some debate. But there is no doubt the Victorian of the Year recipient, director of Odyssey drug rehabilitation centre and a former teacher at Winlaton Youth Training Centre, was branded unreliable in police circles.

Eventually the Attorney-General released a code of conduct for Victoria's bail justices. It was a thinly disguised swipe at Ms Allsop and her ongoing relationship with Gangitano, a relationship she refused to abandon.

'He was always a perfect gentleman in my company,' she said. 'I know he was no angel but I believe he was trying to change.'

But, for Alphonse Gangitano, gossip about whether he was having an affair with a bail justice was the least of his problems.

FOR a man who liked to look and act like someone always in control, Gangitano was becoming increasingly reliant on others: he needed a lawyer because, for the previous four years, he had been facing a string of criminal charges and he needed a driver because he had lost his licence for refusing a breath test.

But what he needed most was friends, and powerful ones, in the underworld. Restaurant owners and waiters might have waved and smiled at 'Phonse', but the men who make life-and-death decisions about career criminals were showing less affection towards the big man with the vicious temper.

Some police believe Gangitano's death certificate was signed, but the date left blank, when he murdered popular crime identity Gregory John Workman on 7 February, 1995.

According to police documents, Workman and Gangitano, after attending a wake at a Richmond hotel, went to an underworld party in Wando Grove, East St Kilda, to raise bail money for an armed robber.

Gangitano was drunk and, as was his form, looking for trouble. He tried to pick a fight with a gambling associate then, about 4am, he pulled a pistol on another man and had to be dragged away.

About 4.40am, a woman heard what she thought were fire crackers above the noise of the party. She later told police she went outside and saw Gangitano, holding a pistol, standing over Workman, who was lying on the ground, bleeding profusely.

Workman had been shot eight times with a .32 semi-automatic pistol. He died several hours later.

Two sisters made detailed statements implicating Gangitano and he was charged with the murder – the first serious charges levelled against him. For years police had wanted to nail him, but despite his growing reputation as a gangster his criminal record showed only minor offences.

Born on 24 March, 1957, Gangitano was the only son of a decent family involved in the travel and real estate businesses. An uninspiring student at De La Salle, Marcellin and Taylors College, he developed the reputation as a vain, arrogant bully who could be charming, but with a violent streak.

Fellow Marcellin student, Bill Birnbauer, who went on to become an award-winning journalist with *The Age,* recalled that Gangitano was a bash artist who used the king-hit with brutal results.

In April 1976, he appeared at the Malvern Magistrates' Court charged with offensive behaviour and for the next five years drifted through the courts on a series of 'kiddie crimes' – vandalism and street offences. At that stage he was a hoon flexing his muscles, but in 1981 he was found with a firearm and over the next few years the young hood became steadily more violent. Backed by his gang, he developed a reputation for bashing police. He would see a young copper off duty at a disco and ask, 'Are you in the job?' When the young man nodded, Gangitano would lash out with a big punch without warning.

Over three years he was charged with hindering police, assault by kicking, assaulting police, resisting police and other crimes of violence. But each time the charges were thrown out and each time he would walk out of court a little bit cockier.

A confidential police special circular warned police of Gangitano and his team. 'They approach members and assault them for no apparent reason. They are all extremely anti-police and are known to be ex-boxers. They often frequent in a group numbering approximately fifteen. They single out up to three off-duty police and assault them, generally by punching and kicking them. On most occasions in the past members have been hospitalised due to injuries received from these persons.' Gangitano was described as 'EXTREMELY VIOLENT AND DANGEROUS.'

In the early 1980s, Gangitano started to use his muscle and his mates to stand over nightclubs. He would arrive and tell owners that unless they paid protection money he would begin bashing patrons. More often than not the owners would pay for peace.

He also began to get a toe-hold in the booming illegal gambling scene, and had a slice of a profitable baccarat school in Lygon Street.

He was seen regularly at race tracks, owned racehorses and harness-horses, and was listed in police files as a suspected race-fixer in Victoria and Western Australia.

Police believed he sold guns from a nightclub in Brunswick. He began to associate with some well-known older criminals, including the man purported to be the best safe-breaker in Australia. He was graduating from hoon to hood.

In 1987, the ambitious young man went into partnership with an older Italian criminal in a scheme to open a casino in Fitzroy. It was to be a restaurant downstairs and a plush gaming venue upstairs.

According to police records, Gangitano ploughed $300,000 of his own money into the plan. He didn't know that police had set up a surveillance post across the road. The casino lasted just two days; police closed it down. It hurt the young thug's pocket, but again he escaped prosecution. This became part of the Gangitano myth. Did he stay out of jail because he was paying off police, because he was cunning or just lucky?

The older he became, the more brazen he seemed. According to police, 'good' criminals try to hide their success. They know that the more they flaunt their wealth, the more likely they are to attract police and tax department interest. But Gangitano loved the spotlight. He would wander Lygon Street as if it were his kingdom and playing the role of a young Godfather, nodding to restaurateurs and chatting with fellow hoods.

Undeniably good looking, he dressed well and acted as nonchalantly as a man without a care in the world.

He became more closely involved in the boxing scene and had strong links with the camp of world champion Lester Ellis. Long-time boxing rival and fellow world champion Barry Michael was bashed and bitten by Gangitano and his associates at a King Street nightclub in 1987.

Gangitano was vicious, but also unpredictable. Once, a policeman was eating with a woman other than his wife in Lygon Street when he took offence at the bad language at a table behind him. He turned around and demanded they keep the language down. The off-duty detective only then realised he had confronted a group of thugs, including Gangitano.

The policeman fully expected the incident to become violent and was surprised to hear Gangitano castigate his team for their behaviour. The hoods left and the head waiter arrived with the most expensive bottle of wine on the menu. It was a gift from Alphonse, to apologise for his friends' language.

The same man was known for bashing people for little or no reason. He shot a criminal in the knee at a family wake and was believed to be involved in several other shootings.

In the underworld, no-one is beyond intimidation and Alphonse could also be the prey as well as the hunter. His long-time enemy was

Mark Brandon Read, the standover man who had his own ears cut off while in Pentridge Prison's infamous H Division. In the late 1980s, Read took on Gangitano's gang and demanded payment. The long-awaited confrontation was on the cards when Read walked into one of Gangitano's haunts in Lygon Street.

The earless standover man was dressed well, but under his leather jacket was strapped several sticks of gelignite, equipped with a fuse. In his mouth was a lit cigar. The threat was too much. According to underworld legend, when Gangitano heard Read was waiting for him and prepared to blow the club sky-high, he slipped through iron security bars in the lavatories and ran away.

A group of criminals once planned to use land mines to kill Gangitano at his eastern suburbs house but abandoned the plan because of the likelihood of other people being killed.

When Read was due for release in 1991, after spending five years in jail for shooting a criminal and burning his house down, an associate of Gangitano's went to H Division to try to strike a peace deal. But, at the same time, police knew that Gangitano's people were offering a $30,000 contract on Read.

It might have been a coincidence, but Gangitano decided to leave Australia in July, 1991, around the time Read was due out of Pentridge.

He returned in January, 1993, weeks after Read was back in jail in Tasmania for shooting another criminal. Police phone taps showed that Gangitano had been in constant contact with his Australian criminal connections while in Europe. Read was later to claim he received regular four-figure payments from Gangitano to stay out of Victoria. Several taskforces from the Victoria Police, National Crime Authority and Federal Police worked on Gangitano, but had come up with nothing.

For a time it looked as if the man who loved to play the gangster was beyond policing. But when he opened fire on Greg Workman in St Kilda, the game changed. There were witnesses and there was a corpse.

For the police, this promised to be the big break.

Gangitano knew he was in big trouble and went straight to his legal team. A high-profile lawyer called the homicide squad: Would they like to interview his client about the demise of a Mr Workman? Homicide detectives said he could wait. They would conduct their inquiries and interview people when they decided. They wanted Gangitano to swing in the breeze while they gathered evidence.

They knew they would never get a confession, so they had to have a watertight case.

The key was the two sisters who witnessed the crime. Both identified Gangitano as the trigger man. One saw him led away from the dying man by another gangster. Others confirmed the argument at the party and others told lies. The case looked good, and the police moved in to charge the gangster.

But as they celebrated in anticipation of putting Gangitano away for twenty years, their case was already unravelling.

The sisters had been hidden away under witness protection. They should have been safe and beyond influence, but it all went wrong. Police documents described the women as 'fearful for their safety and in an extremely fragile state'.

The women began to lose confidence in the police when, despite being promised protection, they were driven down Lygon Street and actually spent a few nights staying in the heart of Gangitano country, Carlton.

They complained that they were treated like criminals, refused wine with meals, not allowed to go to a hairdresser, and refused permission to buy food instead of living on takeaway fast food.

They were moved to Swan Hill, where they nearly ran into an associate of one of Gangitano's best friends. Police moved them to Warrnambool and put them in a cabin at a caravan park. It was hardly five-star accommodation. Worse, they were left alone, and told there was a twenty-four-hour hotline they could ring if they needed help. Three times they rang and three times the phone rang out. Alone and frightened, they contacted a friend of Gangitano's in a bid to make peace. Big Al's friends jumped at the chance and organised the girls to be driven from Warrnambool to a Melbourne solicitor's office.

While police believed their star witnesses were safely tucked away in country Victoria, on 6 March, 1995, both women were making taped statements in a lawyer's office recanting their original police statements. It was not the police witness scheme's finest hour.

The women were secretly driven back to Warrnambool. Two days later, police discovered their case was mortally damaged. On 20 May, the sisters flew from Melbourne to England and said they would refuse to testify in the murder case. It is believed Gangitano paid for the flights and all expenses for their extended 'holiday'.

Police dropped the murder charges against Gangitano and were presented with a $69,975 legal bill by his defence team. Police negotiated and paid a reduced fee. By withdrawing the charges before a trial, police left themselves the opportunity to re-charge if their case improved.

Late in 1997, the sisters slipped back into Melbourne. The police had another go, quietly working to get them to make fresh statements so Gangitano could be charged again.

But Workman's friends had little faith in justice being done through the legal system. According to police sources, several months after the murder, criminal associates of the dead man made contact with Gangitano's offsiders and asked, 'If we kill him, will it start a war?'

At that time, Alphonse still had enough friends to protect him but, in the following year, his power base eroded. His behaviour became more erratic. Stories surfaced of him fighting with old gaming associates, of money problems – and even rumours of a drug habit, which was proven wrong after his death, when a toxicology report showed no signs of drugs in his system.

He was alleged to have fallen out with three brothers who control a large segment of the Lygon Street 'mafia'.

The opening of Crown Casino had dried up much of the illegal gaming industry that had been a milking cow for Gangitano and his friends. And while he had beaten the murder charge (at least temporarily), he was under legal siege. Although not facing heavy charges, he was subjected to a series of draining legal problems. Charges of assault, refusing a breath test and possession of a firearm began to bite.

He spent time in jail on some charges and was bailed on a night curfew on others. He couldn't prowl his patch late at night and began to lose control. The illusion that he was above the law, that he had paid off the police and that he would never go to jail, was shattered.

The standover man was beginning to be stood over by the law. But even as his empire crumbled, Gangitano worried about his looks.

When reporting for bail he noticed the police Polaroid picture on his file was less than flattering. He had a professional shot taken and brought it to the police station when he next had to report and had it exchanged for the harsh photo.

Even though still in Tasmania's Risdon prison, Chopper Read knew what was likely to happen to his enemy. A month before Gangitano's murder, Read predicted the Carlton criminal had been marked for death.

'Al is not long for this world, I fear,' Read confided from his cell.

Read said he was concerned that Gangitano's enemies might wait for his own release from prison before killing the gangster.

'I have heard that some would like to have me out so that I would be blamed for any misadventures that may befall the unfortunate Mr Gangitano,' he said.

But, later, Read said Gangitano had only weeks to live. A television reporter wanted to organise an interview with Gangitano and Read when the latter was released from prison in February, 1998. 'Not possible, darling,' Read said. 'He'll be dead before I'm out, I'm afraid.'

Read, a crime author, had planned to dedicate his next book to Gangitano with the words, 'To Al, get yourself a sense of humour'.

After the killing, Read said: 'Alphonse was betrayed from within his own camp. There were plenty of crocodile tears at his funeral. Ultimately people like Alphonse are killed by their friends, not their enemies. His mistake was that he could no longer tell the difference.'

The fact that Read was in jail at the time of the murder did not discount him as a suspect. Detectives interviewed two of Read's closest associates, 'Dave the Jew' and Amos Atkinson, in relation to the murder. 'The Jew' was purported to be an underworld killer and Atkinson had once held thirty people hostage in Melbourne's Italian Waiters' Club in a crazy attempt to free Read from jail.

Both men said they could not help police with their enquires. 'The Jew' denied he was at all violent, although police found an axe in his bedroom.

In September, 1997, crime commentator 'Sly of the Underworld' said on the breakfast program of radio station 3AW that a well-known Carlton gangster had fallen out with former allies and was likely to be murdered. Gangitano contacted 'Sly' through an intermediary and said it was nonsense. 'We laughed about it,' Gangitano said.

When police searched his house after he was killed, they found a transcript from the radio segment that predicted his murder.

Although Gangitano has been publicly identified as a heavy gangster, some police believe his reputation was bigger than the man.

But certainly he was probably the highest-profile criminal in Victoria in the 1990s, mostly due to his own efforts to make sure he was. All major criminals knew him. Gangitano, also known as 'Al Granger' and 'Al Gange', gave his occupation as property developer. Police claim his income came largely from drugs.

Aged forty, Gangitano was old for a standover man and he needed to graduate from thug to organiser, a move that seemed beyond him.

Still good-looking and fit, he wanted to be a part of the nightclub scene, as a patron, a standover man and an owner, although his court-ordered curfew made that impossible.

Gangitano was reputed to have a financial interest in several nightclubs in Melbourne and some entertainment spots in Carlton. The Liquor Licensing Commission banned him from having any involvement in one club because of his criminal background. He was alleged to have extorted money from fast-food vendors in the city nightclub belt.

When arrested by police after one assault, he yelled, 'Do you know who I am?' A police baton across the back of his legs answered the question.

'He was dangerous, unpredictable and violent,' said a policeman who watched him, 'but he was well short of the elite.'

Many professional criminals were surprised at how Gangitano brought police and public attention to himself by indulging in glorified pub brawls and bashings while they were busy making serious money.

Gangitano was always security conscious, but almost no-one is immune from a professional hit, especially one performed 'on the inside'. Police believe that many of Alphonse's so-called friends knew he was about to die.

He was shot dead in his home after the first day of his committal. There was no sign of a struggle. It seemed that Gangitano welcomed his killer into his home. The fact he must have known his killer is little help to police, because he probably knew all Melbourne's gunmen.

For police investigating the murder, it is not so much a case of trying to find enemies of the deceased, but of eliminating potential suspects from those known to have a grudge against him.

A man with a savage temper who is quick with his fists and a gun makes enemies. Many patient men in the underworld hold grudges for years, waiting until their target loses influence, and age dulls the survival instinct.

One policeman said of Gangitano: 'He was not wealthy and good criminals dropped off him because he attracted trouble and police interest. The elite use crime to make money. Alphonse wanted to be seen as a crime boss, but at the end of the day he was just another thug with a bad temper.'

Form No. **260**

# CRIMINAL HISTORY SHEET

?1337/80—P364

Fingerprint—Records Section,
Information Bureau,
Police Headquarters,    JMP
Melbourne

| Fingerprint Classification | 25/4 Cr/Ct O1O/O11 22/12+ Temp1Class. | Date 16th February, 1982 |
|---|---|---|

Photo
Book Numbers....VSP.FSL.80/801.

| I.B.R. No. ..T.G.625..... | Docket No. ..663/81. | Gaol No. |
|---|---|---|

Date of birth 22.4.1957    Record of Convictions against   GANGITANO: Alphonse John

@ Alphonse Gagitano @Al Granger @ Alphonse.John.Ganuitano.@.Alfons.John.Gangitano.

| Court | | Date | | Offence | Sentence |
|---|---|---|---|---|---|
| VICTORIA, Malvern (Print) | M.C. | 2 | 4 76 | Offensive Behaviour. | Adjourned 12 months on $50 G.B.Bond as Alphonse John Gangitano. |
| Heidelberg (N/Print) | M.C. | 9 | 11 76 | Insulting words. | $30 def. days.as Alphonse John Gangitano. |
| Prahran (N/Print) | M.C. | 30 | 1 81 | Unlawful Assault. Wilful Damage. | $150 with $30 costs def. 9 days. $50 def.2days.as Alphonse John Gangitano. |
| Melbourne (Print) | M.C. | 5 | 3 81 | Unlawful Possession. | $200 def.7 days.as Alphonse John Gangitano. |
| Melbourne | M.C. | 3 | 4 81 | Assault(3 charges). Asslt.by kicking. Assault in company. (2 charges). Resist Arrest. Hinder Police(2 charges). ) | All charges Dismissed.as Alphonse John Gangitano. |
| Melbourne County Court | | 2 | 11 83 | Affray. Assault Occasioning Actual Bodily ( 7 counts). Assault Police (3 counts). ) | All counts Acquitted.as Alphonse John Gangitano. |
| Melbourne County | | 13 | 6 84 | Affray. Assault occasioning actual bodily harm. Assault police. Resist arrest. ) | All counts Nolle Prosequi entered by Director of Public Prosecutions as Alphonse John Gangitano. |
| Melbourne | M.C. | 13 | 12 84 | Drunk. Indecent Language. ) Offensive Behaviour. Threatening words. | Dismissed. $250 default 5 days on each charge. Withdrawn.as Alphonse John Gangitano. |

46

# Friday

## Trick or treat in a dead-end street?

*Like many 40-year-olds with children,
he still required a mortgage.*

BIG Al was happy. He was going home to his new house in Templestowe after a day in court, and for the first time in four years he could see past the annoying charges that had helped erode his standing as a feared crime figure.

His lawyers had told him that the first day of his committal at the Melbourne Magistrates' Court on charges of affray and assault had gone well, and that made him relaxed. He was now confident of a good result, and the court proceedings themselves held no fears for him. After all, he had been in and out of courts since he was a teenager and had an astonishing record of beating charges ranging from illegal possession of a firearm to murder.

This, he hoped, would soon fade into just another inconvenience. He would soon be free to go back on the city streets he treated as his fiefdom.

Bail conditions had stopped him being out after 9pm, making it hard to do what he did best – cutting an intimidating figure around nightclubs.

To the man known to the system as Alphonse John Gangitano,

sitting in the dock listening to police and witnesses describe him as an organised crime figure and a violent gangster was an occupational hazard. In fact, he had come to enjoy the notoriety.

Not that he was pleased with his constant legal problems. Only a day earlier he had confided to his friend, Bail Justice Rowena Allsop, that he wanted the committal to be over as quickly as possible because he was worried about mounting legal bills. Legal Aid rarely defends clients in Zegna suits.

Gangitano was dropped home by his long-time driver, Santo, on that Friday afternoon, 16 January, 1998. Walking down the sloping drive to the front door of the house in Glen Orchard Close that he'd bought six months earlier, he could see three of the four security cameras he'd installed as soon as he moved in.

The system was set up to cover the front of the house, the back, the drive and the street. In the front garden were the foundations for the big brick fence he had ordered built to deter prying eyes. It would have been the only front fence on his side of the road. A security intercom had also been put in.

Gangitano's home was not the best of the twenty-seven houses in the dead-end street, but it suited his purposes best. On the low side of the street, on a sweeping left-hand bend, it was perfectly placed for a man who wished to know who was coming and going in the neighbourhood.

The double-storey brick, thirty-square home was built on a sloping block, and so the downstairs rooms and the front door could not be watched from any distance. But the upstairs windows faced the street, giving the householder a perfect view of the road to the corner – and of anyone entering the area.

The houses were built in the 1980s in what real estate agents describe as a 'highly sought-after cul-de-sac'. Lawns, bulbs, silver birches, small shrubs and open gardens are the style of the street.

There were few places where unwelcome observers, or a gunman, could hide.

Gangitano, who bought the property in late 1997, wanted a secure house in a no-through road to foil police raids and surveillance. He had been the subject of much interest from the National Crime Authority, the Federal Police and the organised crime, drug, racing, gaming and vice squads of the Victoria Police. That was why he wanted a house that could protect him from police. Ironically, however, the greatest threat probably came from someone close. From someone he trusted, on his own side of the law.

There were other ironies. Such as the fact he'd bought the house, not from the proceeds of organised crime, but from the sale of his deceased parents' Eaglemont home. Like most 40-year-olds with children, he still required a mortgage.

The house was comfortable without being opulent. But upstairs in the walk-in robe were up to thirty suits, leather jackets and expensive fashion accessories. If he was having money troubles, it didn't show in his clothes.

One of Gangitano's favourite rooms was the study. Books on the shelves included one on Al Capone. On the walls were pictures from his days as an influential figure in the fight game – one of Melbourne boxer Lester Ellis, a framed poster of the 'Raging Bull', Jake La Motta, and a famous photo of the most famous of them all, Muhammad Ali, standing over the prone body of Sonny Liston.

If Gangitano had studied the Ali-Liston photograph carefully he might have learned a valuable lesson. Liston was the biggest and baddest of his time, seemingly unbeatable. But when his powers waned he was manipulated by others and finally died in sordid circumstances probably linked to organised crime.

WHEN Gangitano came home he was alone. His de facto wife, Virginia, and their children, had gone to her sister's St Kilda home about 1pm that afternoon.

He removed his expensive, imported grey suit and draped it over the banister before going upstairs for a sleep. Even though he was on a court-designated curfew, he maintained his nocturnal habits of sleeping during the day.

The sort of business that Gangitano specialised in required night work. For more than a decade he was regularly sighted in gambling dens and the nightspots of Lygon and King streets.

From the early 1980s he had stood over some nightclubs and had needed to be seen to maintain a brooding, violent presence to encourage prompt payments.

But after twenty two years in the crime world, Gangitano was under pressure. The impulsive, charismatic and violent gangster was a police magnet. His high public profile made him a target and he was having trouble distinguishing friends from enemies, a weakness that can be deadlier than most diseases.

Police views on Gangitano varied greatly. Some saw him as a big organised crime figure. Others saw him as a self-inflated street thug and a parody of a gangster. All agreed he was a pain in the neck.

Predictably, perhaps, Gangitano's relatives were – and still are – furious at the media picture of him as a violent crime figure with probable drug connections. They claim he was anti-drugs and 'would go ballistic' at the thought of anyone close to his family becoming involved.

They acknowledge he was a criminal. Illegal gambler? Yes. Standover man? Yes. Killer? Perhaps. But drug dealer? Certainly not. It is, of course, a common refrain among criminals and their supporters, who like to flatter themselves and persuade others that what they do is excusable. Or, at least, not as bad as what others do.

In the 1990s, Victoria moved from the wowser state to embracing gambling, from small-time slot machines to 'high roller' rooms in the massive Crown Casino complex. For decades politicians had failed to give police strong laws to let them to seize illegal poker machines and close known gambling dens, but when the Government decided it wanted a slice of the gaming action it suddenly found the spine to introduce new laws that wiped out large sections of the illegal industry almost overnight.

The Government's move to take over traditional racketeer territory eroded Gangitano's financial base. At the same time, police investigations also began to cut into his protection business. He described himself as a 'property developer' in court documents and in his will as a 'gentleman'. His only legitimate income came from renting a Lygon Street property that had been owned by his parents and was now shared with his sister.

Certainly Gangitano was under huge financial pressure. He was paying lawyers hundreds of thousands of dollars a year. He even flew one lawyer overseas to take a statement from a potentially damaging witness.

In a sense, he was trapped by his carefully-crafted image as a mobster. He saw no choice other than to act in the same violent way he had all his adult life.

Gangitano's murder of Gregory John Workman after a drunken argument at a party in 1995 brought him under the greatest pressure of his life. If he believed he was above the law he was to learn otherwise the hard way. He had to pay to have two star witnesses move overseas and, meanwhile, many of his associates moved to distance themselves from the loose cannon of Lygon Street.

He was, by the New Year of 1998, dangerously exposed and running out of friends. But he wasn't losing any sleep over it on the Friday afternoon. Just after 3.30pm he headed upstairs to the main bedroom. It was a pleasant day outside, with the temperature about 23 degrees. But upstairs it was warm enough that he turned on the fan near the bed before dozing off.

SIX hours later Gangitano woke and went downstairs. The telephone rang. It was Tony, an old friend from Brunswick, who wanted to know how his case was going. 'He said he was confident ... he was in good spirits and was joking,' Tony was to say later.

As they chatted, the telephone beeped to indicate a second call coming through. It was Virginia, saying she would be home in around an hour.

He took two more calls, one from a Victorian criminal and one from a well-known criminal associate in Perth.

If anything was worrying Alphonse he didn't let on over the telephone. But, according to associates, he rarely spoke at length, believing the line and his house were bugged by police. He would always go outside if he wanted to say anything he wanted to remain confidential.

Few of his criminal associates were welcome at Alphonse's home. One of his closest criminal lieutenants was to claim he didn't even know where Gangitano lived, and it was made clear that business and family were to remain separate worlds.

'He always tried to insulate Virginia and the children,' an associate said.

Virginia knew he was a criminal but he never spoke to her of how he made his money. She was given weekly housekeeping and the job of caring for the children and the home. Difficult questions weren't encouraged.

Those who knew Virginia say she was anything but a gangster's moll. She had met Alphonse twenty-three years earlier when she was only sixteen and he was a big teenager who was quick with his fists. She had seen him grow from a loud schoolboy lout into a handsome and recognised gangster. They had lived together for fifteen years.

Fair-haired, attractive and devoted to her children, the well-educated product of Genazzano Catholic College, whose friends included at least one policeman's wife, had long ago decided to stick with the man she had loved from schooldays.

Despite her man's desire to keep business and family apart, at least one old friend felt free to visit late at night, apparently without invitation.

Graham Allen Kinniburgh, a trusted confidant of Gangitano, had excited police curiosity for at least three decades. To them, the older, experienced Kinniburgh and the younger, more excitable Gangitano made an odd couple.

Kinniburgh, then 56, stayed in the shadows while Gangitano enjoyed the limelight. The older man dressed in staid, middle-of-the-road casual clothes while the younger preferred designer suits.

Gangitano had a reputation as a hothead who could become violent at the wrong times, often leaving his lawyers to try to clean up the mess. Kinniburgh was far more controlled, although as a younger man he could flare up, and had once broken a policeman's nose. But he had matured into a man who saw that no-one profited from pub brawls and fist fights.

Kinniburgh lives in a prestigious part of Kew and has clearly been successful at his chosen occupation. What that occupation is remains a mystery. Why he was dubbed 'The Munster' is also unknown.

Like many successful people, Kinniburgh is admirably security conscious. His double-storey house is protected by video cameras and his privacy ensured with a high brick fence.

But on the Friday night in question Kinniburgh tore himself away from the considerable comforts of his own home. He had a few drinks with an associate – and fellow friend of Gangitano's – called Lou

Cozzo, at the Laurel Hotel in Mt Alexander Road, Moonee Ponds. Some time after 10pm he left the hotel and, instead of driving home, he went further east, to Templestowe, to visit his friend.

Kinniburgh said later that when he arrived, around 10.50pm, Gangitano told him he was about to meet someone and asked the older man to make himself scarce for a while.

Kinniburgh decided to go off to the local shop to get a packet of Benson & Hedges cigarettes. The Quix convenience store in Blackburn Road is 800m from Gangitano's home, less than two minutes' drive away, yet Kinniburgh was to claim he was gone for thirty.

ALPHONSE Gangitano sat at the small, round kitchen table facing the hallway. It was a sensible spot for a man expecting visitors, whether enemies or friends.

By moving his head slightly to the left he could look down to the front entrance. In summer he would keep the front door open but the security mesh door locked. The mesh was sensibly designed so you could see out but not into the house.

Alphonse had been out of bed for more than an hour, but with the temperature around eighteen degrees at 11pm he hadn't bothered to get dressed and remained in his blue underpants.

Whoever arrived at the house late that night must have been well-known to Alphonse. He would have seen him and opened the door of his own accord. And, whoever it was, the host was relaxed enough to stay in his underpants when his guest arrived. Alphonse sat back at the kitchen table.

What happened next is a matter of some conjecture. But one certainty is that the visitor suddenly pulled a gun.

One theory is the killer, a trusted friend of the victim, went to the house with a plan to murder him as part of a cold-blooded gangland execution devised with the blessing of others.

But there is a strong suggestion that the killer was a subordinate of the crime figure, a soldier Gangitano felt had ambitions to be a general, and that they had a fatal argument.

Observers had noticed a cooling in the two men's once close relationship, even though they had been seen shaking hands earlier that day. Like Gangitano, the visitor, aged about 40, was known as a hot head who, when pushed, would pull a gun and use it without heeding the consequences. In which case there were two loose cannons in the kitchen, but only one had a gun.

Alphonse realised too late that he'd lost control. He jumped up and ran a few metres towards the laundry as the gunman fired. He could not get a gun – repeated police raids meant he would not risk hiding a firearm at his home. His only chance was to escape through the laundry door, but there was a slight problem. It was blocked by the family clothes horse.

It was just what the gunman needed. His first shot missed, but the second wounded his victim. It was easy to finish him off. He showed the same measure of mercy that Gangitano had shown his own victims for twenty years.

ABOUT one minute before Kinniburgh walked into the Quix store, Gangitano's partner Virginia happened to walk into the same shop to buy ice creams for the children. Two security cameras, the size of cigarette packets, sat blinking in the shop. One faced the counter, the second pointed towards the door.

Security tapes from the cameras confirmed that Virginia and Kinniburgh were in the store making their separate purchases.

Police believe the two may well have driven past each other. It is not known if Kinniburgh recognised the Gangitano family's burgundy Telstra sedan as they passed in the night.

As Virginia turned into Glen Orchard Close and neared home she saw a car with square headlights complete a U-turn and cruise slowly away.

As she swung into the driveway and opened the remote-controlled double garage door, she noticed the front sensor light was on, indicating someone, or something, had passed within the previous forty seconds.

The children raced to the front door, but the heavy mesh security door was locked. They rang the bell, waiting for their father to let them in.

Virginia opened the door with her keys. She found her children's father lying face down. She saw the blood and the wounds and realised he had been shot, but because his body was still warm she had a desperate hope that he could be revived.

She ran to the phone and called the emergency number to get an ambulance. Just then, Kinniburgh arrived from his thirty-minute trip to fetch cigarettes.

He tried to roll the big man over to administer first aid, failing at first because of his bulk, but finally shifting him. Virginia remained calm, passing on instructions from the operator to Kinniburgh to clear the patient's airway while an ambulance was despatched.

Ambulance tapes clearly record the anguished mother trying to keep her children away from the horrible sight of their father in the laundry while relaying the first-aid instructions.

But the best surgeons in the world could not have saved him. He had bled to death.

MANY of the men police hoped could shed some light on what happened on that warm night in Templestowe have remained silent.

A close friend who has told anyone who will listen that he misses 'Big Al' and that he would love to know what happened, turned up at the homicide squad, freshly showered and with a top criminal lawyer in tow.

He refused to answer any questions.

Graham Kinniburgh also refused to answer police questions, adopting a code of silence he must have learned when he associated with painters and dockers long before he moved to leafy Kew.

Hundreds of people, many with colourful criminal histories, have been interviewed by police, Many have expressed anger, grief and sorrow for the death of their old friend. Few have provided facts.

Some tried to suggest police may have murdered Gangitano, but there is no evidence to back the theory. As a criminal figure Gangitano was on the way out, and he went out ... feet first. Forty-year-old street thugs are a dying breed. Alphonse proved it.

Gangitano would never have opened the door to police unless they had a search warrant, and none had been drawn. Any policeman contemplating turning killer would have known the house may have been bugged or under surveillance by another law enforcement body.

Pages and pages of death notices appeared in the *Herald Sun,*

newspaper of choice for the criminal classes, who supply many of the
lucrative massage parlor advertisements that once belonged to *Truth*
newspaper. Many were placed by the vaguest of associates and vicari-
ous hangers-on who wanted to be connected, no matter how
tenuously, to a Melbourne crime event.

Nine months after the murder police offered a $50,000 government
approved reward for the arrest and conviction of the people responsible for Gangitano's murder. Detective Inspector Dave Reid of the
homicide squad said that in the circles that Big Al frequented, greed
could prove to be a more powerful motivator than comunity spirit. 'It
is a lot of money for not a great deal of work,' he said.

Chief investigator in the case, Detective Senior Sergeant Charlie
Bezzina, said police were more advanced than many believed. Clearly
police were satisified they had established the identity of the gunman.

But knowing, and proving can be a world apart.

Usually, after a crime figure is murdered, some form of underworld
revenge is expected. But, following Gangitano's death, there has been
a peaceful silence.

It is as if both his friends and enemies have decided he died of
natural causes.

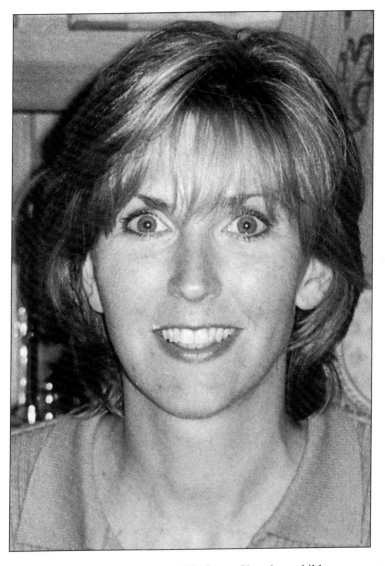

Jane Thurgood-Dove ... shot dead in front of her three children.
The Victorian Premier Jeff Kennett personally intervened to double
the reward to $100,000 to solve the case.

Suspect … a police computer image of the getaway driver in the
Thurgood-Dove murder.

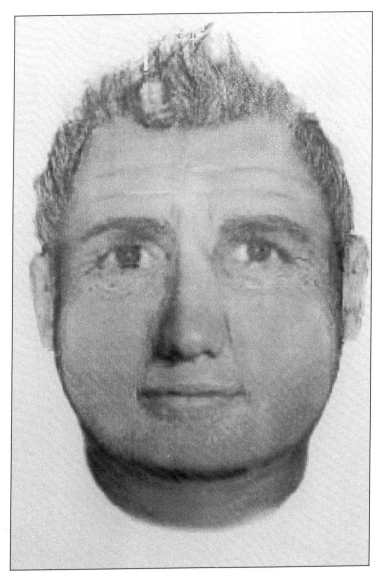

Pot-bellied killer ... the man who chased Jane Thurgood-Dove
around her car before shooting her in front of her children.

Australia's worst rail disaster … Granville, 1977.

83 dead, 213 injured … and looters stole tools from the rescue trucks.

Ron Williams … a battler taken in by a cold-blooded killer.

Alex MacDonald … murdered Williams to take his identity.

The Commonwealth Bank at Port Douglas … MacDonald's hostage plan failed for the strangest reason.

The Chinese Vice Premier, Zhu Rongji, enjoyed Port Douglas.

Armed robber's kit … number plates, cash and pain killers.

The cool cat in the hat … Alex MacDonald, wearing his distinctive hat, robs Airlie Beach bank in Queensland.

Derek Ernest Percy … bad, but not mad.

Yvonne Tuohy was murdered as a man called Armstrong was about to walk on the moon.

Shane Spiller … took on a killer with his tomahawk, but it wasn't enough to save his friend.

Shane Spiller as a little boy … a killer stole his childhood and blighted his life.

Kathleen Downes ... stabbed to death in a nursing home. Her killer has never been found.

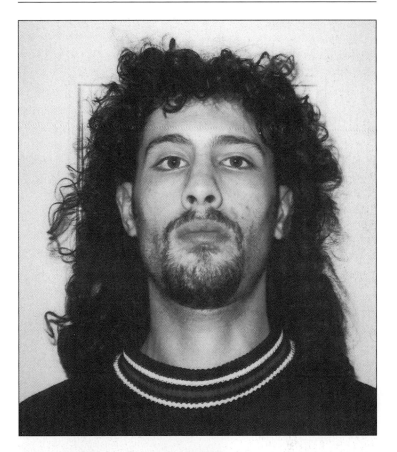

Hussein Issa (above) … drug dealer and idiot. Captured on a secret video trying to bribe police. It didn't work. He went to jail.

Rocky Iaria … buried twice, six years apart.

# CHAPTER 5

# A week later

## Burying the Black Prince of Lygon Street

*'He is one of the few criminals in Australian history to be known simply by his first name.'*

OUTSIDE, the Mercedes and BMW coupes circle in the afternoon sun like sharks, cruising for parking spots among shoals of lesser vehicles jamming the usually quiet streets in West Melbourne. They're late models in dark colors, mostly black or midnight blue, and run to sharp personal number plates and mobile phone aerials tilted rakishly, like dorsal fins on sharks.

The whiff of menace and money – fat rolls of cash money – wafts from the drivers, their hard faces blank as they join the silent crowd gathered at the church door next to a big, black Cadillac hearse parked near a pile of wreaths banked against the bluestone wall.

Not everyone here is a big shot and many mourners are clearly not from Melbourne's underworld, but they dress the part. There's a generic quality about the gathering that strikes a watcher.

There are men old enough to be grandfathers who move confidently through the crowd, escorted by young blonde women who are not their grand-daughters.

There are young men, with their hair cropped short, tied back in tight pony-tails or slicked back, hard and shiny. They mostly wear dark suits, gold jewellery, lightweight slip-on shoes and sunglasses. Many are heavily muscled, with the bulk that comes from weight-lifting, and perhaps steroids. They tend to favor permanent scowls, and would look at home on nightclub doors, as some no doubt do. If they don't smoke, they chew gum. Some do both.

One hardboiled character dragging on a borrowed Winfield has on the compulsory dark suit, but with fawn slip-on suede loafers. He wears no socks, but it doesn't matter much. His ankles are tattooed almost solid blue and green.

Across the street, marooned on a traffic island, the cameras of the media contingent are trained on the crowd. Those who hold the equipment keep their distance, perhaps remembering the ugly scenes at the funeral of Robert 'Aussie Bob' Trimbole in Sydney in the 1980s, when angry mourners attacked cameramen and journalists.

This is the scene at St Mary's By The Sea Catholic church around 1.15pm on Friday, 23 January, 1998, as the minutes crawl towards the start of a funeral service for a man who died a week earlier the way he had lived: violently and fast.

His name is, or was, Alphonse John Gangitano, and he is one of the few criminals in Australian history to be known – even by people he'd never met – simply by his first name. Like Squizzy. Like Chopper. Like Neddy.

Alphonse, also known as Al, was shot several times in the laundry of his Templestowe home by an assassin still officially unknown, and likely to remain so, but who must have been well known to his victim.

An assassin trusted enough, it would appear, that he was let into the house unchallenged before he produced a weapon and squeezed the trigger at close range.

Many of the details of the shooting are a mystery. So is the question of how a boastful schoolyard bully, who left school more than twenty years ago with nothing more useful than a bad reputation, managed to support himself and his family in relative luxury most of his adult life.

Gangitano often claimed he was a 'property developer', but that was probably just another example of the mischievous sense of humour his friends and supporters claim for him, exemplified by the fulsome praise heaped on him by one of his more unusual friends, bail justice Rowena Allsop, who addressed the packed church at the funeral. Ms Allsop, who has been heavily criticised for her close association with Gangitano, was asked to speak by the dead man's family. She delivered a ringing tribute in which she compared his wit with Oscar Wilde's, gushed about his silk ties, cashmere overcoats and 'the lingering scent' of his aftershave, and noted his consuming interest in John F. Kennedy and Napoleon.

She said her friend had been 'like a king commanding a court, with his friends laughing at his old jokes'. She said she was touched by him turning up at the Children's Hospital last Christmas with a bag of toys for the children in the cancer ward.

Others, however, detected a darker side to Gangitano's gregarious character. He might well have developed properties, they say. And no doubt he sometimes arranged for holes to be dug – but not always to pour foundations.

If the man in the coffin wasn't a gangster, he acted like one. And he was certainly buried like one.

A fitting exit, some might say, for the Black Prince of Lygon Street.

MELBOURNE is Australia's Chicago, but with a touch of London's old East End 'manor' tradition about it. A tradition of almost feudal loyalty to local 'crime lords' going back to the solidarity of the old working class inner suburbs in John Wren and Squizzy Taylor's day.

Unlike the criminal subculture in other cities, Melbourne's underworld has a tradition of big occasion funerals, preceded by an avalanche of newspaper death notices. Many of these are effusive and ostentatiously long, implying that money is no object. Some are 'crocodile tears'. A few are downright tongue-in-cheek, and contain coded jokes and messages.

Police searching for clues to gangland slayings are known to comb the death notices carefully. Indeed, some are rumoured to write the occasional contribution themselves. Gangitano wasn't the only one with a mischievous sense of humor. One notice read 'The impression you left on me will stay eternally in my heart. Jim Pinarkos.'

Pinarkos' headless body was found at Rye beach in July 1989. He died from an arrow through his heart. The murder was never solved.

Whatever the reasons, Gangitano's farewell was one of the biggest underworld funerals in Melbourne since the murder of master bank robber Raymond (Chuck) Bennett in the magistrate's court in 1979 and of Bennett's arch enemy, the notorious gunman Brian Kane, in a Brunswick hotel some time later.

The ritual ran over a week, starting with twenty two death notices for Gangitano in the underworld's favourite newspaper, the *Herald Sun*, on the Monday after the murder.

The number of notices more than doubled to forty eight on Tuesday, led by a joint tribute from Gangitano's widow and their daughters, and his sister Nuccia, and including several from prominent underworld figures.

It peaked on Wednesday, with sixty eight notices, including one from Charlie Wootton, a reclusive but well-known and much-respected gaming identity whose past links him with the blood-spattered history of the painters and dockers union.

As a teenager in the 1950s, Wootton reputedly disposed of the empty shotgun shells left when an 'unknown' gunman shot Freddy 'The Frog' Harrison on the wharves.

Dozens of men saw the Frog get croaked, the legend goes, but it was never officially solved. Like the others, young Charlie Wootton developed amnesia, a condition that still affects police investigations today, including this one.

In the seven days before his burial there had been two hundred and nine death notices for Gangitano. This was a bonanza for Rupert Murdoch's classified advertising coffers – and a measure of the generous underworld protocol that makes a hero of a man dismissed by some as a thug who didn't have the brains to be a 'Mr Big'.

Criminal groupies who hardly knew the dead man put notices in the paper as though they were great friends. But columns of newsprint aren't the only measure of Gangitano's posthumous popularity. At least eight hundred people, and possibly a thousand, turned up to the funeral service, filling the church and spilling outside.

So why the big deal?

One reason could be that Gangitano was, in his own way, a 'crossover' criminal. He was from a respectable Italian family – not one, according to police sources, that automatically connected him with organised crime from birth, as with some Calabrian and Sicilian peasant clans for whom kidnapping, extortion and violence are facts of life. He went to school with other middle-class boys, and could just as easily have become a lawyer or an accountant if he'd studied, which he didn't. Schoolmates recall that he was always aggressive, but that his father was outraged when he secretly tattooed his arms, and forced him to have skin grafts to remove them. When forced to leave Marcellin College, he did his last year of school at Taylors' College. Classmates there remember that even then, he was lazy, manipulative, on the make and constantly accompanied by the first member of what was to become his gang.

The picture that emerges is of an egotistical young bully whose nature made him gravitate towards a life of crime. His charm and his looks attracted attention. So did his vanity and appetite for extreme violence, especially when the odds were in his favor.

But whereas more traditional Italian organised crime figures kept largely to their own, the more urbane Gangitano slipped easily between the Calabrian and Sicilian crime syndicates, other ethnic crime groups, and mainstream Australian criminals connected with the painters and dockers union. In the end, this willingness to deal with all comers might be what got him killed.

A former associate from the boxing world – who did not attend the funeral because of a violent disagreement many years ago – recalls being present when Gangitano spoke at length to the notorious Sydney standover man Tom Domican, with whom he evidently had a warm relationship.

Others describe Gangitano's links with one of Perth's heaviest criminals, the convicted heroin trafficker John Kizon, named recently in connection with the late Laurie Connell, millionaire race-fixer and the most ruthless of the 'WA Inc' corporate robber barons.

Domican and Kizon were reportedly among several interstate criminals who flew to Melbourne to attend Gangitano's funeral. They were joined, rumor has it, by an Asian contact who counted Gangitano a close-enough friend to travel to Australia for the service.

In his private life, Gangitano was unlike the strictly-controlled members of the traditional Italian groups, where marriages are often organised, often between distant relatives from the same region in Italy. He did not marry, but lived with Virginia, a private school girl who was not Italian. Her sister, Fiona, a handsome and distinguished-looking woman, added a touch of class to the proceedings by giving one of the readings during the service.

But, for all his wide-ranging contacts, Gangitano was best-known and – at least on the surface – most admired in Melbourne's little Italy, Lygon Street.

There, according to one of the many death notices placed by people who had met him, he was 'an icon' in certain sections of the community.

All of which has a bearing on the huge turn-up at his funeral. It seems St Mary's By The Sea in West Melbourne, close to the Victoria Market, is the church of choice for Melbourne's mafia.

It was a case of history repeating itself. Hairstyles, hemlines and cars change, but among the older people in the congregation were some who have attended more than one big mafia funeral there.

When one of Victoria's earliest godfathers, Domenico 'the Pope' Italiano, died in 1962 he was buried from St Mary's. So were Vincenzo Muratore and Vincenzo Agillette, killed little more than a year later in the power struggle caused by Italiano's death.

They were all given elaborate funerals, early proof of the potency and loyalty of the Italian organised crime groups that had taken control of Melbourne's fruit and vegetable markets.

But none was more elaborate than Gangitano's. From the taped music to the singing of *Ave Maria* by his friend, Simon Pantano, it was a lavish production from start to end.

Of course, not everyone present was in mourning. Apart from a core of family and close friends, the crowd comprised mostly those who felt obliged to be there, and hangers-on attracted by the publicity.

One reason for the big crowd, joked a well-known criminal lawyer afterwards, was the number of undercover police there to execute outstanding warrants on elusive criminals drawn from cover for the occasion. Another, he said, was the number of lawyers trying to collect overdue fees for court appearances for some of the colorful identities in the congregation.

A former detective who first ran against the young Gangitano in nightclubs in the early 1980s, and was respected by him, injects a sombre note.

'I hope a war doesn't go on over this, because the biggest losers are their kids,' he says. 'I have seen the toughest men, but all their lives consist of are a series of battles with the law and with their criminal counterparts. No kid deserves to have their father taken away like this.

'But it's happened to Alphonse's kids, and now there's probably someone out there scheming to kill some other kids' father.'

So, whodunnit? There were rumors. That the Albanians did it. That the Lebanese did it. That the Lebanese rumor was started by someone wanting to cover the real killer's tracks. That it was an inside job, performed with the blessing of people close to him. Any, or none, of these theories could be correct, although the smart money is on the inside job.

Rumors spread at the funeral that the mystery man who was at the house the night Gangitano was killed was a criminal well-known on racetracks. And he wasn't the only visitor Gangitano had that night.

Police have their job cut out to sort the red hot from the red herrings.

A cryptic message from a well-informed underworld source says the shooting granted the dying wish of an old man ... and that the process of spreading disinformation about who and why it was done began 'before the gun was chosen'.

A postscript. In August, 1992, another man called Al – Alfonso Muratore – was shot dead outside his Hampton home, twenty eight years after his father Vincenzo was shot outside his house in the same way, less than a kilometre away.

Afterwards, a potential witness told police why he couldn't co-operate with them. 'You can put me in jail,' he said, 'but they can give me the death sentence.'

Nothing's changed since then.

IN THE SUPREME COURT OF VICTORIA
IN ITS PROBATE JURISDICTION

1144772 ℞

1998 No.

In the matter of the Will of **Alphonse Alfred John Gangitano** deceased

Application by:

Virginia

Plaintiff

ORIGINATING MOTION FOR A GRANT OF PROBATE MAY 1938

Date of document:
Filed on behalf of the Plaintiff
Perillo, Adami & Frank                    Solicitor's Code: 467
Solicitors              -8 MAY 1938         DX 81105 Footscray
209 Nicholson Street                          Tel: 9687 3384
FOOTSCRAY 3011                            Ref: V. Adami 980043

**This is an application by the abovenamed Plaintiff for the grant by this Honourable Court of probate of the Will dated 20th May, 1993 of the abovenamed deceased.**

Particulars of this application are as follows: OVER

(1)   *of the deceased*

Surname:                 Gangitano
Given Names:             Alphonse Alfred John
In the will called:      As Above
Last residential address:    Glen Orchard Close,
                             Templestowe, Victoria, 3106
Last known occupation:   Gentleman
Date and place of birth: 22nd April, 1957
                         at Fitzroy, Victoria 3065
Date and place of death: 16th January, 1998 at
                         Templestowe, Victoria 3106

(2)   *of the plaintiff*   WAS found dead on

Surname:
Given Names:             Virginia
In the will called:      As above
Residential address:     Glen Orchard Close
                         Templestowe, Victoria 3106
Occupation:              Home Duties
Relationship to deceased: Defacto wife

**This application is made by the Plaintiff as the Executrix appointed in the Will of the deceased.**

. . . *Perillo, Adami + Frank* . . . . . .
PERILLO, ADAMI & FRANK
Solicitors for the Plaintiff

# CHAPTER 6

# Jaidyn's world

## Broken hearts and stunted dreams

*'She was only thirteen,
but she had big norks'*

WHERE does it really begin and end, the pathetic story of Jaidyn Leskie? Not when he's born, although the portents are ominous enough: the birth is the week of the Port Arthur massacre.

Not the night he disappears from a house in Moe in June, 1997, starting a search that runs longer than the one for a prime minister thirty years before.

Not when the tiny body floats to the surface of a lake on New Year's Day, 1998. Nor when the sordid squabble over where – or whether – to bury the remains is settled, so he can be laid to rest at last.

The truth, elusive in all this, is that the black farce played out for more than six months was only the public part of a story that started long ago, and which isn't finished yet. It is not only the story of a battered baby, but of where he came from ... from a place of broken families and broken hearts, shattered trust and stunted dreams.

It's an ugly soap opera with real blood and real bruises. It's a tragedy, a morality tale, and a love story gone wrong. Like all dramas, it turns on sex, betrayal and death. It goes something like this ...

IT'S the late 1960s. She is the policeman's daughter in a mountain town in far East Gippsland. He works in the timber mill, the district's only industry apart from sheep and cattle. If it's not love, it's near enough, even if her parents aren't too keen on the idea.

Which is how Pam ('don't use my maiden name, for my dad's sake') comes to be married at nineteen in the old Presbyterian church in the main, and only, street of Swift's Creek in 1970.

Despite the rumors, she is not pregnant. It's not until nearly two years later, in the Omeo hospital, that she has her first child. They call her Katie.

Married life is fine – for a while. To hear Pam tell it, as soon as she's pregnant, her man chases women, drinks, and belts her. 'I ran into that many cupboards and brooms,' she laughs mirthlessly twenty-five years later. 'Once I told the truth about how I got a black eye, and nobody believed me. Even his own mother told me to get out. She'd put up with the same thing for ten years herself.'

Between drinking and fighting, there are reconciliations. Bilynda is born three years after Katie, at Bairnsdale. Then comes a son, Glenn. But babies don't make it better, nor does the first of many shifts – this one to Myrtleford in 1977.

There, he goes to work in the bush at 3am on Mondays, returns on Friday nights. She dreads weekends. One Monday she hires a van and flees to a family friend at Mooroopna, then rents a house in Bendigo. He finds her, begs forgiveness, promises to give up drinking. He does – for six weeks.

She works in a motel at night. He works on her best friend, an amorous alcoholic with plenty of kids and no man. Katie, now eight, one day asks why Daddy was in bed with Aunty B. It's a tough question. Pam answers it by dumping all his gear on her ex-friend's doorstep, including his guns. Aunty B. doesn't like guns 'because her father shot himself', Pam is to recall with grim pleasure. 'I told her, "if you want him so bad, then you can have his stuff, guns 'n' all".'

Pam is to leave her husband three more times. The last time is a month before her tenth wedding anniversary. Her father moves her to Lakes Entrance, warns her that if she ever takes the bastard back, he'll never talk to her again. This time, she listens.

But, seventeen years on, she pays her children's father ('I call him the sperm donor, not my husband') a grudging compliment. 'He did some awful things,' she says, 'but I will say he always had a job. Still has.'

She doesn't add that it's more than can be said for her three children, or most of those that hang around them. She doesn't have to. It's a fact of life. In her world, they learn the facts of life early. All of them.

KATIE renames herself Kadee around the time she first leaves home. She's fourteen, a rebel, and stays seven weeks with friends, then goes home because 'Mum would buy me smokes, and the other people wouldn't'. This is after they've returned to Myrtleford, the fifth of fifteen moves in twenty years.

Kadee turns fifteen around the time they move to Heyfield. She leaves Maffra High School in year nine, bolts to another town and lands 'the second best job I've ever had', in an old people's home: 'I got $75 a fortnight and thought I was rich.' It lasts nine weeks. Until the day (she says) her boss argued with Kadee's grandmother on the golf course. Arguing seems to run in the family.

Kadee's favourite job is sorting rubbish in a recycler's yard, but that does not last long, either. In fact, the most constant thing in her life is the social security payments. They've been far more reliable than most of her men. Which is where the family's recent troubles really start.

Kadee is sixteen when she leaves home for the second time. She takes the train from Nathalia, her mother's eighth home in as many years, to Moe, where she'd met a girl on a previous visit. 'Everything I owned was at my feet,' she says, 'and I had nowhere to go.' She finds the girl, and arranges to stay in her flat. Three nights later they go to a party, armed with a flask of Jim Beam.

'We spotted three guys. Gave them marks out of ten. One was gorgeous, and we gave him bonus points because his fly was undone. Another got seven, but he was married.' They give only three points to the third ('he was feral') but when Kadee goes outside later, he follows and chats to her. His name is Brett Leskie. They spend that night and next day in the flat.

Two days later he dumps her. A week later she gets back with him, takes him to Nathalia on the train to see her mother, flaunts her independence by sleeping with him on the couch. Pam doesn't like the sixteen-year-old Brett ('I thought he was a selfish little mongrel'), and, naturally, that's enough to make Kadee want to keep him. Pam notices him looking over Kadee's kid sister, Bilynda. 'She was only thirteen, but she had big norks,' is her summary of the situation.

The pair go back to the La Trobe Valley. Kadee moves in with the Leskies, then share-farming at Yallourn North. She pays $25 a fortnight board, helps milk the cows four nights a week and Sunday mornings. She and Brett draw the 'de facto dole' because it's bigger.

It's a wonder it lasts five months. After the split, Kadee moves in with 'a big-time junkie' in Moe who beats her up, then she goes back to her mother at Nathalia. They move to Moruya, in New South Wales, where Pam later has the stroke that paralyses her down one side and puts her in hospital for months. After three weeks, Kadee gets itchy feet and goes to Lakes Entrance.

She runs into Brett Leskie at the local speedway car races, spends two nights with him at the caravan park where she's living. 'I tried like mad to get pregnant to him,' she says, 'because then I thought he'd have to stay with me.' He leaves. She doesn't see him for eighteen months.

A few weeks later, she does get pregnant – to a drug addict who doesn't know about the baby boy born later, in late 1991, back in Moruya. They all move to Sale: Pam, Bilynda, brother Glenn, Kadee and baby Harley. They stay with friends. It doesn't work. How could it?

While in Sale, Kadee chances on Brett in the street. He looks at the baby. She doesn't tell him it's not his. Later, he comes around. It's pension day. Kadee buys a bottle of rum for the occasion: 'I thought if we get pissed and get back on together, that's a start.'

This time she does get pregnant, although she later miscarries. Brett's mother, Elizabeth Leskie, says they have to get married. Kadee, happy, borrows a debutante dress that's too small, and has it altered. The Leskies buy the rings from a pawn shop in Morwell and set a date three weeks away, 24 October, 1992.

A Baptist minister marries them in the front yard of the Leskies' brick veneer on their new share-farm at Denison, on the flat irrigation farming country near Sale. The reception is a barbecue in the backyard. Kadee recalls spending the afternoon driving Brett and his mates around in her car 'getting pissed and stoned'. Just another weekend, really.

She says Brett is drunk by 5pm, and unconscious in bed, alone, by 8.30pm. Kadee drives to Sale, buys beer and spends her wedding night drinking with a female friend.

The 'honeymoon' is spent on the farm, putting a new motor in Brett's car. Not long afterwards, says Kadee, Brett's parents kick him out for 'doing donuts and burnouts' in front of their house. They go to his sister's at Morwell, then rent a house at Yallourn North.

Brett, she claims, starts to 'dress up to the nines' and stays out late while she is home with her baby boy. She suspects he is seeing other women, and cries herself to sleep each night. She demands he leaves her enough marijuana to stay stoned all day, to kill the loneliness. She is pregnant again with her second child. Kadee has problems, but lack of fertility isn't one of them.

They argue at their joint 21st party in June 1993. They go to Lakes Entrance to try to patch it up. Kadee, eight months pregnant, says she finds Brett embracing Bilynda, now sixteen and still with 'big norks', in a back shed. He insists there's nothing in it, but that night he tells her he's 'fallen out of love' with her. She abuses him, tells him to leave.

He takes Bilynda with him. Two weeks later he returns with a carload of mates. Kadee's version of what happens next is that when she stops him removing his stereo from her mother's car, he assaults her. Two weeks later she gives birth to his daughter, Shannan.

Kadee promises revenge. If it takes her ten years, she says, she will split her husband and her sister. As it happens, it takes her only four.

CUT to early 1997. Brett and Bilynda have had two children, Breehanna and Jaidyn. Kadee, by this time with a third child by a third man, is also coping with the knowledge that her daughter, Shannan, has leukaemia. She finally hatches her plot.

Kadee knows if she can get Bilynda interested in someone else, she'll leave Brett. Kadee picks one of Brett's friends, a self-taught mechanic and panel-beater who runs a panel shop with Brett in Moe under a CES grant scheme. She calls him Grishka, but most call him Greg. She can't spell his surname – Domaszewicz. Sometimes they call him 'Doma'.

'I stooged Brett with his best mate,' she is to recall with characteristic bravado. 'I kept tipping Boo (Bilynda) off about Grishka. We had a code so I could tell her when he was down the street without Brett knowing. Brett would even mind all the kids while we went down the street. Grishka knew I was using them all as puppets, pulling the strings. I said to him, I didn't care if he stayed with Bilynda or not, as long as he split them up.'

Eventually, Brett Leskie has an argument with Bilynda and leaves town, then heads to Kalgoorlie.

This allows Bilynda to openly carry on her affair with Greg Domaszewicz, who seems fond of her 14-month-old son, Jaidyn, and often looks after him. For a while, Kadee is happy, or as close to it as she gets.

Two months later, Jaidyn goes missing.

# CHAPTER 7

# The Lime Funeral

## How Rocky Iaria was buried twice

*As a crook the boy makes*
*a pretty good fruitpicker*

ROCKY Iaria's mamma believes in miracles. Long after giving up hope her boy will turn up alive, she prays his body will be found so she can lay him to rest properly, with tears and wreaths, a headstone of Italian marble and all the rites of her religion.

She waits more than six years from the night Rocky disappears, never losing faith. Then, on 19 February, 1998, Mrs Iaria gets her miracle ...

It's a Thursday morning, cloudless and still, another in the endless succession of fine days in the drought-stricken countryside, but perfect for weddings and funerals.

The gravedigger at Pine Lodge lawn cemetery, a peaceful spot on the Benalla road in the flat country east of Shepparton, trundles through the cemetery gate in a tip-truck. There's a funeral later that day; he has to open a grave so that the recently-deceased Derwent Phillip Pearson — known all his life as Jim — can be buried with his wife Dulcie, who left him behind in early August, 1991.

He reverses the truck to the Pearson grave, which is near a tree at the rear of the cemetery, well away from the road. Then he starts the yellow Massey Ferguson tractor with its front-end bucket and backhoe, and begins work, the rattle and hum of the diesel motor echoing across the flat paddocks.

The soil has settled a little in the six-and-a-half years since Dulcie Pearson left her Jim, but it's easy digging with the backhoe. The operator knows from practice just how deep to go without hitting the coffin below. It's all worked out: the first coffin into a double grave is buried two metres deep, leaving plenty of room for the second to sit above, with a few centimetres of earth sandwiched between the two.

That's the way it's supposed to be, anyway. Which is why the gravedigger is surprised, he later tells police, when the jaws of the backhoe strike something odd only 'a couple of feet down'. He gets off the tractor and peers into the hole.

He works the levers, then stares and feels a flutter of apprehension. Poking through the loose earth is something swaddled in black plastic. The steel jaws have torn the plastic, and stinking slime oozes from the tear. For a moment, he thinks there's been some ghastly mistake: perhaps someone has buried a baby in the wrong grave.

It's the wrong grave, all right. Whoever buried the thing wrapped in plastic made a mistake. They picked a fresh grave where the ground was already disturbed, but they didn't realise — or didn't care — that one day it would be reopened. Otherwise, it could have been the perfect crime.

The gravedigger doesn't know any of that yet. He calls a supervisor, who tells him to proceed carefully. He does. He jiggles the foul-smelling thing into the bucket of the front-end loader and places it gently on the truck.

As he does, the plastic tears some more, and he sees the leg of a pair of beige-colored jeans. It's then he knows it's a job for the police. He kills the motor and reaches for his mobile telephone again.

ROCKY Andrew Iaria would have turned twenty-seven in 1998, as his father, Antonio, recalls sadly when asked about the fourth of his six children.

Iaria senior is a leathery little man with the marks of many seasons on his face.

He speaks fractured English, learnt after arriving from Calabria at age fourteen, and doesn't say much. His wife, Raffaela, says little more, but her eyes glisten with tears as she spreads on the table a handful of photographs marking milestones of her boy's short life.

Here's Rocky the toddler. Then the cheeky schoolboy, the cocky teenager, and the sharply dressed best man at a cousin's wedding, his curly hair short at the sides, shoulder length at the back, tumbling over the rented tuxedo as he looks at the camera with a faint smile on his angular young face.

The wedding picture is the one his mother chooses for the memorial cards given to mourners at the Requiem Mass when they re-bury Rocky — in his own grave, this time — at Myrtleford on 3 March, 1998.

In another snap, taken when Rocky is about seventeen, he sports a windcheater with the words 'Already A Legend' on it, a gold ring on his index finger, a cigarette, and a nonchalant look. He looks like a kid who wants to be a tough guy.

The impression is reinforced in another picture, released by police. Eyes narrowed, he's blowing out a plume of smoke and wearing a sharp checked bomber jacket. The same one he wears the night he goes missing in September, 1991.

By that time Rocky's twenty, and in big trouble, just like a real tough guy. But he isn't that tough, he isn't that smart, and he doesn't realise the trouble is big enough to get his head blown off with a shotgun. How can he? He's only a kid.

Rocky Iaria was born and bred in Shepparton, where his mother moved from Myrtleford after she married Antonio in 1966.

Raffaela Iaria will never forget the day she bought her bridesmaids' dresses for the wedding. It's the day Shepparton closes down for the funerals of two local teenagers, Garry Heywood and Abina Madill, abducted on 10 February, 1966, and found, murdered, sixteen days later. It's a crime that shocks Australia, and is to echo down the years until the killer, the man they call 'Mr Stinky', is caught almost two decades later.

The young bride can hardly guess that she, like the dead teenagers' parents she pities that afternoon, will later also suffer the agony of not knowing a child's fate.

Not just for sixteen days, but for more than six years. In the 1990s, however, neither her son's disappearance nor the discovery of his body is to rate much more than local headlines.

One reason for this is that as violent death becomes more common, reaction to it wanes. Another is that for a long time Rocky Iaria's disappearance is only that: any public interest in the mystery fades with time and the lingering suggestion that he might have run away. Third, the taint of a criminal connection hangs over the case. And, finally, the missing man belongs to people who tend to keep their tragedies private — and to settle grievances their own way.

The Iarias live, for a while, on a small orchard at Shepparton East, before moving into the town when the children are small. They work hard but keep, in many ways, the peasant mindset of their forebears. They belong to a tight-knit local Calabrian community which, by the 1960s, dominates the Melbourne wholesale fruit and vegetable market.

Some families flourish more than the Iarias. Such as the Latorres, who work hard and become well-known and relatively prosperous figures in the market scene.

By the late 1980s, Mario Latorre, born in 1942, has a fruit business at Epsom, near Bendigo. His brother John Latorre, born in 1959, is a stallholder at the wholesale market in Melbourne. Their younger brother, Vincent Paul Latorre (not to be confused with an influential relative, also Vincent Latorre, now of Werribee) stays on the farm at Shepparton.

Vince Latorre loves fast cars and he finds the money to buy them. In the late 1980s he owns, according to local police, two customised 'Brock' Commodores, instantly recognisable to anyone interested in cars. It's hardly surprising that Rocky Iaria — ten years younger, also car crazy, and a seasonal farm worker — gravitates towards Latorre, a fellow Calabrian who hires farm workers he can trust in a business where edible fruit and vegetables aren't the only produce.

Rocky not only works for Latorre. He hangs around with him and another colorful Shepparton East identity, Danny Murtagh, who has married into a local Italian family.

Keeping such company isn't wise for young Rocky, according to police intelligence, which in 1989 puts some of the locals high on a list of suspects for a series of burglaries and robberies of wealthy

Italians. They don't come much wealthier than Stephen Monti, a millionaire tomato grower from Bendigo, who returns to his home in Napier Street, White Hills, on the evening of 16 May 1989, to find his back door blocked, his front door open and the house ransacked.

Gone are a clock radio, a camera, a video recorder, watches and leather jackets — but what really hurts is that Monti's open fireplace is smashed and the safe that had been bricked into it is gone. Few people know the safe exists, let alone what's inside, but Monti tells police there was about $300,000 cash, 110 ounces of gold and expensive jewellery. Estimates of the total value of the haul range from $500,000 to $700,000.

For several reasons, the best being a tip-off, police suspect the Shepparton crew for the Monti heist. One reason for this is that Vince Latorre's distinctive Brock special is seen near Monti's house. In fact, a truck driver with a keen eye for cars notices it four times on the day of the robbery.

The truckie, one Stuart Andrew Young, is later to testify in court to seeing the car at Goornong (between Shepparton and Bendigo) early that morning, then at a McEwans hardware store about 11.30am; there are two men in the car and a third getting into it after buying some 'jemmy' bars, the house-breaker's tool of choice. Later, Young sees the car in a side street near Monti's home. And, about 3.30pm, he sees it turn into the Epsom Fruit Works, owned by Mario Latorre.

Young isn't the only witness. It seems to others that Rocky Iaria, or someone very like him, is keeping lookout in Napier Street around the time of the burglary. Unfortunately, he tries hiding behind a post that's thinner than he is, which makes him look both ridiculous and suspect.

If it is Iaria dodging guiltily behind the road sign — as the Crown later claims — then as a crook the boy makes a good fruit picker.

THE execution of the Bendigo burglary might be amateurish, but there's nothing amateur about the information that prompts it, nor the size of the prize. It is deemed a major crime and therefore a job for the major crime squad, a group later disbanded amid official misgivings about the activities of a few of its members.

The official line on what happens next is, in the words of one policeman, that the squad 'commenced an investigation that identified two suspects at Shepparton'. Meaning that at dawn one morning soon after the Monti job a crew of major crime detectives uses a sledge-hammer to open the door of the unit Latorre then lives in with his wife, Angela Robinson, and their small son. It's a heavy-handed affair, and Latorre later complains about the detectives frightening his family. Meanwhile, at the Iarias' house in Orchard Court, Rocky also cops a rude awakening.

The pair are questioned in separate rooms at Shepparton police station. Latorre is twenty-nine, heavily built and quiet. He agrees he was in Bendigo on the day of the burglary, but says he was visiting his brother.

In the next interview room his employee and alleged accomplice, barely nineteen, has a little more explaining to do; the police have found goods that look suspiciously like Monti's at his house. Rocky claims he bought them from a stranger selling 'hot' stuff.

Despite the denials, the detectives put together what they judge is a strong case, which is set to go to court in early 1991. But a funny thing happens on the way to trial. The police, it seems, aren't the only ones doing their homework; someone else believes, or is told, that Vince Latorre might know where the Monti loot is.

This is why — about 1.30am on Thursday 20 July 1989 — Latorre is abducted from his flat by two men wearing masks, caps and overalls. They tie and gag his wife and leave her in the flat, bundle him in a car, bound and blindfolded, and drive into the bush. There they bash and interrogate him for more than an hour.

Latorre doesn't talk. Either he is brave, or it's true he doesn't know what's happened to the loot because he didn't do the burglary, or he's even more frightened of someone else than he is of the thugs working him over. Whatever the reason, the abductors get nothing from him.

Bleeding and battered, he's driven back to Shepparton and shoved out the door near his unit, still tied and blindfolded. He has to be taken to hospital.

Local police soon hear of two men who'd been staying at a Shepparton motel the night before. An alert receptionist tells them she assumed the pair were police special operations group members because they were dressed in dark blue overalls and baseball caps, and acted as if they were planning some sort of raid.

Local police trace calls the men made from the motel room. Curiously, some of the calls are to detectives — one in Melbourne and one in Bendigo. The local police aren't sure if this is linked with Latorre's idea that a third person was lurking in the background where he was bashed. Latorre thinks his assailants stopped working him over to consult someone else, but he can't be sure.

Like the mysterious telephone calls, Latorre's suspicions of a third person being involved in his abduction come to nothing. What does happen is that two standover men, Chris Dudkowski and Robert Punicki, are arrested, charged and convicted of the abduction and assault of Latorre, among other offences.

The pair, who have been well-known bouncers at Shepparton hotels, are described by police as 'opportunists' acting independently to find the Monti money. Dudkowski and Punicki go along with this. They are especially discreet after one is warned in jail he'll be 'knocked' (killed) and an inquisitive lawyer 'loaded up' with bogus drug charges if there is any loose talk about anybody else being involved.

Allegations of such activities have no bearing, of course, on the subsequent disbanding of the major crime squad, despite speculation to the contrary. If there is any background involvement by rogue cops in the abduction and bashing of Latorre, it is unclear who they are.

Not all police work is as surefooted as the Dudkowski-Punicki arrests. Surveillance police working for the major crime squad waste several days watching the wrong Vince Latorre, an uncle of the wanted man who then lives in Doyle's Road, Shepparton, some distance from his nephew.

Despite such bumbling, the major crime squad is confident when Latorre and Iaria finally face the Bendigo County Court on 11 February 1991. But not all jury members, after a hearing that stretches into early March, are so sure of the police case. Result: a hung jury.

At the time, Rocky Iaria is happy enough to avoid a conviction, even if it means facing another trial later that year. But the truth is, if he'd been found guilty and gone to jail he'd probably be alive today.

It's a tip-off — allegedly anonymous — that gets Rocky killed.

The official version of events is that someone telephones Bendigo police to say a relative of Iaria's, a tobacco farmer near Myrtleford, has a video recorder stolen in the Monti burglary. A detective goes to the farm and identifies the machine as Monti's. The relative says he bought it for $150, while Rocky was present. It's the link the prosecution needs to tie Rocky to the burglary.

Which it does. On 6 September 1991, just seventeen days before the second trial is set to start.

ROCKY is driving around that Friday afternoon, in his white XW Falcon. About 3pm he ferries cold drinks to his older brothers, who are pruning fruit trees, then comes home to the house in Orchard Court his parents have put up as surety for the $50,000 bail to guarantee he will front at the new trial.

In the lull before the evening meal, he kicks a football around the back yard with two of his brothers, Nick and Fiore, still schoolboys.

His mother calls out to ask him if he will be home to eat with the family. He asks his brothers to tell her he'll be home 'about 8 or 9 o'clock'. Then he gets into the Falcon and drives off. They don't see him again. Ever.

He doesn't meet his brother, Paddy, at a parking spot near the lake where young bucks gather on Friday nights. It's not the first time Rocky has stayed out all night. But it is the first time he doesn't telephone early next morning to tell his parents he's all right.

They're worried. On Sunday they visit a local detective at home ... accompanied by Vince Latorre. The detective is wary; he suspects they are trying to use him to make it look as if Rocky's disappearance is not just jumping bail. He soon changes his mind.

He talks to Latorre and the Iarias separately. Latorre, he is to recall, shrugs off Rocky's disappearance, saying he doesn't know where he is, and suspects Rocky has 'pissed off because he's shit frightened of the second trial coming up'.

But Antonio Iaria is ashen with fear for his son. He thinks the boy is dead, that he would never run away without telling the family, and in any case he wouldn't jump bail because it would cost the family their house. The father's distress is convincing.

The detective sends the family to the police station to file a missing person's report. Iaria's disappearance isn't made public until two days later, when the *Shepparton News* runs a small story saying police 'fear for the safety' of a local man after discovery of his car the day before in the carpark at Benalla railway station.

There's speculation Rocky has fled the district on the train, but his family knows it's not true, as much as they would like it to be.

Two weeks later, on 23 September, the new trial begins at Bendigo. Latorre, facing the jury alone, is quickly acquitted. Evidence involving Iaria is inadmissible, and so the case against Latorre doesn't stand up, just as predicted.

Latorre returns to the vast, white ranch-style house built on the orchard he has bought in Central Avenue, Shepparton East, near the old place where he and his brothers grew up. Close, too, to his friend Danny Murtagh, who has come under police notice for stealing farm machinery and other offences.

For the Iarias, there is an appalling silence that is to last more than six years. Grieving for their boy, but not knowing what has happened, they hire a lawyer for court hearings to lift the $50,000 bail surety on their house. Eventually, they sell out and move to Myrtleford, away from cruel rumors in Shepparton that they have hidden Rocky interstate or overseas.

Now, at least, they have a grave to tend. But will it end there?

SUSPICIONS linger in Shepparton about who killed Rocky Iaria. When the autopsy showed he died of a shotgun blast, it made some people think hard about a gun handed anonymously to police in 1993.

It was a sawn-off single-barrel shotgun, found in an irrigation channel at Shepparton East. It was identified as a Stirling ... registered to Danny Murtagh. Questioned, Murtagh asserted the gun had been damaged in a fire, then given to an unknown person, who might well have sawn it off and thrown it in the channel.

Police have not proved the gun is linked to Iaria's murder, but believe it could be a vital clue in any future trial. Unfortunately, they don't know who handed in the weapon — and it has since reportedly been destroyed in a clean-up of Shepparton police station.

Chances of finding who handed in the shotgun faded when the officer in charge of Shepparton CIB, a Detective Sergeant Barry Stevens, made a public appeal on local television in which, inexplicably, he described the weapon as a 'long-barrelled firearm' handed in during a gun amnesty. Meanwhile, strange things happen in the orchards and farms around Shepparton.

Police were set to move against a local gang suspected of stealing irrigation equipment from an Italian farming family at Tatura in 1997, when a neighbor talked of giving evidence.

Days later the neighbor's entire tomato crop — a year's work worth tens of thousands of dollars — withered and died. It had been poisoned. The theft case collapsed through of lack of evidence. 'I don't want a bullet in the back of my head,' a potential witness told police.

The thieves are feared, but they have their own fears, too. Especially one, a man many in the district believe was behind the Monti burglary — and consequently, the murder of Rocky Iaria.

The old Calabrian way of seeking revenge, says a man who knows the main players, would not simply be to kill the person suspected of murdering Rocky Iaria.

It would be to kill that person's son, when the boy turns the same age Rocky was when he died. It has already been decided, he says.

# CHAPTER 8

# Stares and whispers

## The mystery of Muriel Street

*Police are no closer to establishing a
motive than they were on the day
Jane Thurgood-Dove died.*

IT was a happy family home. Right up until the moment a pot-bellied coward with a pistol killed Jane Thurgood-Dove in front of her children as they cowered in the family car. That was in November, 1997.

Weeks later the home was only a house, one of the plainest in a street of weatherboard houses as simple and tidy as its name. Muriel Street, Niddrie, less than half an hour from the city but, dozing in the spring sunshine, it could pass for a street in almost any country town.

Outside number five, the flowers had gone from the footpath. The flood of letters and sympathy cards delivered to the rickety letter box leaning over the wire mesh fence had been carefully filed away as a private memory to a very public death.

The family's blue heeler dog barked and thumped its tail at passersby as it peered hopefully beneath the picket gates in the drive, where the yellow paint police use to mark crime scenes was already fading.

There remained one reminder of the awful thing that happened here at 3.50 pm on Thursday, November 6: a hole in the wall, ugly as a missing tooth, where police had taken a board to examine the bullets lodged in it. There were other, more subtle, changes. Muriel Street had become a place of stares and whispers. As locals drove past, their eyes flicked sideways at the murder house, fascinated and a little fearful.

When facts are thin, theories fill the void. Police admit, after thousands of hours of investigation, they are no closer to establishing a motive than they were the day Jane Thurgood-Dove died. But many of the people who live there believe the murder had nothing to do with the victim or her husband, Mark. They believe it was a case of mistaken identity. And they think they know who the real target was.

The circumstantial case for this is intriguing.

The Thurgood-Doves' house is the third from the corner, on the left heading west from Hoffman's Road. It is two doors from St John Bosco's parish school, church and presbytery, which covers twelve house blocks. Then there is a cross-street. The third house from this corner – still on the left heading west – is number thirty nine. It belongs to a family that some locals suspect was the hitman's target.

Most people in the street are original 'settlers' from the early 1950s, and are now grandparents. Jane Thurgood-Dove was one of few women in the street with school-age children.

One of only three young mothers living on her side of the street is Carmel Kypri, who has occupied number thirty nine with her husband Peter since the mid-1980s. Peter Kypri has renovated their weatherboard – making it one of the best houses on the street – and keeps it spotlessly tidy. But in some circles he is not popular.

The reasons for this are buried deep in muttered conversations. Muriel Street folk are a friendly lot, but Peter Kypri isn't, they say.

But it's not only neighbours who dislike Peter Kypri. Much heavier people have disliked him enough to plan his murder.

Enter Philip Peters, a greedy, crooked lawyer who claimed Kypri had cost him $200,000 in an insurance scam that went wrong. Peters was taped plotting Kypri's abduction and murder 'because the bastard has pinched $200,000 of stock'. Peters told associates he arranged for Kypri to steal computer equipment from his (Peters') office so he could claim insurance, but then found the policy was void because he hadn't paid the premiums. Peters was very unhappy.

In a police operation codenamed 'Soli' detectives foiled the murder plan and saved Kypri's life. They succeeded because the man Peters recruited to kill Kypri became a police agent and provided evidence that resulted in the conviction of the former solicitor.

Peters' plan was for his partner, known as 'John', to lure Kypri into a bogus $200,000 marijuana deal, drug him with a sedative, and take him to a farmhouse at St Arnaud in central Victoria, where he would be tortured in a hidden cellar, then killed. Peters ordered John, a butcher by trade, to cut Kypri's body into pieces for easy disposal and to prevent identification.

The police transcript reads in part:

John: 'Yeah, well, you said that the other day, and you know, it makes sense. How's he gonna be killed? You said you were gonna do it.'

Peters: 'Well, I thought you might do it, John. You know how to cut up sheep.'

John: 'Yeah.'

Peters: 'There's no difference.'

Operation Soli revealed that Kypri had more than one enemy. Peters claimed, in one of many secretly-recorded conversations, that another gangster had taken a contract out on Kypri's life.

Peters: 'He was going to vanish totally.'

John: 'As in totally dead, dead?'

Peters: 'Dead, dead. Well, he has pinched so much from so many people that the world – you would get a medal ... Yeah, well, Danny has, I believe – no, not has, had – put a contract out on him ... I made some inquiries and Danny had apparently put a contract out on him two years ago.'

John: 'Yeah.'

Peters: 'The bloke took Danny's money, then told Kypri.'

John: 'They're not going to find the body, are they?'

Peters: 'Nuh, Nuh, they're not gonna find anything.'

John, who later gave evidence against Peters, said in an interview with the authors that Kypri was an unpleasant man with many enemies and deliberately gave the impression he was connected with the underworld.

'He always said he carried a gun. I didn't see it, but he showed me the bullets. He was a calculating type, and a loner. He had the reputation that if you needed anything done, he could do it.' When John visited Kypri's home in Muriel Street he learned that the family had its own alarm code. If Peter Kypri saw a strange car in the street, he would give a particular whistle. This was the signal for his wife and children to lock themselves indoors immediately.

Kypri took other elaborate precautions. He always backed his vehicles into the drive, ready for a fast getaway, and insisted visitors not block his escape route by parking in front of his car.

John has since left the shadowy world of Peters and Kypri. But, when he saw the picture of Jane Thurgood-Dove, it reminded him a little of Kypri's hairdresser wife, Carmel. 'They had the same facial features and same hairstyle. Carmel's hair was more fawn than blonde, but they were very similar.

'And when I saw her on Australia's Most Wanted the hairs on the back of my neck stood up.'

A policeman who knows Kypri well says he 'would have plenty of enemies'. Another said he would like to be known as a mover and shaker and would relish his local notoriety. 'He'd be loving it.'

But neighbours claim the Kypris became even more cautious about the family's security in the months before the murder. Whereas they once let their two children play in the street, the pair began to be driven to and from the local secondary school, were rarely seen outside and often taken away from the house for hours in the early evening.

Carmel Kypri runs a hairdressing business from a converted garage at the rear of the property. Her husband has dozens of brand new tyres stacked in the drive, in the spot where he once kept an expensive boat that neighbours say was stolen and burned.

The house has a heavy mesh security door through which a visitor can barely see the occupant. All that can be seen of Carmel Kypri when she comes to the door is the glint of large gold earrings through the grille.

Mrs Kypri agrees with her neighbours that Jane Thurgood-Dove's murder was 'probably' a case of mistaken identity. 'If it wasn't meant for her it makes you wonder,' she says. 'It has made us wary. My husband says to watch out when we come into the drive, to look around the place.'

She volunteers that 'it's a pretty "old" street. There aren't many young mothers here … me, her and Sue down that end.

'They (the Thurgood-Doves) seemed like a close-knit family. When I first heard about it I thought it might be road rage, but then I heard they'd been watching her.

'I keep the door locked. Maybe it was for us. Who knows? But you can't let it stop your life. The kids still go to school.

'If it's going to happen, it's going to happen, but we try not to worry. We are a bit more wary, that's all.'

The puzzle facing police is this. If Jane Thurgood-Dove was the wrong woman, how could professional hitmen who stalked their quarry for two days make such a fundamental blunder?

The truth is that so-called 'professional' hitmen are often criminal misfits who will kill strangers for a few thousand dollars, risking a life sentence for no more money than a competent burglar can steal by breaking into a shop.

Homicide files contain many proven cases of incompetent killers who have hit the wrong person. In 1984 a harmless citizen called Lindsay Simpson was executed by career criminal Ray 'Red Rat' Pollitt at Lower Plenty. The target of the hit was drug dealer Alan Williams, Simpson's brother-in-law.

Another criminal's brother-in-law, Norman McLeod, was shot dead as he left his Coolaroo home on his way to work in July, 1981. The unknown gunman mistook McLeod for his brother-in-law Vincent Mikkelsen, one of three men charged and later acquitted of killing painter and docker Leslie Herbert Kane.

Meanwhile, investigators are striving to unravel a case that promised in the first hours to be another 'domestic' murder, but which now baffles them.

When Jane Thurgood-Dove was murdered, police acted within seconds of the first call that shots had been fired near the school in Muriel Street. The first officers on the scene called in the homicide squad. The on-call section, crew five, was sent.

The detectives' first priority was to secure the scene and ensure the victim's distressed children were looked after. It was two hours before they went to the Campbellfield packaging factory where the dead woman's husband worked as a foreman.

Homicide detectives chose to deliver the message personally for two reasons. One was that they are experienced at dealing with shattered relatives of murder victims. More importantly, they wanted to observe first-hand Mark Thurgood-Dove's reaction to the worst news he'd ever hear.

When a woman with no criminal connections is murdered, the first person police want to talk to is her husband, de facto or lover. Most murders are 'domestics', with people killed either by – or for – someone close to them. The most common motives are jealousy and greed.

Just before knock-off time at the factory, detectives went quietly to the boss's office and made discreet inquiries.

Had Mark slipped out during the day? Had he been moody or distracted? The answer was no. Mark Thurgood-Dove was a man with no secrets.

The firm's trusted foreman was then called into the office and told the terrible news. Police went to talk to the most likely suspect, but what they found was a devastated man who had lost the woman he loved.

Victims rarely take secrets to the grave. Detectives scour their personal history for any clue. In such cases, possible murder motives are often easily established. Was the marriage on the rocks? Was the victim's life heavily insured? Were there financial problems?

But not this time. In the first few weeks, detectives found nothing to indicate that Mark and Jane Thurgood-Dove were anything other than the loving couple they appeared to be.

But police knew that if they dug deep enough there would always be secrets to be unearthed. Perhaps more than one.

It is the human condition.

# CHAPTER 9

# Sweet Jane

## Two men loved her – but who killed her?

*The dead woman's sister and a friend
claimed Jane had told them
... of an unspecified 'dark secret'*

IT was the first time in his ten-year career that the senior constable had been in on the big one. It was, in fact, one of the few times he had been to police crime headquarters in St Kilda Road at all.

But the plodding policeman from the suburbs wasn't there because of his ability as an investigator. Far from it. He was on the wrong side of the desk ... and he had a lawyer with him.

In the stark homicide interview room on the ninth floor, a video recorder was cued to record not his questions, but his answers. The policeman knew word for word the formal caution recited to him by a homicide detective, which told him the same thing his lawyer had drummed into him before they arrived: he did not have to answer any questions, but that anything he did say could be used against him.

Confused and disturbed, he took his counsel's advice and stayed silent. For the lawyer, it was standard practice. But, for detectives, a 'no comment' interview raises suspicion. A long-held police axiom is that, in practice, silence is usually the refuge of the guilty.

Which is why, when the senior constable left the building with his lawyer, the men in the dark suits in the homicide office believed they might have the first tiny break in one of the most distressing – and baffling – murders in their experience.

Jane Thurgood-Dove was pretty, young, a wife and a mother. She lived in an ordinary house in an ordinary street. When she was shot dead on her doorstep in front of her three children on Oaks Day, 1997, it grabbed a city's attention.

Two men – probably paid killers – had stalked her for days around the north-western Melbourne suburb of Niddrie. Their car had been seen the previous day about 9.30am near Essendon North Primary School, soon after she dropped two of her three children at school. It was also seen several times near her home on 6 November, the day she was killed.

She pulled into the driveway of her weatherboard house in Muriel Street at 3.50pm. A silver-blue VL Commodore sedan immediately parked behind her, blocking her blue four-wheel-drive.

A pot-bellied man who looked to be in his forties jumped from the front passenger seat and chased the terrified woman. He shot her in the head at least three times with a large-calibre handgun as her children cowered in the car.

The man got back into the Commodore, which was driven by a younger, thin-faced man, who reversed the car so abruptly that the fat gunman had difficulty closing the door.

The car sped off, dodged around a couple of corners and was set on fire a few blocks away in a deserted side street near some parkland. From the burnt-out wreck, police recovered a brown parka, which was found to have been stolen from another Commodore in Carlton only a few days before.

In cases like this, when the victim is seen as blameless, sympathy and outrage swell. The Victorian Premier, Jeff Kennett, intervened to double the $50,000 reward requested by police. It was a timely and popular gesture, but it wasn't to make any difference to the investigation.

Few of the seventy-odd murders committed each year in Victoria attract the wide interest, let alone concern and sympathy, that Jane Thurgood-Dove's violent death did.

But there is no sentiment in a murder investigation. While thousands of people who did not know the victim were saddened by her death because of the coverage it attracted, homicide detectives had to confront her grief-stricken husband, family and friends with the reality that – until proven otherwise – they were all potential murder suspects.

Even the police's timing when they told Mark Thurgood-Dove of the murder was contrived. They set up the meeting at the Campbellfield factory where he then worked so that they could study him for any hint of a staged reaction.

From day one, Thurgood-Dove was the main suspect. Not because there was a scrap of evidence against him – but because that's where an investigation must start when there is no obvious lead.

In the months after the murder, the shattered husband's life was examined minutely. The conclusion: that he is a decent man, still shattered by his wife's death, battling to care for their three children.

If it wasn't her husband, who did kill Jane Thurgood-Dove?

Soon after the killing, a detective going through her possessions found papers connected to a uniformed policeman.

It was, at that stage, only one of hundreds of details to be checked. The policeman, like scores of people vaguely associated with the dead woman, was routinely contacted.

When he was first approached by detectives, just weeks after the killing, he admitted he knew the Thurgood-Doves socially. Then he surprised them by volunteering that he had harbored deep feelings for the married woman for years.

Colleagues said the senior constable was 'different', a loner who lived by himself. In a profession known for bold personalities, he was shy.

In a force of ten thousand sworn members, only a handful chase serious criminals for a living. The senior constable who knew Jane Thurgood-Dove has a spotless record – and a short arrest sheet.

They met in the most mundane circumstances. He used to buy the sausages for his station's barbecues and became friendly with one of the butchers, who was related to her.

They began to move in the same social circle. He became friendly with Mark and Jane Thurgood-Dove and, although romantically involved with another woman, became obsessed with the young mother. The policeman began to orchestrate social gatherings just to be in her company. About 1994, Mrs Thurgood-Dove became uncomfortable with her admirer's fixation. She tried to distance herself, but they continued to cross paths. It was inevitable. They lived only streets apart.

In the frantic weeks after the murder, detectives spent hundreds of hours chasing dozens of dead-end leads. Despite their determination and the public's outrage, they were no closer to an answer than the day Jane Thurgood-Dove was killed.

So when the senior constable revealed his love for the dead woman, it was the only fresh development. For want of any stronger lead, investigators put the man under the microscope.

When he realised he was part of a murder investigation, he went to the Police Association for help. He was given the number of a barrister called Tony Hargreaves, a seasoned lawyer who has helped many police in trouble – and who has also represented Laurie Tanner, husband of Jennifer Tanner, the woman shot dead in suspicious circumstances at their Bonnie Doon farmhouse in 1984. But that is another story.

In January, the barrister Hargreaves and his nervous client went, by invitation, to the homicide squad, where the policeman exercised his right not to answer questions.

Some investigators saw the policeman as a suspect, though not the only one. They calculated there were at least two other tenable theories.

One was that the housewife was the victim of mistaken identity, that bumbling hitmen killed her instead of another young woman married to a known criminal who lives in the same street and who had already been the target of an aborted murder plot.

The second theory was that the gunman was the father of a violent criminal connected right to the end with the late Alphonse Gangitano, although a motive has not been established, and it appears a long shot based mostly on physical description.

Police have said the senior constable was one of about twelve people to be seriously questioned about the murder. But, for forty-eight hours in January, the policeman was the one in the frame.

Then came a twist. The policeman walked into St Kilda Road headquarters – alone, this time, and prepared to answer questions.

Yes, he said, he loved Jane Thurgood-Dove and had once wanted her to leave her husband. But he had not killed her. He explained his whereabouts around the time of the killing.

He emerged as an ordinary uniformed policeman without the criminal contacts to find and hire someone prepared to kill for money. Detectives decided that he had no more resources to organise such a crime than the average bank teller or public servant.

Within days of the policeman being formally interviewed, the police gossip network had spread the story. The man spoke to his station colleagues, telling them he had been questioned and had nothing to hide.

Senior police fended off media inquiries. They said the case was open, and they were not close to a breakthrough of any sort.

Months later, Channel Seven's *Australia's Most Wanted* program broadcast a police-generated story on the Thurgood-Dove murder in an attempt to provoke a public response – and fresh leads. Such co-operation with the media is usually a sign that an investigation is at a stalemate.

The basis of the TV story was a claim by the dead woman's sister, Sue, and a friend, Judy Fenner, that Jane Thurgood-Dove had told them, separately, of an unspecified 'dark secret'.

Days later, the *Herald Sun* published a page one story describing the unnamed policeman as 'the prime suspect'.

The head of the homicide squad, Detective Chief Inspector Rod Collins, took the unusual step of publicly denying that the policeman was a suspect. The policeman, deeply distressed, declined to speak to the authors of this book. He even refused to answer the door of the unassuming suburban house where he lived only a few blocks from the Thurgood-Doves'. In fact, senior police ordered welfare sections of the force to monitor the man's welfare, believing he could be suicidal.

Some police believed he shouldn't have been kept on operational duties while he was depressed, because it meant he had access to firearms. Others, however, felt that removing him from his job could have tipped him over the edge.

For outsiders, it seemed a juicy development: a distraught admirer of a dead woman in a murder case going nowhere. But police have to build evidence, not theories. Ultimately, a coroner or a Supreme Court jury must decide the truth.

The best hope for a breakthrough is for an unknown car thief to surface. The thief, that is, who stole the car the killers used – and, probably, another Commodore a few days earlier.

Months after the murder, with time and leads running out, detectives gave up hope of a thief with a conscience coming forward.

Which is why, in addition to the $100,000 carrot, the chief commissioner of police has offered to make a deal with anyone on the periphery who can name the killers and stand up in court. Such a person will be given not only the cash but a 'clean slate', a pardon for their part in the crime, if any.

Meanwhile, in the quiet suburban streets where Niddrie borders Essendon, two men who still live less than five hundred metres apart nurse shattered lives behind shuttered windows.

Both are in mourning for the woman they love. Both keep pictures of her. There is no evidence, police insist, that either had anything to do with her death.

But someone did. And they are still out there.

# CHAPTER 10

# Monstrous but not mad

## Australia's Hannibal Lecter

*'He is the nearest thing
to a robot I have met'*

HE was Victoria's longest-serving prisoner, yet in the eyes of the law he remained an innocent man. He was declared mentally ill, yet was repeatedly denied treatment in a psychiatric institution.

In August 1998 the forgotten man of the prison system, Derek Ernest Percy, was put under public scrutiny for the first time in twenty-nine years when his unique case was reviewed in the Supreme Court. It was the first time since 1969 that he'd been given the chance to argue why he should start his journey to freedom and why society no longer had a reason to fear him.

Hundreds of more notorious criminals have passed through Australian jails in the past three decades, and few people remember Percy. The police who arrested him have long since retired, his defence lawyer has moved on to be a respected Supreme Court judge, and many of the jails that had held him had since been closed. He was a model prisoner, seemingly content to play carpet bowls, collect stamps and browse though the cricket statistics he kept on his personal computer.

Yet many in the criminal justice system feared the day this

seemingly harmless man would be given a legal opportunity to push for his release. On Derek Percy's first day in a cell Neil Armstrong walked on the moon, John Gorton was Prime Minister, Australian troops were fighting in Vietnam and a bottle of milk, home delivered by the local milkie, cost 19c. Derek Percy was twenty-one.

Percy has been in prison since he was arrested for the murder of Yvonne Elizabeth Tuohy, a twelve-year-old girl he abducted, tortured, sexually assaulted and killed on a Westernport beach, near Melbourne, on 20 July, 1969.

On the fifth day of his Supreme Court trial in March 1970 he was found not guilty on the grounds of insanity and sentenced to an indefinite term at the Governor's Pleasure.

Three psychiatrists gave evidence of his 'acute psycho-sexual disorder.' A jury found it impossible to believe that a sane man could have done what Percy did to young Yvonne Tuohy.

It was in the days when only the defence could raise the issue of the accused's sanity and it was also in the days when capital punishment was still on the statute books.

Ronald Ryan was the last man hanged in Australia in 1967. Percy would have been a candidate for the noose if he had been found both sane and guilty.

The defence of insanity was usually raised only by the defence as the last throw of the dice in murder cases.

Grieving relatives of Yvonne Tuohy were assured on the steps of the court that Percy was so twisted he would never be released.

In the 1960s and 1970s the difference between being found not guilty on grounds of insanity by a criminal court rather than guilty was more an argument in semantics than of treatment. The terms 'patient' and 'criminal' amounted to much the same thing. No matter what the court found the sane and insane were taken by prison van and dumped in Pentridge.

But in the 1980s treatment improved and inmates who, in the eyes of the law were insane, were moved to psychiatric institutions. All, that is, except Percy.

Many were given long-term leave and were no longer seen as dangerous. In 1998 all forty-seven Governor's Pleasure 'clients', were told their cases would be reviewed in the Supreme Court to see if they should be freed. One, James Henry Patrick Belsey, who had lived without incident in a Melbourne northern suburb, died only weeks before his case was to be heard. He had been diagnosed with inoperable throat cancer several months earlier.

Belsey stabbed and killed Senior Constable Charles Norman Curson on the steps of Flinders Street station on 8 January, 1974, but years later he became balanced enough to live quietly, spending his days helping the aged and infirm with their mundane chores.

The changes to the law have been seen by politicians, judges, police and psychiatrists as humane, progressive and just. The Mental Impairment and Unfitness to be Tried Act took decisions on Governor's Pleasure cases away from politicians and into the hands of judges.

By the mid-1990s about half the Governor's Pleasure clients lived in the community on extended leave and were no longer seen as a danger to anyone. The rest remained under the supervision of government psychiatrists with varying levels of security.

But, through it all, Percy was the exception. He stayed in jail and seventeen internal reviews all said he remained as dangerous as the day he was arrested.

GROWING up, Derek Percy was hardly in one area long enough to make friends, but he had always been so self-absorbed the moves did not seem to worry him — at least outwardly.

He was the oldest of four boys, one of whom died from diphtheria as an infant when Derek was ten. His father was an electrical mechanic and the family moved from Sydney to Victoria when Derek was eight.

Percy senior was employed by the SEC and was often moved from post to post around Victoria. In ten years, the family lived in Melbourne, Warrnambool, and in Victoria's high country. Derek went to seven schools, was brighter than average, and wanted to be an architect.

He seemed a little cold and aloof, but that was put down to the shyness that came from living on the move. No teachers or schoolmates became close enough to him to consider him as anything but ordinary.

As a child he gravitated to solitary activities. He enjoyed stamps, building up a collection of more than ten thousand, and he inherited his father's love of yachting, although he preferred to sail on his own. When he was arrested he owned a Moth-class yacht. He loved to read and, like many teenagers, he took to keeping a diary to record his innermost thoughts.

For Percy, the diary was probably more important than for most kids because with his family's constant moving he didn't have a close friend to confide in.

When he was seventeen his parents stumbled on his diary and began to read. What they saw left them horrified. Their quiet, intelligent oldest son was having bizarre sexual fantasies. Worse, many of the fantasies involved children.

His parents took him to the local, overworked doctor. According to a prison report written years later they were told not to worry as the writings were 'just a stage of growing up.'

'No other action was taken,' the report said.

After Derek finished year eleven his father bought a service station near Newcastle, and the family moved again. The boy enrolled in his final year at Gosford High, but he gave up, tired of starting again at a new school.

His new plan was to get a job in a drafting office, but he soon found he was under-qualified, and started working with his father in the family service station for five months.

At nineteen, he decided to join the navy and was accepted within a week of lodging his application. For the next eighteen months he was stationed at three bases in Victoria and NSW. With an IQ of 122, he was offered the chance to complete officer's training. The navy felt he had a future. He took orders well, was bright and loved the sea.

No-one knew that he was still keeping his diary, and far from 'growing out' of his sadistic sexual fantasies. They were getting worse.

YVONNE Tuohy was quite grown up and independent for a twelve-year-old. During the week she would play with kids from her school, but at weekends she would see the Melbourne families that came to Warneet to relax on the Westernport beaches.

Her parents owned the local shop and ran the boat hiring business, so they knew all the locals and regular holidaymakers by name.

Yvonne liked to explore with a young Melbourne boy, Shane Spiller, who came to Warneet with his parents most weekends. Apollo 11 was circling the moon when the pair asked their parents if they could go for a hike along a peaceful strip of a Westernport beach on a winter's Sunday afternoon. It was 20 July, 1969, in an era when parents were not concerned by their children being out of sight. It was a fine day with enough sun around to encourage the children to get some fresh air and make their own fun.

Frank Spiller was up a ladder painting the side of the family's weatherboard weekender when his son suggested a walk with Yvonne. The Spillers liked to leave Melbourne at the weekends to spend their time at Warneet, less than an hour from their eastern suburbs home. It was such a nice spot that years later Frank and his wife, Daphne, were to retire there.

Daphne Spiller cut sandwiches for the kids, and Shane grabbed his little tomahawk to cut wood for a billy tea on the beach.

The country girl and the city boy walked down a vehicle track, past a small car park to Ski Beach. Shane noticed a Datsun station wagon with a man sitting behind the wheel. 'I had a feeling that day he was bad news,' Shane Spiller was able to recall almost thirty years later.

In the car was Derek Percy, who had a weekend leave from Cerberus Navy Base. He had gone to the Frankston drive-in the previous night, slept in his car and driven to Cowes. On his way back he pulled into Warneet. For years, he was later to admit, he had been having dark thoughts about sexually molesting and killing children, but he was to claim he didn't believe he would ever act on these impulses.

When the kids reached the beach they remained undecided for a few seconds whether to head to a friend's farmhouse or to the nearby township. Confused, they walked in opposite directions for a few moments, then turned to walked back to each other. They were only metres apart when Percy appeared and grabbed Yvonne. The sailor produced a red-handled dagger and menaced the girl and ordered Shane to come to him, but the young boy pulled his hatchet from his belt and waved it above his head to keep the him away.

'We were there for a long time while he was trying to entice me to him. I don't know if it was minutes or seconds,' he was to say of a scene that is burned into his memory.

Percy held the knife to Yvonne's throat, forcing the young girl to try to beg her friend to give up. 'Come back or he'll cut my throat,' she is alleged to have said.

Instead, Shane ran off through 200 metres of scrub to get help. As he neared the road he saw the attacker drive off with Yvonne in the car. He screamed, but a family having a picnic nearby ignored him, later telling police they thought the kids were just playing. One of the parents was later to approach young Shane to apologise. Three decades later, he still could not forgive them.

According to police, Shane Spiller's actions saved his life and ultimately helped catch the killer. They say if he had not gone for help Percy would have killed him as well as Yvonne Tuohy. With no living witness, he may never have been apprehended.

Police said the youngster was an excellent witness who remembered details that led them to Percy. He described the killer's car and sketched a sticker he had seen on the back window. It was the navy insignia.

BIG Jack Ford, then head of the homicide squad, and his team raced to nearby Cerberus Navy Base and found Percy washing blood from his clothes. They also found his diary. After reading chilling details of what he intended to do with children they were in no doubt they had their killer.

According to police this may have been a random attack — but it had been planned in the killer's mind over the years. Again and again he would fantasise about abducting children and he would write in detail of how he planned to kill them. As the hours passed, Yvonne's parents still hoped the crime would be abduction — even a rape — but not a murder. But when Ford returned to Warneet it was to bring the worst possible news. He walked up the path to the Spillers' house where the Tuohys were huddled together, waiting. Frank Spiller was outside and asked if there was any hope. Ford shook his head and silently ran a finger across his own throat to indicate the child was dead.

Shane Spiller was a model witness. He gave the police the lead, then on the same night he walked through the navy base car park until he identified the killer's station wagon. Later, at a police line up, he had to walk up and touch the man who had planned to kill him.

Nothing was too much trouble for the young boy. He posed with his tomahawk for press photographers and didn't miss a court date, giving evidence bravely and honestly, even when he believed a relative of Percy continued to stare and intimidate him inside the court, trying to bully him into a mistake.

At the end of the ordeal grateful police had their sketch artist draw a picture of the boy and gave him a show bag of gifts as a thankyou. Then they then just moved on to the next case.

But Shane Spiller couldn't move on. The bright, observant little boy didn't recover. He was afraid of the dark. He was concerned that Percy would break out and come looking for him.

Family and friends believed that time would heal the wound. They were wrong. Time turned into an angry, festering sore.

He began drinking at fourteen, sought psychiatric help at eighteen. In an era before victim counselling Shane Spiller became increasingly bitter that no-one seemed to understand his pain, fear and loneliness.

Half a lifetime later his friends say, 'He's in a pretty bad way.'

In 1998 police found Spiller, who had tried to lose himself in country NSW, and told him that despite what had been promised, Derek Percy's case was to be reviewed. The man who had stolen Shane Spiller's chance of a normal life was going to be given the opportunity to salvage his.

'It's really knocked me around, mate. I still get nightmares. I spin out. I'm going through a rough trot now,' Spiller was to say afterwards.

The news brought to the surface fears that were never truly hidden. But it also gave him the chance to talk about the ugly things that had festered inside him. Police finally put him in touch with counsellors. He was told that he was not weak, not strange, just a victim who, understandably, couldn't cope.

'I think about it every day of my life, mate. I've searched for help. I think I'm starting to get it now.'

He said he'd been good friends with Yvonne. 'We couldn't have been closer. She meant so much to me. I've never had a decent relationship since then.' Shane Spiller lives on a disability pension, has been unable to hold down full-time work, and keeps a pick-handle next to his bed.

He admits to long-term battles with alcohol and drugs.

'What happened stuffed me. I think I could have had quite a successful life if it wasn't for that.'

He said for years he was frightened Percy would come after him. 'In the line up at Russell Street (police station) I had to pick him. I had to walk up and point right at his nose. The look he gave me. I can still remember it.'

Five days after the killing Percy was interviewed by prison psychiatrist Dr Allen Bartholomew. 'Bart', as he was known in prison and police circles, had known most of Victoria's maddest and baddest and he had seen the worst and the most bizarre the human condition could provide.

He was as close as you could get to being unshockable.

Percy told Dr Bartholomew he had been watching the two children when he was 'overcome by a feeling — almost a compulsion — to do things to kids.' He said that over the previous four years he had weekly fantasies of sexually molesting and killing children. 'These thoughts worried him but he did nothing as he never thought he would be game enough to do it,' the psychiatrist later wrote.

Dr Bartholomew had learnt through dealing with 1500 criminal cases that time was on his side. His experience was that if you sat back you could develop a relationship with even the worst offenders and, with patience, learn their inner secrets.

But not with Percy. His few comments five days after the crime were to be his most animated. No-one could have known the window into his dark psyche was already closing.

AFTER a year in jail Percy described himself as 'a loner, not lonely', but Dr Bartholomew still hoped that over time he would be able to learn more about the distant killer.

'He demonstrates no behavioural evidence of any psychosis and his talk is rational – demonstrating reality-based thinking. He is rather retiring, having little to do with other prisoners, and only superficial relationships with the staff.

'I am quite unable, at this stage, to offer any prognosis regarding the prisoner, but clearly he is a potential danger to the youthful community. At present one can only wait and observe, and later attempt to further investigate the prisoner. I hope that he may be allowed to remain in G Division for the next few years — he is a rare and interesting case.'

An experienced parole officer observed him in the early days and stated: 'He is intelligent and his conversation follows a detailed, but matter of fact, cold format. He evidences no emotion and he describes his activities as if he was carving up a Sunday joint of meat.'

Most people who enter the jail system as adults without having been through the youth training system find it terrifying, but Percy adapted quickly, which was not surprising considering his lifelong capacity to withdraw into himself. 'Prison is all right if you go along with it and do what you are told and it's all right — like the navy,' he was to say during a review.

He had reasons to remember the Navy fondly. After he was charged he received $1270 in back pay and a fortnightly pension cheque while in jail – making him one of the most affluent prisoners in the system.

Much later he was able to invest his pension fund in gold, build a bank account of almost $30,000, and buy a personal computer.

His interests included playing the guitar, making model boats he put in bottles, reading science fiction and maritime novels, and playing tennis. He was quiet and described by the chief of the division as 'a model prisoner (who) consistently receives excellent reports for conduct and industry.'

It might have appeared that Percy was changing, but he wasn't. A routine search of his cell on 28 September, 1971, showed that he was still writing down bizarre and sadistic thoughts.

Prison officers found detailed plans of what he wanted to do with children. They found pictures of children hidden in the cell. The brutal and graphic writings belied his passive exterior.

'Thus at about September 1971 the prisoner was behaving in a manner very similar to the year or more prior to the killing with which he was charged: apparently normal behaviour to the ordinary onlooker but a grossly disturbed sexual fantasy life,' Dr Bartholomew recorded.

As the years passed Dr Bartholomew and other psychiatrists started to doubt if they would ever break through the walls around Percy's mind. In April, 1975, he wrote: 'He is efficient, undemonstrative, quiet and never forms a relationship with anybody. Because of this withdrawal from inter-personal contact, it is impossible to have any worthwhile knowledge of his feelings and his mental state. His answers are stereotypes and safe — non informative.

'I have to say that I can think of no valuable indices for release, and tend to wonder whether any really exist other than old age and or gross physical disability.'

The following year Dr Bartholomew described Percy as a 'colourless and somewhat withdrawn individual. His behaviour is above reproach but what thoughts go on in his mind I have no idea. Any endeavour to become to some extent involved with him is repulsed. He must be seen as a danger to children.'

He would talk to Dr Bartholomew about matters such as Test Match cricket, but refused to open up about his personality.

'I suspect, but cannot prove, that this prisoner has a rich (and morbid) fantasy sexual life but that he has learnt that it is to his own advantage that he covers it up. The prognosis is not good and I cannot see him being released for a long time yet,' he wrote in 1977.

Professor Richard Ball, who gave evidence at the first trial, re-interviewed Percy in January 1977. 'He volunteered nothing and extracting information was like pulling teeth.'

'I doubt that he is entirely without sadist fantasies.'

In 1979 he revived his teenage hobby of stamp collecting and the following year he started tertiary computer studies. He had earlier started group therapy for sex offenders, but after nine months he drifted back into his own world.

He did not want to leave a protection division in Pentridge because he had been in jail long enough to know what happened to child killers in mainstream jail. Computer nerds who cut up kids were easy prey for real crooks.

By 1980 he could be seen wandering around his division with a screwdriver, trusted to do electrical work in the jail. In his eleventh year in jail his supervisor wrote: 'One can't help but feeling that there is, in fact, much under the surface that he chooses not to reveal.'

He was then moved to J Division in February 1981 and for the first time Dr Bartholomew was prepared to write what many had suspected for years: Percy had beaten the system. He was not mad and had never been so. 'He is not formally psychiatrically ill, and is not in need of treatment at this time.'

Another psychiatrist, Pentridge Co-ordinator of Forensic Psychiatry Services, Doctor Stephens, wrote: 'Percy is sexually grossly disturbed and should never be released from prison.'

In 1984 Percy told his mind minders he did not dwell about the killing of Yvonne Tuohy. 'His memories of what occurred are now faded, but that he used to feel some concern for his victim's parents, but hardly thinks of them any more.'

In the same year Dr Stephens said Percy needed to be able to offer an insight into himself if he was ever to be understood. 'I doubt whether he ever will and expect that he will remain in jail until he is made safe by advanced old age or physical disease.'

According to a parole report Dr Stephens thought Percy was 'a highly dangerous, sadistic paedophile who should never be released from safe custody. He is not certifiable neither is he psychiatrically treatable and he is totally unsuited to a mental institution. If Percy is ever so transferred he will in all probability earn some degree of freedom as the result of reasonable and conforming behaviour. The consequences of such freedom could well prove tragic.

'At this stage it remains the combined opinions of Dr Stephens and the writer that Percy be contained in a maximum security environment for the rest of his life.'

By 1985 he had not seen his family for two years. He appeared not to care. The only time he showed emotion was when it was suggested that he would be transferred to a country prison. 'Percy, whose face was inscrutable, the eyes cold and mesmeric, suddenly displayed emotion. His lips trembled convulsively as he emotionally stated that he did not want to move from J Division because he had "his computers there".'

He started to write computer programs to help intellectually disabled children learn to read and was visited once a month by a volunteer social worker. Bob Hawke was Prime Minister, Alan Bond still a national hero and Christopher Skase had a solid reputation and sound lungs when Percy had served fifteen years in jail. A prison report in 1985 said 'It has been mentioned that he is suspected of committing other child murders and if ever taken off the Governor's Pleasure list may be charged by the police with other murders.'

One of the original homicide detectives, Dick Knight, who was to go on to become a respected assistant commissioner, remained convinced that Percy had killed before he attacked Yvonne Tuohy. He argued that no-one could have committed the Westernport murder 'cold' and that it was likely he was responsible for earlier crimes.

Files from around Australia were reviewed and unsolved child killings examined. Percy was considered a suspect in the abduction murders of Christine Sharrock and Marianne Schmidt on Sydney's Wanda Beach in January, 1965, the three Beaumont children in Adelaide in 1966, Alan Redston, a six-year-old murdered in Canberra in September, 1966, Simon Brook, a young boy killed in Sydney in 1968 and Linda Stillwell, 7, abducted from St Kilda in August, 1968. Thirty years later the questions remained unanswered.

Dr Stephens said Percy was a dangerously abnormal personality, but not mentally sick in the accepted sense.

He was moved against his will to Beechworth prison in July 1986. At first he was unhappy because he did not have access to his computer and did not like the cold weather. He said 'he wasn't holding his breath' waiting for a release date. The penny had finally dropped.

Six psychiatrists interviewed Percy and none found signs of treatable mental disease.

Dr Richard Ball, by then Professor of Psychiatry at Melbourne University, saw him again in February 1988. He reported that Percy refused to talk to others and spent most of his time either quietly reading, listening to the radio or resting, staring into space.

'In a formal sense I suppose he could be regarded as without psychiatric illness,' Dr Ball wrote.

Professor Ball said he didn't believe Percy's statements that he couldn't remember what happened over the killing. He said he offered Percy the chance to take a truth drug, purely to judge his reaction. He refused the offer. 'I think this man has always been very secretive about his fantasies and his actions. It is very clear of course that for many years prior to his apprehension he had successfully hidden these from public scrutiny, even when living in a communal setting such as the navy.

'I have the feeling that this man is dissimulating and is just not prepared to admit his feelings and impulses.'

As a test Professor Ball decided to put Percy under pressure, bringing up horrible details of the torture and murder he had committed. 'He did not appear distressed in any way. There was no evidence of sweating, raised pulse rate, his respiratory rate remained unchanged, his colour was no different, his eye contact remained exactly the same. I might simply have been talking about the kinds of cheese that one eats.

'I think he must be regarded as having an abnormal personality with major sexual deviation and I cannot assure myself that this has changed for the better.'

Professor Ball added that the problem might get worse, not better. 'I suppose one needs to consider the possibility that sometimes age withers control rather than decreasing drive.'

By 1988 Percy's parents had retired to live in a caravan park and his younger brother operated the family's car air-conditioning business in Queensland. The parents went on an extended holiday, travelling around Australia.

Percy told prison officer he no longer had fantasies about children and wanted to be released. He said talk of him being involved in other child murders was a fixation of the media.

He still received an invalid pension from the navy and had saved $9000. Visits from his family became less frequent and he had not seen his brothers for five years. The mail chess games with his closest brother stopped years earlier.

He smoked, did not take illegal drugs and was considered fit. His transfer to Beechworth failed due to some 'hassles with blokes over a number of things.' He returned to Pentridge seven months later. In September, 1987, he was moved to Castlemaine jail.

His favourite television program was *A Country Practice*.

He began to age, lose his hair and develop the defeatist attitude of a man who has realised he may never be freed. 'That's what jail does to you,' he said.

His one outside friend, volunteer social worker, George McNaughton, retired and lost contact. In September ,1988, he was stabbed in the chest by another prisoner at Castlemaine who falsely believed he had killed the inmate's niece. Percy escaped serious injury.

He followed a vague interest in following Fitzroy in the football and kept an interest in Test cricket.

In 1990 Dr John Grigor from Mont Park Hospital suggested Percy be moved from prison and treated with drugs to suppress his sadistic sexuality. It was the first hope for Percy in years, but it failed to eventuate.

In 1991 he was described as an 'oddball, but no trouble whatsoever.' Prison officers said he mixed only with fellow sex offenders who, like him, refused to take responsibility for their crimes.

In his sixteenth review his interviewer tried a different approach to get through the 'cold and remote' veneer. For years Percy would answer all questions with a detached, rehearsed response. This time he was caught off-guard. 'Why do you think society takes such a dim view of people murdering children?' he was asked.

Then Percy did something he had rarely done in twenty years — he laughed.

'Why, there would be nobody left, would there?' he spluttered.

Wrong answer.

The interviewer wrote in his conclusion, 'Percy presents as an unacceptable risk and as such should be confined in the safe and, above all, secure custody of a correctional facility indefinitely.'

In 1992 psychiatrist Dr Neville Parker reviewed the case. He said Percy was not insane and the Supreme Court jury had got it wrong. 'There was nothing at the time to suggest that he was psychotic when he committed the crime, nor that he had ever had a mental illness.'

He said he didn't believe there was any treatment that 'could hold out any hope of changing this man's very perverted sexual drives.'

By 1992 he had effectively given up hope of ever being released, believing psychiatrists had preconceived ideas about him.

In 1993, when asked about his crime, he said he didn't think about it and said his victim could have been 'hit by a bus a week later and died.' He refused to join any therapeutic programs. The interviewer said Percy's only apparent regret was the crime had 'stuffed up' his life.

Professor Paul Mullen wrote in 1993 that Percy was sane. 'The wisdom or otherwise of the court's finding in Mr Percy's case may be open to question but it is not open to modification.'

He said it was unsatisfactory that Percy was still in a jail but there was no secure facility suitable for him outside of the prison system.

By 1994 he had more than $25,000 in bank accounts and investments in gold. His navy pension was forwarded to the family business.

He played cricket once a week at Ararat and worked with his computer.

In 1995 Attorney General Jan Wade said she wanted to know if there were any moves to transfer Percy to a hospital because of the 'need for the strictest security at all times.'

In 1997 he was developing a computer program to retrieve cricket statistics and remained an avid newspaper reader. According to his prison review: 'Currently the objective with Mr Percy can only be for reasonably humane, long-term detention.'

After spending five years in Ararat he was involved in carpet bowls and organised intra-prison competitions, but only at a superficial level. He was still, in 1998, marooned on an emotional island the way he'd always been.

He'd had what was described as a 'remarkably uneventful prison history.' He had no friends and had made no efforts to deal with his problems.

He outlasted his investigators and most of captors. He outlasted three of the jails where he was an inmate: Beechworth, Pentridge and Castlemaine have all been closed.

His prison record showed he was one of the best-behaved inmates in Australia. In November, 1995, he was fined $60 for having too many educational tapes in his cell.

A little earlier he had been transported from Ararat to Pentridge for an assessment. He was taken in a private prison van that had windows. He was, noted an observer, 'clearly elated by this experience as it is perhaps the first time Percy has viewed the open country side in almost twenty-five years.'

## WHAT THE JUDGE SAID:

FINAL judgment of Justice Eames, delivered on 30 September, 1998:

'The notes seized from Mr Percy's car after the killing of the young girl disclosed that her abduction and death were not spontaneous events, but occurred very much as the notes anticipated that such events might occur.

In 1971, in his cell, it was discovered that Mr Percy had comprehensive notes describing even more horrific fantasies concerning abduction, imprisonment, torture, rape and killing of children. Also located was a collage of newspaper photographs of children, with obscene additional artwork in Mr Percy's hand.

The notes are of the most horrifying nature, which, again, I consider it unnecessary to describe in detail.

Mr Percy had written a complex chart, with first names given to proposed victims, in which he traced a pattern of conduct which would take place over many years involving the rape, torture and killing of named children.

Among the first names of the children referred to in these 1971 notes were some names which coincided with those of children of a family known to him, which family he had occasionally visited at the time of his arrest.

There were, too, some other references in the notes which suggested that the perverted fantasies did relate to those children, even if other names used were those of imaginary children. I have before me a statement by the father of those, now adult, children, urging that Mr Percy not be released.

Mr Percy did not give evidence to me, and his assertion to those who interviewed him — that he no longer holds violent sexual fantasies — has not been tested.

There is no doubt, whatsoever, in my opinion, that both at 1969 and at 1971 Mr Percy was indeed a very dangerous man whose release from custody would have been inconceivable. The question is whether he remains such a dangerous person.

In my opinion, an examination of the 1969 and 1971 material, together with knowledge of the facts surrounding the killing, tend to confirm that not only was Mr Percy very dangerous at the time, he remains so, because the underlying sadistic condition was then, and remains now, deeply entrenched. He has received no treatment of any kind which might have changed that situation. He has shown no real interest in having such treatment. He has demonstrated no significant remorse or anxiety, at least none which I find credible, as to the circumstances which caused him to kill.

Because I am satisfied that Mr Percy holds those fantasies, then, in my opinion, the conclusion is irresistible that he remains as dangerous now as he was in 1969 and 1971.

Prior to, and during the course of, my hearings several articles appeared in the newspapers which speculated that Mr Percy may have committed more killings than that of Elizabeth Tuohy. There is no evidence before me to support that assertion.

Amongst the materials placed before me was a statement by Detective Senior Constable K. S. Robertson of the Victoria Police, dated 5 May, 1970. In that report Robertson referred to an interview conducted with Mr Percy about the deaths and disappearances of other children, both in NSW and Canberra. I did not hear any evidence from Mr Robertson. At its highest the statement of Mr Robertson records Mr Percy's agreement that on other occasions prior to the death of Elizabeth Tuohy, whilst on beaches in New South Wales, he had sordid thoughts towards children and his agreement that he might have committed other offences had not the children been in the company of their parents.

The note records that police had no evidence to connect Mr Percy to any other killings. Only one item of 'evidence' was advanced. When questioned about one killing in Sydney he is recorded as having said: 'I could have done it but I can't remember.'

TELEPHONE 350.1322

All communications to be addressed to—
The Psychiatrist Superintendent

SOCIAL WELFARE DEPARTMENT
PRISONS DIVISION

PSYCHIATRIC CLINIC
H. M. PENTRIDGE PRISON,
COBURG, 3058

9th April, 1975

The Secretary,
Parole Board,
Social Welfare Department,
1 Macarthur Street,
MELBOURNE.

C O N F I D E N T I A L

Dear Sir,

re:  Derek E. PERCY

The abovenamed prisoner has been an inmate of G.
Division since my last report (26.2.74).

In no way has he changed in his behaviour, and his
declared mental state is unchanged.

He works well in the Division; he is efficient,
undemonstrative, quiet and never forms any meaningful degree
of relationship with anybody.  He is the nearest thing to
a robot I have met for a long time.  Because of this withdrawal from inter-personal contact, it is impossible to have
any worth-while knowledge of his feelings and his mental
state.  His answers are stereotyped and "safe" – non-
informative.

At this time I have not been able to have the
prisoner re-tested by a psychologist as I placed the matter
on a low priority basis, and other matters have been deemed
of greater urgency.  However, as soon as practicable I shall
arrange further testing.

Clearly at this time the prisoner cannot be
considered for release from H.M.P.Pentridge – other than to
some other place of security – and I can see no brief for
recommending that he leave G.Division, and he has expressed
no desire to leave.

I might add, as a footnote, that I am somewhat
exercised as to what criteria one needs to ever recommend
release, either absolutely or to lesser security.  It has
been noted in the literature that good institutional behaviour
is no guide to the safety of releasing.  This is a matter
that will no doubt cause anxiety to the Board in the years
to come, but at this stage I have to say that I can think
of no very valuable indices for release, and tend to wonder
whether any really exist other than old age and/or gross
physical disability.  This is, perhaps, a matter worthy
of discussion at some time.

Yours faithfully,

(A. A. Bartholomew)
MBBS, DPM, DPR, M.R.C.Psych., F.A.N.Z.C.P., M.A.Ps.S.
Consultant Psychiatrist in Charge
Hon. Senior Associate, Forensic Psychiatry,
Dept.Psychiatry, University of Melbourne.

# CHAPTER 11

# Riding with the enemy

## Inside the Bandidos bike gang

*Kulakowski gave the nod and they*
*trashed the place and bashed the bouncers*

IT was the spot a film director might pick for the opening scene of a
bikie movie. Bleak, damp Ballarat, with the first morning of winter
only hours away. Two angry, suspicious men and two detectives from
the organised crime squad, collars turned up against the biting cold,
meet near an isolated hamburger stand in a desolate car park.

Out of sight, armed police watch, ready to move if things turn ugly.
The stakes were high. Melbourne police had called the meeting to stop
what was destined to be a full-scale bikie war. Trouble had been
fermenting for just over a year and the organised crime squad knew
that if nothing was done to prevent the slide towards armed confrontation, killings would follow.

The police wanted to get together representatives of two warring
bike groups: the Vikings, who for years had been the tough gang that
controlled Ballarat, and the Bandidos, predators with a world-wide
reputation for violence and drugs. The outlaw motorcycle world is
always filled with tensions between groups, but usually there is a
balance between the bravado of drug-enhanced macho aggression and
the basic instinct of self preservation that ensures an uneasy peace.

But it doesn't take much to upset the fine balance and turn a stand-off into a running war. The balance was destroyed in Victoria when the two heaviest bikie groups agreed to divide the state like a ripe peach, leaving the remaining gangs dangerously exposed.

According to police intelligence, The Hells Angels, long the bikie power in South-East Australia, agreed to allow the Bandidos to expand into regional Victoria on the condition the Angels' power remained unchallenged in Melbourne. The two gangs still had their skirmishes, including the occasional drunken bashing, but in general the pact held.

The Bandidos were expansionists from way back. They moved into country centres and used their national numbers to take over local bikie groups. Join us, or get beaten to a pulp, was the general message. This resulted in country club-houses being signed over, an increase in membership and new drug distribution opportunities.

They were not the only gang in the take-over business. In 1993 a man was shot dead and several others tortured when the Rebels took over the Warlocks in Geelong. In the bikie world, the strong devour the weak. Rather like the stockmarket, but with guns and real blood.

In April, 1995, the Bandidos took over the Broke Brothers in Kyabram. Only three Broke Brothers joined, the rest were 'retired'. The next month the Bandidos absorbed the Ballarat gang the Loners. The Loners and the Vikings had been the local gangs for years and although they hated each other they managed to co-exist in an uneasy peace. The Bandidos also opened a Geelong chapter in July.

In May the Bandidos decided to take over the Vikings, but the local gang refused the 'offer'. This led to a series of increasingly violent incidents over the following year that convinced police a gang war was almost inevitable.

In April, 1995, the Vikings' Ballarat clubhouse was sprayed with gunfire. In response several Melbourne outlaw motorcycle gangs vowed to support the Vikings. In May, a bike shop owned by a Bandidos' member was fire-bombed. In November, a Bandido was the victim of a hit-run. The car that struck him was believed to have been driven by a Hells Angel. In February, 1996, a car containing Vikings members was shot nearly twenty times in a drive-by shooting.

A man was systematically beaten with a baseball bat, another was bashed, and teams of armed bikies were seen driving through Sebastopol, near Ballarat, with shotgun barrels stuck out the windows. Police searched the house of one bikie and found twenty-one sticks of gelignite and three shotguns, members of one gang were surrounded in a hotel and one bikie was beaten up at a Ballarat intersection in front of members of the public. One bikie group began to compile dossiers on rivals, including photos, home and business addresses, and known movements.

When facing a violent feud, police often try to broker a peace deal behind the scenes. There are no sensational headlines and no spectacular arrests, but many underworld figures owe their lives to quiet police intervention before guns do the talking.

But on that Friday night, 31 May, 1996, only the Vikings wanted to talk to Detective Senior Sergeant Graham Larchin and Detective Sergeant Rob Sodomaco from the organised crime squad. In the darkened carpark the two Vikings office bearers told the detectives their club wanted to exist in its own right and their members would respond with violence only if attacked.

The Bandidos didn't even bother to turn up. Police telephoned them the following day, still trying to negotiate peace. The Bandidos responded with their own demands: they wanted guarantees that police would not attend, or even monitor national bike runs or fundraising concerts. They had their own plans and a peace deal with the Vikings was not part of them. The detectives concluded the bikies believed they were a law unto themselves.

Detectives reported back to senior officers that the Bandidos effectively wanted to be able to deal drugs without any police resistance. At that point the police decided conciliation and community policing had failed. It was time for old-fashioned detective work.

The target committee of the state crime squads met and declared Bandidos a major organised crime target and a priority investigation.

Over the previous thirty years target policing had usually failed against bike gangs. Police success against bikies has involved opportunistic investigations into individual crimes, not long-term exposure of the organisations themselves.

The trouble has been that outlaw motorcycle gangs around the world have proven almost impossible to infiltrate. In one case in the US, the undercover policeman was accepted into the bike group, but he turned and ultimately became worse than the criminals he was sent to pursue.

Despite concerns over the long-term chances of success, police set up Operation Barkly, the secret investigation into the Bandidos. In mid-1996 the Covert Investigation Unit briefed two of its best undercover men. Their mission: to do the impossible. That is, get inside the gang, be accepted as brothers and provide evidence that would stand up in court against Queen's Counsel's cross examination.

Wes and Alby were born. They were two unemployed men in their late twenties on the fringes of the criminal world. Wes was to have a criminal record involving drugs. They were then set up in a rented house in Ballarat. Both were keen to make money and were happy to go outside the law to do it.

To what length the police department went to provide false identities for the men must remain secret, as these methods will be used again. Suffice to say Wes and Alby were to go deeper undercover than any police in Australia had ever been before.

THE carefully sculptured image of the Bandidos as a group of renegades who dropped out of society to share an interest in bikes, booze and broads is anything but true. The bikie world actually mimics mainstream society where money and power open doors and those who do not obey the rules are eventually shunned.

At a struggling chapter like Ballarat the fee for members was $105 per month plus $1000 to join, putting it in a league just behind an exclusive club such as Royal Melbourne Golf Club.

According to police the fees for members at the Prospect chapter in Sydney were $600 a month — seemingly steep dues given that most of the members were supposed to be unemployed battlers on the dole. Most of each month's dues were divided between the national defence fund, local legal fees, the central chapter and clubhouse rent. Members leaving the club were also expected to 'donate' their Harley Davidsons to the Bandidos. This was no glee club.

One young member without a job said he had just bought a top of the range Landcruiser for $60,000 and a Harley for $30,000. 'Paid cash,' he bragged. The gang had set up chapters in Geelong, Ballarat, Perth, Brisbane's hinterland, Griffith, Hunter Valley, Sydney, inner Sydney, Prospect, NSW north coast, inner Brisbane and Cairns.

With almost 300 members in Australia and connections with the overseas organisation, they had the power to intimidate and apparently had access to unlimited weaponry to back up any threats.

Police say the Bandidos used a shoulder-fired anti-tank rocket launcher to kill two and injure seventeen at a Copenhagen Hells Angels' party in 1996. According to police, one of the suspects later travelled to Australia for a national bike run and complained that he couldn't hear for two weeks after he fired the rocket.

The Bandido Motorcycle gang was formed in Texas in 1966 by Donald Eugene Chambers, who was later convicted of killing two men who allegedly ripped off the gang in a drug deal. According to the FBI, the first Australian chapter was established in Sydney in 1983.

The FBI found the Sydney chapter was opened to give the gang access to Australian chemicals, banned in the US, that could be used in the production of amphetamines.

For fifteen years police have regarded the Bandidos as the most violent bikie gang in Australia. In 1984 the Bandidos and the Commancheros opened fire on each other in what became known as the Milperra Father's Day massacre that left six bikies and a fifteen-year-old girl dead. The gangs gave the impression it was a romantic battle over 'turf'. It wasn't. It was over drugs.

According to US authorities the Bandidos is one of 'The Big Four' international bikie organised crime groups. It has one of the best counter-intelligence systems and is considered the hardest to crack.

It was not the only international bikie group to establish strong links in Australia. Lax rules in relation to chemicals used for speed, such as P2P, meant this country was regarded as ripe for colonisation. The US Hells Angels were provided with huge quantities of P2P from their Australian connections, smuggled into America in pineapple tins. An American hitman was intercepted at Melbourne airport after police received information he had taken a contract to kill a local detective.

The federal government tried to ban international bikie leaders from entering Australia, but many still managed to arrive, some legally, and others under false names. Police around Australia were alerted in 1998 to look for an international outlaw bikie boss, wanted for questioning in the US over a series of murders and bombings linked with organised crime.

The FBI contacted the Australian Bureau of Criminal Intelligence and asked for assistance after receiving information that the international president of the Outlaws Motorcycle Club, Harry Joseph Bowman, might be hiding in Australia.

Bowman, one of the FBI's top ten most wanted criminals, was reported to be 'armed and extremely dangerous.'

According to the FBI: 'Bowman heads the Outlaws operations in more than thirty cities in the United States and twenty chapters in at least four other countries (including Australia). Bowman may be guarded by members of the Outlaws.

'Harry Joseph Bowman, international president of the Outlaws Motorcycle Club, is wanted for his alleged involvement in violent racketeering acts (that) include murders, bombings, drug trafficking, extortion, firearms violations, and other acts of violence.

'Bowman was allegedly involved in the murders of two Outlaws members and may have participated in the murder of a rival motorcycle club member. The indictment alleges that he ordered the bombings of rival motorcycle clubhouses.'

The FBI has offered a $50,000 reward for information leading to his arrest.

The Outlaws were formed in Chicago in the 1950s and Bowman, known as 'Taco' took over as National President in 1984. US authorities say the gang has been heavily involved in distributing cocaine in Florida, and has developed strong drug connections in Colombia and Cuba.

US police claim the Outlaws were responsible for at least 115 murders over thirteen years, and another twenty-nine murders in Canada. 'The Outlaws have also utilised explosives and bombing devices in carrying out acts against perceived "enemies",' an FBI investigation found.

'The Outlaws engage in extensive witness intimidation and jury tampering efforts which closely parallel other outlaw motorcycle gang tactics.'

WHEN Victorian police decided to try to infiltrate one of the Big Four, they knew the tactic had failed around the world. Any chance of success rested with the ability of the two undercover police selected for the job.

Alby and Wes moved to Ballarat determined to keep a low profile. Being too keen would have ruined their chances. They had to develop trust with a gang of men who seemed determined to trust nobody.

The Bandidos say they are no longer part of society. 'This is why we look repulsive. We're saying we don't want to be like you or look like you,' according to their code. Their motto is 'God forgives, Bandidos don't.'

But bike gangs can't live in isolation. They need cannon fodder: men who want to be near the tough guys and bask in dubious reflected glory. These are the people seen to be disposable. They are used to guard buildings and run errands. In return they attend parties and can buy drugs at a cheaper rate.

When Wes and Alby drifted into town they were treated with suspicion at first. But over months they ran into the Bandidos at pubs and drinking holes in the area and the relationships slowly warmed.

To the bikies, the two seemed ideal, men who were prepared to look the other way at the right time and weren't too concerned about the subtleties of the criminal code. In November, 1996, Wes and Alby were invited to the clubhouse at 4 Greenbank Court, Delacombe, for a party.

If it was a test, they passed. It was the first step in a thirteen-month journey that would lead the two undercover police to give up their professional and personal lives to become beer-swilling, foul-mouthed bikies.

They stayed on the periphery before finally being invited to become 'hangarounds'. This put them in a position where they were welcome at any Bandidos' chapter in Australia.

They were in.

Alby arrived as a would-be bikie. He had a Harley Davidson borrowed by the force for the job. Wes bought his from the president of the Ballarat chapter, Peter Skrokov, with $17,000 provided by the police department. 'We got ripped-off,' a police bean-counter observed later.

It might sound glamorous, to leave the mundane routine of most jobs to ride motorbikes and live on the edge. But the edge was doubly dangerous for the undercover operators — one slip could mean exposure and death. They had to remember every lie and stick strictly to the script.

The simplest everyday occurrences could take on new and sometimes frightening significance. Everybody sometimes runs into an old friend or acquaintance in the strangest place. For most people it is merely an unexpected surprise. For an undercover police officer it could be fatal. During the operation one of the police, wearing his Bandido leathers, was filling his Harley Davidson with petrol at a service station. He looked up to see his next-door neighbour from his "other life" filling the tank of the family sedan at the next bowser. To his relief he passed unrecognised.

Wes and Alby were to report, word for word, what they had learnt, including the Bandidos' greeting — right handshake, left arm embrace and kiss on the lips. Ironically, the police agents may have done the bikies they were tracking a huge favour in the long term. Senior police believe the undercovers not only gathered evidence to use in prosecutions, but saved lives with several early warnings of planned attacks on opposition bikie groups. More than once they slipped away to warn of planned ambushes and police were able to set up blitzes, road blocks and other operations to stop the violence. Each time it was made to look as though it was just bad luck that thwarted the Bandidos attacks.

Detective Superintendent Ian Thomas, the head of the organised crime and task force division, said; 'There is no doubt the two undercover police were at grave risk. Their work helped us move in and stop incidents with the potential to turn violent.'

But it was not one-way traffic. The club rule enforcer, the Ballarat Sergeant-at-Arms, Andrew Michlin, approached Wes and Alby and asked would they grow hydroponic marijuana in their home? It was an offer too good to refuse.

Their rented home in Lydiard Street, Ballarat, was filled with state-of-the-art recording equipment. Michlin set up one of the bedrooms as an indoor nursery, complete with lights, watering systems and tubs. It was all recorded.

Wes and Alby were promoted to 'prospects' in August, 1997, and on 21 October they were promoted to full members on twelve months probation. This was personally ratified by the national president of the Bandidos, Michael Kulakowski.

The power and charisma of Kulakowski was undisputed. He was internationally respected in the bikie world, so much so that he flew to the US in July 1996 to be part of peace negotiations to stop a war between the Hells Angels and the Bandidos in Europe that had claimed eleven lives.

A former soldier and rodeo rider, 'Mick K' or 'Chaos' as he was known by his bikie mates, opted out of mainstream society at forty, but he still enjoyed the trappings of success. He drove a Mercedes, owned a $300,000 home and a top of the range Harley Davidson.

The Bandidos already had a strong grip on the amphetamines market and a healthy sideline in marijuana. But under Kulakowski the gang was moving into the lucrative club drugs of ecstasy and LSD.

According to police the Bandidos needed distribution points to move into the new wave of drugs and began to set up 'techno discos' where they could begin to cultivate thousands of new clients.

Senior Victorian Bandidos were observed in Sydney discussing plans to open techno discos in Ballarat and Geelong as fronts to sell ecstasy and LSD as part of the national expansion.

Wes and Alby were able to buy LSD from the Ballarat Bandidos for $5 a tab. Later they were able to buy it for $3.50 from the Sydney chapter as brothers were prepared to undercut brothers. They transferred money to a Bandido-controlled bank account in NSW and the drugs were moved by express post to a designated post box.

The profits were massive, with each tab selling for $7 retail. Each sheet contained 200 tabs and the Bandidos bragged their courier was walking in through Sydney airport carrying a bundle of LSD sheets twenty-five centimetres thick on every smuggling run.

Bandidos were selling LSD with the Sydney Olympic Logo, a Smiley design, love hearts, and Beavis and Butthead stamps. According to the Melbourne undercovers, the Victorian Bandidos planned to move into the party drug scene. Police were later to say that Alby and Wes were involved in more than thirty deals buying marijuana, amphetamines, LSD and ecstasy from Bandidos in three states during their thirteen months living undercover. They were so trusted that Alby became the secretary-elect for the Ballarat chapter, giving him access to the club's financial records.

The Bandidos continued their plans to expand through regional Victoria. The next target was Wangaratta and that meant an attack on the local club, the Tramps. In February, 1996, the President of the Tramps received a letter in the post. It said the Tramps, their friends and children, would be in danger if the gang did not disband and leave town.

In May, 1997, the Broke Brothers tried to reform for a run. About thirty Bandidos from Ballarat and Geelong rode to Kyabram for a show of strength.

But Wes and Alby were able to report the planned attack in time that police gathered at Kyabram in such force they were able to keep the hostile groups apart.

Despite the ongoing violence the bikies continued to refuse to co-operate with police. The Sergeant-At-Arms, Andrew Michlin, made the mistake of allowing police to conduct a search without a warrant. He was busted back to prospect as a punishment.

The power of the group over the individual is complete. A member of the Griffith chapter, Dean Francis Corboy, declared that a member of the Tramps looked the wrong way at him at Wangaratta on 3 October, 1997. He summoned sixty members from Geelong, Ballarat and Griffith for a confrontation at Wangaratta.

According to the Bandidos code, members were expected to just walk out of their jobs and drive. When a brother needs help, whether he is right or wrong, you must support him. But one of the under-covers managed to get the message to police and when the Bandido strike force turned up there 'just happened' to be a major police blitz on in Wangaratta. Wherever the bikies went they were pulled over. Also unexplained was why no members of the Tramps were anywhere to be seen that night.

Just to show their strength the Bandidos started their 1997 National run in Wangaratta on 23 October, with more than 250 bikers from Australia and around the world present in full colours. To make matters worse for a country town with limited police resources it was the break-up day for VCE students. The town would be filled with drunken bikies and drunken teenage girls. It was every parent's nightmare. Police had a meeting with Kulakowski and explained the situation. He agreed to keep control and 'Chaos' sent out the message to his troops — stay cool. The night passed without incident. 'That was his power,' a senior policeman said. The power to make peace, or war, at whim.

The 250 bikies moved on to Geelong and, according to police, went to a popular local nightclub. The owner set up a special room for them but they wanted the run of the nightclub and the manager baulked. Kulakowski gave the nod and they trashed the place and bashed the bouncers. No official complaint was ever lodged.

On 24 October, 1997, some of the gang, including a few international Bandidos, went out to test fire their illegal firearms. One of the overseas visitors had to be dissuaded from opening fire on a passing Geelong-Melbourne train.

The National Run was to prove the highlight of Kulakowski's reign. He had charisma and power, but that won't stop a bullet. On 9 November Kulakowski, Sergeant-at-Arms Bruce Harrison and fellow member Rick De Stoop, were shot dead in the basement of a Sydney dance club. Another Bandido was shot in the head, but survived.

Bandidos from around Australia, including the two undercover police, drove to Sydney for the funeral. In a ritual fit for royalty more than 200 bikies filed past for a brief moment with their dead leader.

It is alleged one of the undercover officers bent over to embrace the deceased leader and whispered into the casket, 'I'm a copper, you know.'

Dead men tell no tales.

But while the bikies were grieving, business is business and life goes on. Wes and Alby were able to buy a thousand LSD tabs from one of the Sydney leaders of the Bandidos straight after the funeral.

With the danger of revenge killings after the death of the three Bandidos, police had to move quickly.

Wes and Alby were called back in so they wouldn't be at risk. On 11 December more than a hundred police in four states made co-ordinated raids. Nineteen people were arrested and drugs with a street value of more than $1 million were seized. They also found chemicals suitable for making amphetamines worth $6 million, and seized firearms, including an AK 47 rifle and pen pistols. The head of Operation Barkly, Detective Inspector Andrew Allen, said 'Some outlaw motorcycle gangs seem to think that the law does not relate to them. I think we have shown that no-one is beyond policing.

'These gangs must learn that if you traffick drugs and engage in unlawful activities, sooner or later you will be locked up.

'While Operation Barkly has made inroads into the Bandidos, history has shown that these gangs must be continually monitored. Some outlaw bikie groups make a public show of supporting charities to clean up their images when the truth is many are heavily involved in major criminal activities.'

Wes and Alby had gathered so much evidence that most of the bikies charged decided to plead guilty. But the main players, such as Peter Skrokov and Andrew Michlin, were destined to spend only about six months in jail, less than half the time the two police risked their lives infiltrating the group.

In 1998, the last of the arrested bikies, Dean Corboy, pleaded guilty in the Wangaratta Magistrates' Court to trafficking amphetamines. He was sentenced to eight months, with six months suspended — an effective jail term of two months.

But justice sometimes moves in mysterious ways. Another court has also passed judgment on the main players. According to police intelligence, the National Chapter of the Bandidos has sentenced the bikies who embraced Wes and Alby to be flogged when they are released from jail. There will be no appeal.

Police say Wes and Alby have received professional counselling so they can re-enter mainstream policing.

Intelligence reports indicate there are still contracts out on their lives.

# CHAPTER 12

# Blood on the tracks
## Australia's worst train disaster

*Not all the scars from
Granville are physical*

GARY *James Case, taxi driver, is looking out the window of his flat in
Bridge Street, Granville, when he sees the Blue Mountains express on
the railway line below. He hears what he describes later as 'two
metallic noises' as it approaches the overhead bridge spanning the
line. The big locomotive spears off the rails, veers, then tips and skids,
dragging the first carriage with it. It has hit the iron stanchion supporting the bridge. Ten seconds later there is a massive 'whoomph'. The
bridge has fallen on two carriages. It sounds like a bomb, and is just
as deadly. A man calls out 'Trust in God, Christ will save you.' Another
is heard giving himself the last rites. It is 8.12am, 18 January 1977.*

SHE was nineteen, crushed beneath steel girders and three hundred
tonnes of concrete and surrounded by the dead and the dying. Yet she
found strength to ask questions that made the policeman want to cry.

Instead, he lied. Fiercely – as if someone's life depended on it.
Which, in a way, the girl's did. He had already saved her once, after
crawling through the tiny, suffocating space in the rubble between the
bodies, fearing that the concrete slab a few centimetres above his skull

could drop at any moment, killing him and anyone else still alive. When he'd found her, seen that her face was turning blue, he risked moving her injured head to let her breathe, and prayed it wouldn't harm her spine. She started breathing, but her legs were pulped, her pelvis smashed and she was bleeding so much it seemed she would soon be just another body among many.

But she wouldn't give in. First she asked him if she would live. Yes, he said. Then she asked if she'd be able to walk again. Again, the rescue policeman didn't hesitate. Then she asked him a question that still touches him more than all the awful things he's seen. 'Will I ever be able to have a baby?' she whispered.

There was a pause, broken by the moans of the injured and the dying entombed in the crushed railway carriage. 'Yeah,' he said gently. 'God can do miracles.'

He said it but he didn't believe it, then. Even when, hours later, they finally inched Debbie Skow's broken body on to a stretcher and out of the horror and into hospital, Constable Gary Raymond thought the brave girl would die.

But he was wrong. Debbie Skow was in a coma for sixty-five days, and endured dozens of operations, but she lived. She eventually walked a little, despite losing a leg. She married. And, many years later, after adopting a daughter because she thought she would never conceive, Debbie had a baby. A miracle, just as he'd said.

There were other miracles at Granville on that summer morning more than twenty years ago, the day Australia's worst train disaster killed eighty-three people on their way to work in Sydney.

Debbie Skow was one of 213 injured, and Gary Raymond just one of many rescuers. Each has a story, though not all can be told.

IT was a Tuesday, a hot morning guaranteeing a scorching afternoon, and Dick Lamb's day off from the police search and rescue squad. He was taking his family to his father's place on the northern beaches. They left home at Milperra in Sydney's western suburbs about 8am, already in shorts and thongs.

Minutes later Lamb pulled the family Falcon into Woodville Road to head through Granville. The radio was tuned to the 2UE breakfast show. Suddenly, the flip chat was shattered by a news flash. A bridge had fallen on a train at Granville; people were trapped. Lamb turned left into Bold Street and gunned the V-8 motor – but not for long. As he approached the railway cutting he saw the void where the Bold Street bridge had been. He jumped out, ran to the edge of the bridge and looked over.

An entire span of concrete and steel had fallen. Beneath it were two passenger carriages, their roofs squashed below the level of the seats.

An overturned locomotive, a wrecked carriage and one eerily unscathed carriage were scattered on the city side of the broken bridge. Other carriages were strung crookedly on the opposite side.

Lamb yelled to his wife to go home for his overalls, cap and heavy boots. He climbed down the broken bridge, dodging three Holdens and a motorbike stranded on it. He was one of the first police at the scene, but not the first helper.

'The first thing I saw,' he was to recall, 'were the local butchers, the Dawson brothers, helping people out of the wreck. They were great blokes. There were people everywhere. Some were lying down. Some trying to get up. Some walking around, dazed, suffering all sorts of injuries.

'There were some ambulance officers already there. I ran under the bridge and looked up at the carriages. I could hear the screaming. People were hanging out of the carriages.'

He scrambled back up the bridge to the road. Car 3410 from Fairfield police station had just arrived. He raced over, pulling his identity badge from his shorts and flashing it at the stunned uniformed police before grabbing the radio to tell headquarters how serious it was, and demanding all available equipment.

Then he ran down to start sorting the living from the dead and dying. A few minutes later he looked up and saw his longtime crewmate arrive in a rescue truck. 'Bruce!' he yelled, waving frantically. At least now they had some proper equipment. And another level head to help bring order to the sickening chaos.

BRUCE Gane usually took the truck home to Moorebank on nights he was on call. If there was an emergency he'd pick up Lamb, who lived nearby, and off they'd go, lights flashing, siren wailing.

That morning Gane got into the truck, as usual, just after 8am, routinely flicked on the police radio and called in. A couple of minutes later he was told to switch to channel four, the working channel for that area. Something was on.

The first messages about Granville were vague. 'They said it was just a footbridge that had collapsed on a train and that there was two or three people trapped. I tried to think where there was a footbridge. They said to go to Bold Street.'

He pushed the big eight-tonner hard. It took ten minutes, and the radio crackled bad news with mounting urgency. When he got there, he was to recall, he saw his mate Dick Lamb in the middle of 'a hell of a mess'.

Lamb ran up a fireman's ladder propped against the cutting and snatched spare overalls, boots and as much equipment as he could carry. He ordered uniformed police to carry more gear down to the crash.

Rescue trucks were starting to arrive from all over Sydney. One, from police search-and-rescue headquarters in Redfern, was driven by Gary Raymond. When he'd first got the call he imagined a goods train with an oversize load stuck under a bridge. Each call painted a grimmer picture.

A policeman who'd seen only the first carriage reported 'a small number injured'. The next report said people were trapped under the bridge. The next demanded the rescue squad urgently. But it wasn't until he saw it himself that Raymond realised how bad it was.

The bridge had fallen on the third and fourth carriages. Bruce Gane went to carriage four, and Lamb to carriage three, where he cut a hole in the roof with a chainsaw and let himself into the charnel house inside.

Logic told him how many passengers must be trapped, but he was still shocked by the number of dead and injured in the seats. He cleared debris, made an opening at floor level and started passing out the living, assisted by a fireman, ambulance officers and other police. The dead, unless they were in the way, could wait.

He was to put it later: 'We had to do the most good for the most number. We were taking out the least hurt first. We had to get them out of danger.'

At one end of the carriage the concrete slab threatened to slump lower at any moment. At the other, tonnes of loose bricks teetered on the flimsy roof. The rescuers worked with frantic care. Any slip could mean death.

LAMB heard the woman's voice through the debris. 'Help me. Please help me.' He crawled along the floor of the carriage. He recalls vividly how the tacks in the railway carpet had sprung and snagged his overalls.

There were bodies everywhere, some with awful injuries, others with barely a mark. Many had been asphyxiated in the crush. He had to crawl over a dead woman to get to the live one. She was bleeding from the nose and had a broken collar bone but, astonishingly, otherwise seemed all right. That was a miracle in itself; it would need another one to get her along the tiny space he'd cleared under the concrete. She was lying face down on the floor, pinned by the caved-in roof. There was no room to move.

Lamb told the terrified woman he had to fetch equipment, and promised her they'd get her out soon. He tried to crawl out backwards on his stomach, but other rescuers had to drag him by the ankles. He was sent into another part of the carriage to help someone else.

Gerry Buchtmann, firefighter by profession, captain of the Nepean volunteer rescue brigade by choice, made good Lamb's promise. He wriggled into the hole under the slab, which had settled to about thirty centimetres above the carriage floor.

The stench of death filled his lungs. A mixture of vomit, blood and excreta that filled that claustrophobic space like an inert gas.

He had to move bodies and debris to clear around the woman, who had the carriage roof bearing down on her. He used a pruning saw, a fireman's axe and pliers to hack away the roof's laminate lining, piece by piece. 'It was terrible stuff to cut.'

She wanted water but he couldn't give it to her in case she would have to be operated on later, in hospital. He wet her lips with ice and a damp handkerchief. Then came the hard part. There was only one way to get her out. He forced his hands under her chest and, gripping behind her breasts, slowly tugged her longways on the floor. It took until after 3pm to get her out.

She vanished into an ambulance, and was taken to a different hospital from other victims. None of the rescuers saw her again for years, but they heard of her.

Weeks later, she walked into Parramatta police station and told a detective she was a Granville survivor. Hundreds of people were claiming the same thing, so the detective put some questions. Asked how she'd been rescued, she said a young man had pulled her out by the breasts. The detective shook his head and showed her the door. Later, he happened to tell a senior officer about the 'crackpot' woman with the crazy story. But the officer remembered hearing how Buchtmann had dragged out a woman who'd since been lost in the system. He ordered the surprised detective to find her.

Distress does strange things. Dick Lamb had described the woman he'd found as 'about eighteen', and Buchtmann guessed she was in her twenties. It turned out she was a mother of five, almost forty. Her name was Margaret Shuttler.

GLEN Summerhayes was driving to work when he heard the first radio reports. As a State Emergency Service officer, and a trainee with the Nepean volunteers, he thought he could help.

At Granville, the police commander took one look at his small frame and sent him into a tiny hole cut into a crushed carriage. A doctor asked him if he could inject morphia, handed him ampoules of the pain killer and a syringe. He crawled along, feeling the still-warm bodies, injecting the living.

One survivor was so caged in that he couldn't touch him, but he managed to thread an oxygen hose to him through the maze of debris.

Rescuers could smell gas. It came from ruptured bottles of LPG used to run the carriage heaters. Summerhayes saw a tradesman crouched inside a carriage trying to start a small chainsaw. He yelled at the man to stop, grabbed the machine and handed it outside to a policeman – who started it, first pull.

'That was one of the miracles of Granville,' he was to say later. 'If it had started underneath it could have ignited the gas and we might all have gone up.'

He found each leaking gas bottle and painstakingly cut it out of the wreckage. On the roadway above, police warned onlookers not to smoke because of the danger of an explosion. Unbelievably, some tossed butts down into the twisted metal below. It didn't ignite. Another miracle.

After lugging the last gas bottles out, Summerhayes collapsed from lack of oxygen. He was taken by ambulance to Parramatta Hospital. Two hours later he discharged himself and hitched a ride back to Granville in a police car. He went back to work under the slab. His memories of what happened after that are hazy, but some things were to stick in his mind.

In carriage three he saw a couple cuddling each other, as if they were asleep. They were dead.

A man in his 70s dressed in khaki shorts and shirt was pinned down by a steel stanchion across his lap. He said, 'Don't worry about me. I'm old. Go and get the young ones first.' Later they slid him onto a spinal board and into an ambulance. No-one there knew that old man's name, or if he lived or died, but they never forget his offhand bravery.

THERE were other brave people. Michael 'Scotty' McInally was one of them. The Blacktown ambulance officer, originally from Dundee, Scotland, was to emerge from the wreckage more affected by the experience than many passengers.

After driving one of the first ambulances to reach the scene, McInally crawled into the fourth carriage. He found a man trapped from the waist down in the mangled metal. He wormed his way next to the injured man – and stayed there for the next ten hours, despite the painful position and the danger.

McInally took off his own safety hat and put it on the injured man's head. He poured orange juice onto a wad of cotton wool and gently swabbed the other's mouth. And he talked to him through the entire ordeal.

The hurt man was Bryan Gordon. He was in his early thirties, and talked about his wife and daughter at home in the Blue Mountains. McInally, ten years older, told him about his own two boys. As the minutes crept into hours they forged a friendship so strong that when the rescuers were ordered to leave because it was considered too dangerous, the obstinate Scotsman abused his superiors and refused to budge.

McInally wasn't the only one to stay. Dick Lamb, Gary Raymond,

Gerry Buchtmann, Bruce Gane and others promised the injured they wouldn't leave them. If the slab fell, they were prepared to die, too.

McInally promised Gordon they'd get him out. But they both knew it wouldn't be until everyone else had been removed, so that jacks could be used to lift one end of the slab a fraction to free his pulped abdomen and legs. He told rescuers they should concentrate on other people because he was so badly hurt.

Gordon was the last to be rescued, around 6pm. Afterwards, McInally staggered out and sat on the railway line, shaky, weak and aching. There was no one to talk to. He drove himself back to Blacktown ambulance station, signed off and went home.

'And that's when the trouble started,' he was to muse, years later. 'That's when I started to remember things I'd seen down that hole.'

It got worse. Three days later Bryan Gordon died, and part of 'Scotty' McInally died with him. He'd risked his life for a stranger, become his friend, then lost him anyway. McInally was to work for another twelve years as an ambulance officer, but never really got over Gordon's death.

Every year, on 21 January, he goes to Gordon's grave.

SISTER Margaret Warby was scrubbed and ready for theatre at 8.30am when word of the disaster reached Parramatta Hospital. She grabbed overalls, hard hat, syringes, morphia and the emergency medical kit, then jumped into a police car.

In a diary she wrote later, she painted a stark picture. 'People are trapped in the third carriage, some crushed and others pinned beneath concrete and giant steel girders ... This is switch-off time. No room for emotions here. I look for survivors and ignore the dead.

'A woman is very severely crushed and only barely conscious. A young man is pinned by his legs. Another man has one of his ears ripped off. I give them pain killers, wrap them up, joke with them. Swear, too, occasionally. The police rescue squad are marvellous. They swear too, heaving and tugging, cutting and burrowing with their bare hands. It's hot and filthy. Oxygen offers some relief for the trapped but they are getting weak.

'I come out with the crushed woman, manning the resuscitator over the wreckage, up the embankment and on to the hospital. Once she is there ... I turn around and go back. No point in sending a young nurse into a thing like this where she'll carry the memory of it for the rest of her life. I've seen it before ... I know how to cope.'

Sister Warby was credited with saving seven lives.

BY nightfall all survivors had been rescued, but for police the job wasn't finished. Not by a long shot. They had to remove the slab to retrieve the dead strewn beneath.

They worked all night and next day. Workmen broke the bridge with jackhammers, cut steel beams with blowtorches, and lifted sections of concrete off by crane. As each piece was winched upwards more bodies were exposed. Each had to be tagged, photographed and carried to the temporary morgue set up in an army tent in the railway yards.

'The worst thing,' Dick Lamb was to recall, 'was facing more bodies each time a slab section came off. It seemed as if it would never end. It played on my mind. The body of a little girl affected us all. Her mother was across the top of her, trying to protect her. A mother's instinct ... '

His voice trails off as he wakens old feelings. His friend Bruce Gane twists a paper cup in his hand, lights another in an endless chain of cigarettes, and stares into the distance.

The last bodies were recovered late on the second day. The exhausted rescuers threw their gear into heaps and started sorting it. It was then they found that onlookers had stolen tools from some of the rescue trucks. Gary Raymond went home drunk. His wife put him in the bath, put him to bed and burned his bloodstained overalls. A year later he was divorced. Not all scars from Granville are physical.

*GARY Raymond is now a NSW police inspector and Salvation Army officer. Margaret Warby and Gerard Buchtmann were among five people awarded the Queen's Gallantry Medal for their efforts at Granville. Glen Summerhayes was one of five awarded the Queen's Commendation for Bravery. Other rescuers were later awarded a Granville medal struck to mark their selfless conduct.*

# Death line 'needed repair'

1 ᴵ MAR 197~

*Railway acc~*

SYDNEY. — A railways track supervisor said yesterday he continually requested the complete relaying of the track near the Bold Street bridge for 12 months before the Granville rail disaster occurred.

Mr. James Alan Nicholson, a supervisor with he NSW Public Transport Commission, also told he inquiry into the crash he was ordered last year ιot to do maintenance work which would interfere vith train timetables.

Mr. Nicholson said he recommended twice in he 18 months before the crash that a speed restricion be placed on trains' travelling under the bridge ιecause of the condition of the track.

He said he put a speed restriction sign on the ιridge last year.

Mr. A. D. Collins, QC, assisting the inquiry: 'When?"

Nicholson: "It was around about the time the ιew timetables were put in.

# CHAPTER 13

# Let's make a deal

## The man who couldn't take no for an answer

*'What about the charges?*
*Can't we work on the charges.'*

AS a successful drug dealer and a would-be corrupter of police, Hussein Issa believed there was nothing or nobody that couldn't be bought at a price.

Issa dealt in the best green (marijuana) that money could buy. His product was in huge demand. He could sell any amount and in his own words: 'Some weeks I make – I dunno, ten grand.'

He had a steady stream of customers who were prepared to pay top prices for his product. The unemployed Brunswick fencing contractor was on his way up. He was rolling in cash.

He was never going to be a drug boss, a crime baron or an organised crime czar, but as long as the grass was green, it seemed to him he would never have to work for a living again.

But in early April, 1996, the Brunswick special duties police became aware of a new super-strong marijuana in the area and began to hunt down the suppliers.

'We were finding this top quality hooch in a number of raids and we began to work on the dealers,' Sergeant David Taylor was to explain later. The marijuana was eventually traced to a hydroponic crop grown inside a Fawkner house where a man was paid $10,000 to protect the property from being ripped off.

It didn't take long for police to find Hussein Issa, one of the main distributors of the drug. He was selling the marijuana for $5000 for around five hundred grams.

It was money for old dope.

Issa, twenty-six, liked the money he made from dealing but definitely didn't want to cop the down side of his chosen occupation. He was absolutely terrified of jail and would do anything, short of going straight, to keep out of prison.

When he was arrested at his girlfriend's Brunswick home in May police found he had $820, a knife, three bongs, plastic bags, foils and one hundred and eleven grams of marijuana.

He had something else which sparked the police's curiosity. A book of cab charges from the 'Office of the Premier and Cabinet, Central Office.' He claimed to have bought them at a local hotel.

Now Issa may not have been the smartest drug dealer in town but he knew the amount of cannabis seized took him into the trafficker category. He also knew he had a three-month suspended sentence hanging over his head over a burglary matter.

If he went to court to face trafficking charges, he would end up in jail. In his panic-stricken state, he decided to try and cut a deal in the police station.

He thought with the amount of money he was making he could cut the police in on the action and they could all get rich together. After all, he reasoned, if he made the police his partners then they would have a vested interest in letting him continue dealing on the outside.

He asked to go to the toilet when he was taken to the Brunswick police station. In the privacy of the gents, well away from the tapes in the interview room, he said to his escort, Constable Nick Lumb, he would pay $20,000 if police would lose the trafficking charges.

'If you just charge me with a little grass, I'll pay you a lot of money, heaps,' he said, while washing his hands.

Police set up a secret camera in the toilets and later Issa repeated the offer. The deal was struck: $10,000 before the case and $10,000 at its completion. Then the grateful crook and what he thought were his new bent mates headed off to get some cash. At Fawkner he went into a house and came out with $5000 wrapped in silver duct tape. Then he went back in and got another $2000 which he handed to the police. In the next few days Issa handed over the $10,000 first payment in dribs and drabs. He was happy, believing he would easily make the money back from dope dealing.

What he didn't know was that every deal, every payment and every word was being recorded. He was taped telling the police he would pass on the names of drug dealers for police to raid if they passed the drugs back for him to sell. It was a new twist on recycling.

He promised the police $4000 for every five hundred grams they gave him. He even urged them to bash the dealers to make sure they passed over their money and drugs.

When he was finally arrested for bribery Issa just couldn't comprehend that his code – that money talks all languages – might not be right. He decided to talk louder. While being escorted to jail after being charged with bribery he made a new offer.

'We're going to work together … I will get you a few – few decent busts. No worries, man, just work with me. Please.'

He saw the problem as being a financial rather than a moral one.

Had he left some police out? Was his offer too small? 'I can come up with, I don't know, at least twenty grand.

'Talk to me, talk to me, I'm trying to work with youse. What about the charges, can't we work on the charges?'

'He simply couldn't work out that not everyone would sell out for money,' Sergeant Taylor said.

'Right to the end he believed if he made the right offer then the charges would be dropped. Even after the committal hearing we would see him in the street and he'd ask if there was some deal we could make.

'He wasn't what you'd call a quick learner.'

In late 1997 Judge Nixon sentenced Issa to two years six months with a minimum of eighteen months over the bribery attempts. In all, he had offered $70,000. The judge praised the police involved, saying 'these police officers can hold their heads high.'

THE BRUNSWICK TAPES – 27 May, 1996.
Brunswick police station toilet.

Sergeant David TAYLOR: 'I'm running the show.'
Hussein ISSA: 'Yes.'
Constable Nick LUMB: 'Tell him what we've discussed, so he's sure.'
ISSA: 'Look. I'll give you ten grand.'
TAYLOR: 'Hang on.'
ISSA: 'I've got ten grand to give.'
TAYLOR: 'So you want – so, you don't want me to charge you for traffick?'
ISSA: 'No, just possession and use … my place, all right. Brunswick. We'll go there, when I get the money. I'll take you in my car. I'll give you the money … '
TAYLOR: 'That's what I'm not happy with mate.'
ISSA: 'Why?'
TAYLOR: 'I mean, you could have – you could have – five blokes at home with a machine gun.'
ISSA: 'No, man. No, I'm not that type. I'll give you, I've got money at home.'
TAYLOR: 'Right. You're asking us not to charge you with a bit of trafficking and to only charge you with a little bit of possession.'
ISSA: 'Yeah.'
TAYLOR: 'And then?'
ISSA: 'That's all.'
TAYLOR: 'Yeah, that's a big ask. Cash?'
ISSA: 'Yeah, yeah, it's cool. $100 bills, $100 bills.'
LUMB: 'And they're not all new ones?'
ISSA: 'No, no new ones, I hate new ones. All the old ones like these ones . My money … I've got $5000 cash at my home.'
TAYLOR: 'All right. And in return for ten grand.'
ISSA: 'No trafficking … '
TAYLOR: 'All right. Then you still give us.'
ISSA: 'Some dealers.'

TAYLOR: 'Some dealers?'

ISSA: 'Yes, I will give that.'

TAYLOR: 'All right. And you give us ten grand tonight and then what after the court case? So how much profit are you making out of dealing?'

ISSA: 'Give me three months, I'll probably make ten grand.'

TAYLOR: 'So in three months time, you'll have another ten grand for us?'

ISSA: 'Another ten grand, yep.'

TAYLOR: 'And that's when you walk away or you're probably going to get a bond then, aren't you?'

ISSA: 'Well, that's what I'm hoping for. That's what we want.'

LUMB: 'Is that a lot of money to you.'

ISSA: 'What?'

LUMB: 'Ten grand.'

ISSA: 'Not really.'

27 MAY, 1996. Edward Street, Fawkner, at 4.20am. Issa meets three police. He tells them he has $7000 in cash and will get the remaining $3000 for the initial bribe. He puts forward the plan to have police raid drug dealers and provide him with the seized drugs to be re-sold.

TAYLOR: 'How much gear are you moving a week?'

ISSA: 'Well, I can move heaps. That's why, if youse help me with a few cheap pounds, mate, you know.'

TAYLOR: 'Well, what – what sort – what are you doin' at the moment?'

ISSA: 'Well, this is what – you can move up to two pounds, three pounds a week. Fifteen grand you can make in a week, you know. And some weeks I make – I dunno, ten grand. Some weeks I make one grand, you know what I mean. It's that type of business.'

LUMB: 'Easy work.'

ISSA: 'Easy. It's easy work. That's for sure.'

Issa enters a Brunswick house and returns with $7000.

31 MAY, 1996, 8.11 pm. Issa and police are in a police car. He sets up a deal by which he believes police will raid identified dealers and pass on the drugs to him to be sold. He identifies a number of marijuana dealers for police to raid.

ISSA: 'I'll say it now, we're going to make money, they deal in pounds, they help me out now and then ... Every pound I can get five grand cash for it. So, if youse got, you know, like four pounds, just think. I dunno, I'll take – even five, I'll be happy with, youse can keep the fifteen.'
TAYLOR: 'We have to raid the house then.'
ISSA: 'Yeah, yeah.'

GROWING in confidence, Issa began to advise on the best way to make drug dealers confess where they hide their money and drugs.

'Hit 'em a bit so they show youse, because I'm sure youse can't find the – the hidden spots everyone – you know what I mean. Everyone's got a hidden spot and ... '
TAYLOR: 'Yeah.'
ISSA: 'Some of these bludgers, they've got at least five grand hidden you know. I know they're not small timers.'
TAYLOR: 'And then – well, say if we raid them.'
ISSA: 'Well, you raid them, you get three, four pounds out of them, I dunno. Youse give it to me, I'll give youse the money in two, three days. Simple as that.'
TAYLOR: 'If we gave you three pounds what ... what would you then do.'

ISSA: 'I would give you the money, what, I'll give youse probably ten grand, twelve grand.'
LUMB. 'Are you in a position to move that amount?'
ISSA: 'Yeah, yeah. Give me two, three days and it'll be gone.'

ISSA told police he was not interested in dealing heavy drugs. 'So with the white, I can't deal mate.'

LUMB: 'So, Sam, if this business relationship works, how long do you think we can do it for?'
ISSA: 'Long as you want. I don't know. I let youse know where there's money and where there's dope all the time mate, don't worry. So long as I get a cut. I'll get – I'll get rid of the gear or whatever youse give me, just I've got to make a bit too, you know ... Well you can make five – five thousand you can make a pound. You give me a pound, I – I'll make a grand, I'll give youse four. One for me, four for youse. Is that fair enough?'
TAYLOR: 'Mate, I reckon that's very fair.'

THE police ask Issa where he thinks drug dealers would hide their money.

ISSA: 'Like some have buried, some have it, I dunno, in drawers or in socks, you know how it is, some in books, some in butter, albums, you know.'
TAYLOR: 'When you gave us the five grand the other night, that was.'
ISSA: 'Yeah, buried, man.'

ON 19 June police moved in and arrested Issa on bribery charges, but the drug dealer still could not accept he was the victim of a sting operation by honest cops. In the police car on the way to the Melbourne Custody Centre Issa tried again, telling police he can't understand why he has been arrested.

ISSA: 'I haven't wrecked anyone else's life. I've been doing everything by the book ... I'll give youse the money, fifty grand. I can't come up with fifty grand. I can come up with twenty grand, maybe in a couple of months, but not fifty.'
Constable Scott RUDDOCK: 'Well, mate, if we take fifty, when are we going to get it?'

ISSA: 'Six months or so, this is too much, man. I've never had that amount.'

RUDDOCK: 'Mate, fifty grand in six months and what are we going to do until then. What are we going to do with you?'

ISSA: 'We're going to work together ... I will get you a few – few decent busts. No worries, man, just work with me. Please.'

RUDDOCK: 'And what do you want for fifty grand?'

ISSA: 'Get all these charges off.' He then complains that the police are getting greedy and $50,000 is too much. 'I can't come up with fifty, no fucking way. Fifty man, no. I can come up with, I don't know, at least twenty grand.'

He then offers cash to be granted bail. 'I don't want to go to jail.'

ISSA: 'Twenty grand, that's it. I can't come up with much more than that, please. Unless youse give me the dope and I'll sell it ... The more dope youse give me, the more money youse will get ... I'll make five grand in three days, four days, but to make twenty grand, it takes me two weeks, three weeks, maybe.'

Later he become even more desperate. 'What does it take for me to get off, I'll – I can do it. Anything.'

He offers to pay the police $10,000 a week while he is out of jail. 'I'll make the money. The money's there, it's just – the druggies, you know, everybody smokes.'

RUDDOCK: 'What makes you think everyone's prepared to take bribes?'

ISSA: 'Talk to me, talk to me. I'm trying to work with youse. Those guys, they don't want to work with me . . . What about the charges. Can't we work on the charges?'

The answer was no.

# CHAPTER 14

# The day we locked our doors
## Still looking for the Beaumonts

*By the next afternoon it was
the nation's biggest story*

JANE Beaumont wanted to be a writer when she grew up. She could hardly have written anything as heartbreaking or haunting as the story of how she, her brother and sister vanished from an Adelaide beach one hot day more than thirty years ago.

The story of the Beaumont children, which has become a long and tangled tale, has lost none of its potency. At its heart is an act of unspeakable cruelty: of parents being robbed of their children and of never knowing their fate; of being tormented, year after year, with theories, rumors and speculation, false leads, false hopes and false prophets.

And, with each twist in the tale, with each turn of the screw for the lost children's parents, Australia has been mesmerised by a story as mysterious as *Picnic at Hanging Rock,* as sinister as *Silence of the Lambs.* It has burned deep into the national psyche, transcending time and place in a way other crimes have not.

It marks, perhaps, an end of innocence for an old Australia when doors were left unlocked and kids went to the beach alone.

Australia's population has grown by millions since 1966. No one under the age of thirty was born when Jane, Arnna and Grant disappeared, and few under forty actually remember it happening. But that doesn't matter. The Beaumont children are as much a part of popular culture as Ned Kelly or Don Bradman, names that echo down the years and have become part of our mythology.

So, when a retired detective claimed in 1997 that a Canberra woman could be Jane Beaumont, it spawned yet another flurry of publicity. This says more about our preoccupation with the case than about the merit of the claim.

If Jane Natarlie Beaumont were alive when the claims were made, she would turn forty one on 10 September. Arnna Katherine would be thirty nine on 11 November, and Grant Ellis would have turned thirty six the same year.

On Australia Day, 1966, they were nine, seven and four. It was a Wednesday and one of the hottest days of a sweltering January. At the Beaumonts' modest war-service home in Harding Street, Somerton Park, Nancy Beaumont gave in to her children's pleas to let them go to nearby Glenelg beach straight after breakfast.

Mrs Beaumont had work to do, her husband, Jim, a travelling salesman, was away, and it seemed safer to send the children on the bus than to let them ride their bikes; more reasonable to let them go early than make them wait for her. She watched and waved as they went out the gate, holding hands, about 8.40 am.

When they failed to return at noon, as arranged, she assumed they had missed the bus and would be on the next one, at 2pm. When they were not, she worried. When Jim arrived home an hour later, they began a search that has never really ended. By next afternoon, it was the biggest story in Australia.

The police were to follow up thousands of leads in the coming months and years, but there has only ever been one firm clue.

Several witnesses had seen the children playing with a tall, thin, blond surfie wearing navy blue bathers. He was never identified.

The search spread interstate, even overseas. A Dutch clairvoyant, Gerard Croiset, arrived in late 1966 amid a huge furore, but his 'visions' failed. Although Croiset died in 1980, his influence has lingered. In 1996, Adelaide businessman Con Polites finally achieved his ambition of digging up a warehouse floor where Croiset thought the bodies could be buried. Stan Swaine was prosecuting a case in a country court the day the children disappeared. Like everybody else, he was interested, but it was not until he took charge of the state's homicide squad two years later that he became involved.

Detective Sergeant Swaine, then forty-one, disagreed with other police that the children had almost certainly been murdered. He thought they might have been taken to be raised by a cult. For a while, the parents, hungry for any hope, grasped at the theory, perhaps earning it more attention than it deserved.

A letter from Dandenong in 1968 lured Swaine and the Beaumonts to drive across for a rendezvous with an unknown person who promised to hand over the children. The supposedly secret meeting had been leaked by other police, and Swaine and the Beaumonts were followed from Adelaide by two carloads of reporters. It did not matter – there was no sign of the children.

A month later, acting on a letter from New South Wales, police searched Mud Island and Swan Island, near Queenscliff, then a spot near Anglesea. In September that year, a ship's crew was questioned and fingerprinted in New Zealand, because the ship had been in Adelaide in January 1966, and in Melbourne in August 1968, when a young girl disappeared from a St Kilda amusement park. No result.

There were many more leads. A sealed shipping container was searched for remains. A blond surfie in Tasmania was heard talking to a child about Adelaide. A Kaniva policeman overheard someone talking about the Beaumonts on a crossed phone line. A Kalgoorlie couple came under scrutiny in 1985 after former neighbors talked of old gossip alleging they had kidnapped the children. Three suitcases full of scrawled-on press clippings about the case were found at an Adelaide tip in 1986. They turned out to be the collection of an eccentric old woman and had been thrown out by relatives after her death.

Nothing indicated the children were alive. Yet, three decades on, Stan Swaine argues they probably are. This might say more about him than about the mystery.

THE man involved for three decades is not so much obsessed as enthusiastic about the case. It is Swaine's hobby. After a lifetime as a detective, he still likes to dabble, and the Beaumont connection always gets him some attention.

In 1997 Swaine appeared at a closed Magistrates Court hearing in which a woman, forty-one, applied unsuccessfully for a restraining order to stop the ageing sleuth approaching her.

His version of events is that, eighteen months before, he was asked by a women's magazine to check out the woman, who claimed to have been brought up by a cult and had herself suggested she might be Jane Beaumont.

He made several trips to Canberra and interviewed the woman. Eager to believe he had cracked the case at last, he seized on the slimmest of 'evidence' – that she has hazel eyes 'like Jane Beaumont's' and that she is roughly the right age.

He says he has seen an extract of her birth certificate, under her present name, but that it was issued after 1966 and he suspects it could be a fake. He cites the bogus identifications obtained by Anne Hamilton-Byrne and others in the cult known as The Family.

The police, however, have no such misgivings, accepting the woman's family's assurances – and her birth certificate – as proof that she is not Jane Beaumont.

Swaine is not convinced. Cults, he shrugs, do unbelievable things. After 900 people poisoned themselves at Jonestown in Guyana, anything's possible, he says.

And, why did intelligent, legally sane people dress in their best clothes, pack their bags and quietly kill themselves in California a few months before, convinced they were being picked up by a spaceship?

Compared with that, and other bizarre incidents, he claims, the idea of children being abducted to be brainwashed and brought up by cult 'parents' is quite plausible.

At first sight, Stan Swaine makes an unlikely private eye. At seventy-two, he is no Philip Marlowe; just an old bloke whose good looks have worn down to a vague kindliness, punctuated with a nervous tic that could be the legacy of being stabbed in the head by a criminal with a screwdriver in 1952, an attack which was nearly fatal for the policeman – and very fatal for the attacker, whom he shot with his service pistol.

He left the police in 1973 to become a private investigator and has been at it ever since. Along the way, he says, his marriage broke up and he lost several Adelaide properties.

Now a pensioner who plays at private eye, he lives alone in a tiny public-housing flat.

Fast chases are out. Swaine does not drive any more and walks with the aid of a stick, nursing a bad knee and juggling a mobile phone, fob watch and insulin syringe kit. He wears a comfy cardigan, sports jacket, tie over nylon shirt and brown pants with a dodgy zipper that threatens to reveal Jockey Y-fronts to match the spare pair drying on the heater in the cluttered flat.

'You'll have to excuse me, I'm a recycled bachelor,' he says apologetically, waving at the books and papers on the dining table that doubles as his desk.

Thirty years after the disappearance the Beaumonts remain big news and Swaine was keen to bask in any reflected publicity.

After flying back from Canberra and an interview with Ray Martin on *A Current Affair* he was pleased with himself. He had been met at the airport by a Nine Network car and a producer detailed to keep him away from rival networks. Then he had been whisked to Nine's studios for a chat with a slightly embarrassed assistant police commissioner and, finally, taken home. There, the answering machine blinked with nine fresh messages, and his mobile phone chirped with interview requests.

'This is like when it first happened,' he said wonderingly. 'I'll be the cynosure of all eyes down at the retired policemen's club, that's for sure.'

He still happily cites the letters sent from Dandenong in 1968 as the basis for his cult theory, ignoring or forgetting the fact that, in 1992, new forensic methods finally proved the letters were a hoax by a teenage boy and so killed any faint chance that the children had ever been held in Victoria.Five years later he was not worried about police dismissing his latest tilt at cracking Australia's biggest case. 'This is not the end of it, mate,' he said conspiratorially. 'All the police have done is look at her birth certificate and talk to people who could be mixed up in a cult, anyway.'

Meanwhile, he is off to the retired policemen's club for lunch. It has been a big week and a most excellent adventure for a bored old man.

Not so for Jim and Nancy Beaumont, perhaps. They both had birthdays a week before the latest false lead – he turned seventy two, she seventy – but all they got was yet another faint hope extinguished.

Chances are, only one person can help them. Somewhere out there is a man who was tall and thin and blond in 1966. Somewhere, in a dusty family album, there will be a snapshot of him in navy blue bathers. Someone, somewhere, must suspect who he is.

Jim and Nancy Beaumont will be always united in grief that only their own deaths will end, but they have lived apart for many years now. They lost their children, and then they lost each other.

*Postscript: A middle aged man who lives in a Melbourne psychiatric hospital has changed his name by deed poll to Grant Beaumont, convinced he was abducted with his sisters more than thirty years years ago.*

# CHAPTER 15

# A rebel with a cause

## Still Peter, not lawless any more

*'This is the first time in forty years
that I don't owe time'*

THEY sat around the board table of the Hawthorn Football Club in comfortable middle-class Melbourne, making their case. They were once the best of enemies, now they found themselves pushing the same cause with equal passion.

Present at the meeting were Hawthorn Chief Executive Officer, Michael Brown, the club's marketing manager, James Henderson, a senior executive from Puma Australia, John Forbes, the respected former police chief commissioner, Mick Miller, and a convicted killer, Peter John Lawless.

The professional policeman, and patron of the Reclink football league, and the career criminal turned football coach, were there to persuade the AFL club to turn over its home base – Glenferrie Oval – to a bunch of unemployed, homeless and drug-addicted men for a regular game of footy.

Mick Miller, the powerful law and order advocate and Lawless, the self-taught jailhouse lawyer born with a name no script writer could better, won the day. And so the Puma Street Hawks had a home. But the moment also marked the private and public rehabilitation of one of Australia's most notorious criminals. Lawless had been out of trouble for seven years, and many police were prepared to mutter the once inconceivable – that he had gone straight, for good.

Some experienced detectives harbor a rough affection some of the criminals they pursue, but Peter John Lawless was never one of them.

'He was a smartarse. One prosecutor is still terrified of him. Lawless threatened him and his family,' one detective recalls.

For Lawless there were no truces, no common ground. For decades the 'jacks' were the enemy and could not be trusted under any circumstances, and he played the game tough and dirty.

Throughout the 1970s the hard men of the underworld, Lawless, Billy 'The Texan' Longley, the Kane Brothers and Chuck Bennett were known, at least by reputation, by all the police in Victoria.

A few years ago Lawless had to deal with a policeman over a routine, non-criminal matter. He squared up and said, 'Do you know who I am? I'm Peter John Lawless.' The young policeman looked at him blankly, not a glimmer of recognition in his eyes. It was then Lawless knew that in criminal terms, he was yesterday's man.

After more than a half a decade out of jail he had lost the grey pallor of the long-term inmate. He no longer had to look straight ahead when a police car went by – and he no longer had to look behind, fearing a sneak attack.

At fifty-eight, with wispy grey hair and reading glasses, he looks nothing like the man who was once for many police the most hated criminal in Victoria.

So where did it all begin? In post-war Melbourne, the young Peter Lawless was an ordinary son from an average family. His housewife mother, Isabel, and his house painter father, Claude, knew their boy was a little wild, but they could hardly guess that he would end up one of the state's most infamous criminals.

By the age of eight the mischievous boy at Tooronga Road Primary School in Malvern had learned the benefits of accurate records. 'I had an exercise book that listed all the houses I could raid for fruit in the district.'

By the time he arrived at Spring Road Central School in Malvern as a skinny twelve-year-old he was ready to rebel, a trait he would keep for another forty years.

'I had a lot of trouble with the boss cocky teacher. I couldn't understand why we were studying Latin and French. I thought it was ludicrous and I didn't try,' he was to explain.

While he was less than impressive in the classroom, failing seventh grade twice, he loved sport, even though he was small for his age. Reputedly an A Grade tennis player as a teenager and a keen footballer and cricketer, he spent more time playing sport than in the classroom. It was a different era, with full employment and a secondary industry protected by tariffs, and teenage boys could swap school uniforms for overalls and be doing a man's job long before they could vote or drive.

Lawless said most teachers ignored him, but there was one he still remembers with respect and affection. He said he had a 'gentleman's agreement' with the teacher who was as sports mad as he was. Lawless said the teacher would turn a blind eye to Lawless's smoking if he turned up to play footy for the school. The teacher, who also coached the cricket and football sides, was an expert at striking deals and pushing through compromises. He was later to use those negotiating skills on a bigger scale. Lindsay Thompson went on to become Premier of Victoria.

More than forty five years on the former Premier remembers Lawless as a small boy who, at the age of twelve, was already an accomplished liar. 'He would look at you straight faced and tell you the most extraordinary stories.

'He arrived one day at 10am and I asked him why he was late. He said his grandmother fell over the letter box and dislocated her left elbow. The story was so strange you felt it couldn't be made up.' But after the third similarly extravagant story the teacher realised his young student, for all his ignorance of books, could think on his feet.

'I knew he had some problems and I took an interest. At the end of one year he knocked on the staff room door, thanked me and presented me with a Parker pen.' Thompson, who knew Lawless had a paper round that put him in close proximity to the news agent's stock, suspected the gift may have been shoplifted. He believed the only way

Lawless would have put his hand in his pocket would have been to hide the pen rather than to pull out his hard-earned shillings to pay for the gift.

The teacher went to the principal and asked advice. 'Keep it, you've got no proof and you'll hurt the boy's feelings,' he was told.

Decades later the then Minister for Education was chatting with a judge, who said a man was to be sentenced the following day for murder. 'He said the man had run his own defence and had done a pretty good job,' he recalled. 'It was Peter Lawless.'

AT the age of fourteen Lawless and formal education parted company by mutual consent. He left school when he was asked to repeat grade seven for a third time, and became an apprentice motor mechanic, later working for a year in the spare parts division. Then he joined his father in the painting business. Although he loved football and made the Richmond under-nineteen squad – 'I had my chances but I didn't take them' – Lawless was in too much of a hurry to dedicate himself to trying to make it on the football field.

He painted during the day but at night he was learning another trade from an older man: how to be a thief. 'There was always something I wanted. I learned the hard way with another guy before I went solo.'

Between 1960 and 1962 the pair pulled a series of safe breakings and burglaries. 'In two years we did all the TABs. He said "that's enough for me" and bailed out. He's now a successful businessman.'

For an unknown break-in artist Lawless embraced the world of crime and became a prolific thief from 1962 until 1964. 'I worked every day, seven days a week, full on. I made a hundred pounds a day.' This was in the days when the average worker made twenty five pounds a week. He broke into shops, supermarkets and cafes and stole cash, cigarettes and coffee. He once pulled eleven jobs in a night and eighty burglaries in two weeks.

He had two men on retainers who would check out likely targets, examine the alarms systems and observe security guard movements, 'I paid them every Friday.'

It was almost the perfect racket. Virtually unknown, Lawless could have set himself for life and then drifted into comfortable anonymity. But, like most crims, he could not quit while he was ahead. There was always another job, another earn. 'I got greedy. My own undoing was going beyond my boundaries. Camera shops and gun shops.'

When he was finally arrested in 1964, Lawless says, he owned a house in Noble Park, had an interest in two car yards and forty thousand pounds in two safety deposit boxes. 'Police asked me if the money was mine. I said I couldn't help them, so I lost the lot.'

But Lawless was a thief with a sharp mind, a solid memory and a healthy ego. 'When I was a motor mechanic, I realised you needed the right tools. When I decided I was gunna be a thief I needed a set of legal tools. I decided I wanted to know what a lawyer knew.'

The boy who couldn't pass seventh grade went on to be one of the best jailhouse lawyers in Australia. He completed three years of a law degree and ended up with a $4000 legal library.

'I was arrested thirty-three times between 1964 and 1969 and lost two cases.'

It was in the days when police could produce unsigned 'confessions' as evidence. While juries routinely accepted police evidence without question, Lawless would always tell juries the statements were fabricated.

'I was "verballed" (the victim of fabricated statements) but I had a retentive memory and I could undo them on their mistakes,' he claimed.

He once produced his unsigned police confession and proved to a jury that a policeman would have been flat out even typing the statement in the stated time of forty-eight minutes, let alone formulating the questions and waiting for the suspect to reply.

'I was unco-operative with the police at all times. I wouldn't talk. I wouldn't sign for property. I wouldn't do anything and then they'd produce these unsworn statements that didn't make sense.'

Despite Lawless's claims that he was railroaded more often than a freight train he does not pretend to be an innocent man. He said that in almost every case he was the right man but the police did not have enough evidence.

'I did nearly all of them. A couple of them I didn't know anything about but most of them I did, yeah.'

He became fascinated by the law. 'I would talk to barristers every chance I had.' But his relationship with his lawyers was always delicate. He was the only major criminal who could boast that he sacked two barristers who went on to become a County Court Judge (Michael Kelly) and a High Court Justice (Daryl Dawson). Even more annoyed with another barrister, Peter Faris, QC, who went on to become the head of the National Crime Authority, he actually punched him in an interview room. 'After that he sacked himself.'

Between 1969 and 1972 he said he went through twelve trials and won eleven. 'The only time I went down I had a barrister. I sacked him during the trial but it was too late.'

In 1972 he was charged with the murder of Christopher John Fitzgerald, who was shot dead in Noble Park. Lawless was found guilty at his second trial after the first was aborted, and formally sentenced to hang, a sentence commuted to life in jail.

More than a quarter of a century later he still maintains he was framed. The star witness in the case was Rayma Joyce, his lover and mother of his daughter. She gave two statements to police, one clearing and the second implicating Lawless in the murder.

For ten years Lawless fought his conviction all the way to the High Court, where he lost four to one. Dissenting Judge, Lionel Murphy, described his conviction as a 'miscarriage of justice.'

The prosecution alleged the two men argued in a car, got out to fight and then Lawless shot Fitzgerald.

In 1982 Rayma Joyce signed a statutory declaration stating her evidence implicating Lawless was false. For the convicted murderer it was the breakthrough he had dreamed of since his sentence. But a month later she changed her mind again and withdrew her sworn declaration.

More than quarter of a century after the killing it is impossible to establish what really happened on Sunday, 24 September, 1972. But it is almost certain that if the Crown was to present a similar case today a conviction would be highly unlikely.

Lawless remains bitter about his conviction but does not blame the woman. 'She was under enormous pressure. They would have taken her children if she did not co-operate. She's changed her story so often that it would be impossible for anyone to believe her now, one way or the other. I get on all right with her. We have a daughter and a grand-daughter together.'

While inside he followed his twin obsessions of the law – in a decade-long fight for a retrial – and sport, running marathons and playing visiting teams at football. 'I've always loved footy, I still do'. He lined up on former North Melbourne rover and VFL President, Allen Aylett, for one game inside Pentridge. 'He asked me what I was in for and I said "murder". I think that was the last game he played.'

He spent four and a half years in the top security H-Division in Pentridge during the so-called 'Overcoat Gang' war involving prisoners bashing and stabbing each other. According to Lawless, some prison officers were prepared to fight fire with fire.

'You would break rocks and then you'd get a belting. You would never know when the belting would come. It was madness, mate.'

Lawless, the jailhouse lawyer, didn't choose sides, but even so, he was drawn into the violence. Only once was he moved to use a home made knife on another inmate. The prisoner told an inquiry Lawless had confessed to the Fitzgerald murder. Enraged, Lawless used a handleless prison shiv to try to stab him. But the blade could not pierce the thick leather jacket the man was wearing. The knife twisted and slipped and ended up cutting the attacker. 'I nearly lost my thumb,' he says, and still bears a long the scar on his hand.

The 'victim' was uninjured.

In 1986, Lawless suffered an aneurism leaving him with limited use of his left side. Typically, he decided to develop his own rehabilitation. He took to playing tennis with his left hand to recover his co-ordination and strength. 'A prison officer I could always beat was able to beat me easily then, but after three months I was beating him again.' The following year Lawless won the Pentridge tennis challenge, using a mixture of right and left handed shots.

In 1987, a change of law enabled him to apply for a minimum jail term. Still suffering the after-effects of his aneurism, he was given a minimum of fourteen years by the Supreme Court, leaving him eligible for almost immediate release.

He was taken to the Governor's Office and asked if he was ready to be freed. 'When I said yes he just told me to fuck off.' With his possessions in two cardboard boxes and $38 in prison savings he found himself in a pub in Bell Street, one hundred metres from the prison.

His then girlfriend, Diane, later to be his wife, came to pick him up by taxi. 'That about chopped out the money. I was shovelled out of the jail with no preparation, I tried the best I could.' Twelve months later, the police who advocates well-known theory involving leopards and spots, were not surprised when Lawless was arrested with three other men, armed with shotguns, trying to rob a Ringwood bank.

'I had been in for fourteen and a half years and the only people I knew were crims.' He said he had 'introduced' two of the stick-up men and was only roped in to a hands-on role in the robbery at the last minute. 'I didn't want to be in on it but I didn't want to let them down,' he said.

The last policeman to arrest Lawless, Peter Butts, then an experienced sergeant in the armed robbery squad, does not buy the last-minute inclusion excuse. 'We had the crew under surveillance and they regularly met at Lawless's house. They took off to do the job from his house.

'I think he didn't realise that police methods had changed a great deal from when he was out previously.'

Butts said he was surprised that after years of fighting so hard to get out of jail Lawless would fall back into committing potentially violent crime.

'For a man of his age to team up with good armed robbers to run into banks was a surprise to me. When he was arrested it looked like his whole world had collapsed. It was like a bad dream for him.'

Butts said detectives also found stolen police identification in a file at Lawless's home.

Although he hated jail time, Lawless admits that being sent back to prison was probably the best thing for him. This time he knew he would be released within a few years and he began to prepare for life on the outside.

He married Diane and when he was released in 1991 he kept a much lower profile. He said he tried to avoid old criminal associates, although 'It is impossible not to run into some of them.'

Lawless was painting a mower shop in the eastern suburbs when an old prison mate walked in and recognised the man in the paint-flecked overalls as one of the biggest names in crime. 'Hey, Peter, I thought they'd never let you out,' the former mate said, by way of introduction.

'He said it in front of everyone there. It was so stupid, I wanted to hit him on the head with a paint tin.' Although out of jail for years, he remains a prisoner of his past. In 1998 his fourteen-year-old granddaughter saw a picture of her kindly grey-haired grandfather in the criminal memoirs of Mark Read, *Chopper From The Inside.* She asked, 'How come I don't know anything about this?'

With two children and five grandchildren, Lawless, who lives under his wife's maiden name, does not advertise his criminal past. Having suffered two aneurisms, two strokes and living with a permanent stiff left shoulder, he has had to learn to cope with his physical limitations.

While Lawless still passionately argues he was wrongly convicted of murder he does not live in the past. He is a keen punter and was even granted a licence to train greyhounds. The standards required to be accepted at in the greyhound fraternity is hardly the same as at the Melbourne Club, but Lawless had to pass police probity checks and pass he did.

But his passion remains football and as an AFL-qualified coach spends much of his time with the Street Hawks. One of his biggest supporters is Puma National Promotions Manager, John Forbes, who met Lawless in Pentridge during a sporting function in the late 80s. 'There was an altercation in the weights room and I ended up being lifted off the ground. Peter stepped in and saved my bacon.

'I told him then and there that I owed him one and that when he got out I'd help him if he went straight.

'You have never seen a bloke work so hard since he's been out. I've got a lot of time for him.'

No-one can look into the future but Lawless appears to have made the jump back into mainstream society. 'I've been out for seven years now. For me, that's like a lifetime.

'In 1958 they brought in the parole system. This is the first time since then that I've been free of it. This is the first time in forty years that I don't owe time.'

It is impossible not to feel the irony of the full-time criminal, who spent most of his adult life bucking the system, now trying to instil team sport discipline into the footballers of the Puma Street Hawks, some of them angry young men with criminal records.

One rainy Wednesday recently after a Reclink game was cancelled two men with a common interest sat in the Michael Tuck Stand at

Glenferrie Oval, chatting like old mates as the trains rattled past. The former chief police commissioner, Mick Miller, who has undergone successful open heart surgery, gently chided the convicted murderer about his chain smoking. 'It will kill you in the end,' he told him.

The former policeman, the career criminal and an ex-boxer turned social worker, Henry Nissen, then pitched in together, sweeping and cleaning the rooms before locking up.

The cop and the robber are not friends and never will be – but they share a common interest in football and people who need help. But in a strange way the two men's careers were linked. Lawless was one of several criminals whose complaints of alleged police illegality resulted in the 1976 Beach Inquiry into the force. The Premier of the time, Sir Rupert Hamer, was looking for a new Chief Commissioner as the incumbent, Reg Jackson, was about to retire. The then Deputy Commissioner, Laurie Newell, was the recommended candidate and the clear front runner.

But Sir Rupert wanted a younger man to clean up any problems in the force in the wake of the Beach controversy. Senior Cabinet colleague and Lawless's former teacher, Lindsay Thompson, knew Mick Miller well. He was impressed with the policeman's braveness and grace under pressure. The two men worked together during the kidnapping of a schoolteacher and six primary school students from the tiny Faraday State School near Castlemaine in 1972. Mick Miller got the job.

Miller says of Lawless. 'Through his football, he has shown himself to be committed to help the socially disadvantaged.' The former commissioner says you judge people on what you see. And what he has seen of Lawless, and men like him connected with Reclink, he supports fully.

'They help the socially disadvantaged and the dysfunctional gain a sense of purpose,' he said.

At one game Lawless gave the players the standard address at quarter time, advising them to play within the rules and not to become upset at the umpire's decision.

'One thing I've learned in this state, is when the whistle blows, that's it. No-one ever changes their mind, it's a waste of time arguing.'

*POSTSCRIPT*

*Lawless spent two years agonising over whether to talk openly about his life. He feared that some people, including his employer, would never accept that a man with his reputation could reform. When he was employed he was not asked about his criminal background, and having legally changed his name by deed poll, he did not volunteer it.*

*Less than two weeks after Lawless's story became public he was called to his office to meet his supervisor. He was surprised when he arrived to find a security guard also present. According to Lawless he was asked if he had ever had another name and then asked about his criminal record.*

*He was then sacked.*

# CHAPTER 16

# The sting

## Conning dirty old men for fun and profit

*She collected husbands – a couple of
her own, several of other people's.*

AT first glance, she makes an unlikely femme fatale. She's fifty, and for anyone half that age she could be a favorite younger aunt, the naughty one who teases you, swears a bit and laughs a lot. But if you were an old man — aged sixty-five to eighty five, say — with an itch for female company, she'd look inviting enough. Especially if she wants to. And if you are old, lonely and rich, she certainly wants to. She's an expert at it.

Marilyn — not her real name — is a mother, a grandmother and a successful small-business proprietor. What her family doesn't know is that she is also rather devious when it comes to serious subjects like sex and money. Her friends call her 'Mrs Swindell', and they're only half joking. Her specialty, these days, is taking dirty old men to the cleaners.

In fact, she has manipulated the sexual harassment laws and the Equal Opportunity Act to relieve a millionaire of $30,000 for seven weeks' 'work'.

This is how she did it.

THE plot, if you can call it that, is hatched in late 1997. Marilyn boasts to her friends that she will extract money, serious money, from 'some old boy' before Christmas. It starts as a joke, and ends as a bet. One she's well-equipped to win.

Marilyn, not to put too fine a point on it, has been around a bit since she left her parents' farm in western Victoria almost thirty years ago.

She was a bright girl — she started school at four, high school at ten — but in that time and place brains didn't mean much if your parents didn't think daughters were worth educating.

The choices, she recalls, were 'nursing, teaching or typing'. She chose nursing. She was good at it, she says. But, later, after leaving the country boy she'd married at twenty ('I was too young; he was too dull' she wisecracks) she gravitated to the fast life, and did a lot of things that would have shocked her respectable folks, had they known.

Not that she was self-destructive. She doesn't smoke, hardly drinks, despises drugs and those who use them; her vices have always been men and money, preferably together.

She is short, stocky and no classic beauty, but people like her. Especially male people. Her assets, apart from a sharp brain, a quick tongue and a steady nerve, are roguish green eyes, a nose just aquiline enough to make her face pleasantly predatory, an infectious smile — and what she describes as the signature feature of the oldest profession, generous breasts.

She collected husbands — a couple of her own, several of other people's. She once ran away to Europe with one of the latter. When the money and the novelty ran out, she left the man with a huge hotel bill and a guilty conscience.

Later, she was visited in Melbourne by two men employed to collect unpaid European hotel bills. She calmly told them that although they had the right address they were out of luck: the woman they were looking for had moved to Scotland. She even wrote down an address for them.

In the late 1980s, Marilyn opened a sandwich and catering shop in Melbourne's eastern suburbs. It was a success, like most things she has done. But, after a few years, it palled, and she sold up.

Then, last year, she went back to nursing. Which is where the story really begins ...

SHE signs on with a reputable agency in early 1997, one that specialises in looking after old people in their own homes. She produces glowing references, a few of which are genuine. The clients love her. They're frail, elderly, lonely and rich. She's bright, cheerful, and wants to be rich. 'I saw the wealth and thought, "I wouldn't mind a bit of that",' is the way she puts it to some of the other nurses.

Her chance comes in October. The agency is having trouble filling a position with an elderly widower in Caulfield. He's in his seventies, but still runs the importing business that has made him a millionaire since he came to Australia as a refugee during the war, when he was one of those shipped across the world on the ship 'Dunera'. Despite his age, the feisty 'Dunera boy' doesn't need a nurse; he wants a 'live-in housekeeper' who, he stipulates, has to be 'under fifty and attractive'.

Three women sent for interviews complain to the agency that he is a 'dirty old man' and that they couldn't possibly work for him. Marilyn, however, thinks he sounds ideal for her plans. The agency tells the client she is forty-seven, attractive and very friendly indeed.

When she gets to the house for the interview she finds a leering gnome with a big belly, a thick accent and a spa bath. It's the spa that makes them both sure they're on a winner.

When Marilyn sees it she coos 'Ooh, what a lovely spa!' The gnome winks at her and suggests she might like to hop in it with him if she takes the job. Sharp business people both, they close the deal immediately.

He insists on driving her to her existing job, nursing an old lady in Toorak. They sit in his big Mercedes Benz sedan, talking. He asks if she'd like to go interstate with him, and dine out every night. She says she would. She brushes his arm and kisses him on one jowly cheek before she gets out. She's baited the hook, and he's taken it.

Days later he takes her to dinner at the Hilton. He reveals he's staying at the hotel because his wife — mother of his adult children — has died only three weeks before, and he doesn't want to sleep at his house yet. Tough as she is, Marilyn is shocked at this callousness; she'd thought he'd been widowed at least six months.

She masks her distaste, and plays the part she has chosen with the ease of long practice. 'Most of the old men like him are afraid of the young dolly birds, because they know that a twenty five-year-old gorgeous blonde must be after their money,' she explains later. 'But a nice, respectable-looking, middle-aged housewife like me is to be trusted.' She laughs ironically.

'That first time we had dinner at the Hilton, I said I wouldn't stay with him. But of course I did. I had a couple of glasses of wine to make it look good and said (here she assumes a mock-genteel accent): "Oh, I feel a bit giddy. I must have a little lie down before I go home." We went up to the room and, of course, as soon as I lay down on the bed he was all over me like a rash.

'Next morning the silly old fool took me down to breakfast. There I am in evening clothes from the night before and he's saying to the staff "Have you met my housekeeper? She's just dropped in to see me this morning. Isn't that nice?" I stayed with him two days. The doormen saw me, and smiled. They knew what was going on.'

After a week of dinners, she moves into the house in Caulfield. There's not much housework. She washes and irons the gnome's shirts and squeezes him orange juice in the morning before he goes to the business. Her main duties are in the bedroom — which, uncharacteristically, she finds increasingly unpleasant. One reason is that the gnome occasionally injects himself with a drug that gives him a four-hour erection.

'The sex nearly killed him,' she is to recall. 'He had to go to hospital one morning and have an ECG. They fitted all these wires and stuff on him. After that he took it easier. He'd just turn over, give my boobs a bit of a pat and go to sleep. I'd sneak off to the other room because it was like sleeping with a pig.'

She kills time during the day by watching television — and entertaining a male friend, who doesn't suspect what's going on because she tells him the old man has a wife.

At first, she schemes to lure the gnome into marriage. But she gives that idea up when she works out that most of his wealth is tied up in a family-owned business effectively controlled by his sons, married men who despise their father's behavior so soon after their mother's death, and are rightly suspicious of the housekeeper's motives.

The pair eat at restaurants most evenings. 'His only friends were waitresses, and that was only because he carried wads of cash and stuffed money into their hands. He talked only about himself. All his business problems, his investments. He told me everything.

'On the way home he would nearly make me sick talking about the girls in the restaurants. "See how they love me!" he'd say. "They can't keep their hands off me." I told the silly old goat they only wanted his money, but he wouldn't take any notice.'

After a month Marilyn senses the old man is already looking around for other women. Top of the list is an Asian girl in her twenties working in a Toorak restaurant. Marilyn deduces that the waitress and her boyfriend are setting up a sting of their own. She decides she has to get in first.

The old man disgusts her in a way she hasn't expected. There isn't a photograph of his wife displayed in the house; he has thrown them all in a box in a back room. She discovers that he has been visiting brothels for years. And that he keeps pornography.

Ironically, after returning from shopping one afternoon, she finds a syringe cap on the bedroom floor that hadn't been there that morning, and guesses he's brought a prostitute into the house.

'I started to hate him. He was suggestive every day. I was sick of the suggestive talk.' She buys a disposable camera, and takes pictures of the pornography, the syringe and sex-drug, and any business documents she can find.

She makes her move in mid-December. He is going to Queensland for Christmas, and has asked her to go with him. She fancies the free holiday, and knows he will shower her with gifts. But there's one problem: 'I knew it won't look good for my case against him.'

The case being sexual harassment. First she goes to a doctor. Not her own — 'he'd know I was up to something' — but one she'd never seen before, in Malvern.

She puts on an act she's still proud of months later. She bursts into tears in the surgery. Tells the doctor, sobbing, that her employer is a monster who forces her to sleep with him and that she can't refuse because she doesn't want to lose the job. She asks for advice and sleeping tablets, and gets both.

Next step, the law. She telephones Maurice Blackburn and Co., a well-known firm in workplace disputes, but they were too busy. Then she goes to a referral centre which recommends 'the best feminist lawyer in Melbourne', a woman at a small city firm that specialises in sexual harassment cases. She makes an appointment for the afternoon of Wednesday, 17 December.

The lawyer is tough, efficient, and dead easy to deceive. She swallows her new client's bogus tale of misery without question. Three hours later, when Marilyn gets back to Caulfield, the gnome is home, waiting. He complains, asking where she has been. She tells him she's been to the city to get him a Christmas present. He brightens, and asks her what it is. 'It's a surprise,' she says, unblinking.

It's a surprise all right. When the lawyer's letter arrives two days later, he is very surprised indeed. And dismayed. The letter outlines a list of alleged offences under the Equal Opportunity Act. The bottom line: $36,000 'compensation' to take it no further.

The old man's sons, themselves married with children, are furious and mortified. They tell him to settle it quickly and to avoid scandal at all costs. He settles for $30,000, on condition the settlement remain confidential.

'I would have taken $10,000,' Marilyn confides later. 'I just hope he reads this.'

She is in a suburban hotel lounge, crowded with pensioners hoeing into a Tuesday special discount lunch before playing the poker machines. 'Look at them,' she says suddenly over the din of dentures grinding half-price wiener schnitzels , waving her arm defiantly at a sea of grey heads. 'They've done nothing in their lives except hang out the washing. At least I've lived a bit.'

The truth is, Marilyn's sting was never only about money. That's why, just before she left the big Caulfield house the last time, she tipped out the owner's expensive cognac — and filled the bottles with a mixture of cold tea and vinegar.

Meanwhile, she wants to make the most of her most marketable commodity. She's looking around for another rich old man with an itch for female company. 'A knight would be nice,' she muses.

AND the gnome? In March 1998 he advertised for a new housekeeper. Three months is a long time when you're seventy-six. Any night could be your last.

# CHAPTER 17

# Queen Street revisited

## No rest for the wicked

*A spoiled and guilt-ridden child inside a man's body*

**DESPITE the extreme nature of his crime, the mass killer appears to be extraordinarily ordinary** – *Dr Jack Levin, sociologist and author*

FRANK Vitkovic was ordinary, but not normal. Few glimpsed the black fantasies squirming behind the mask he held up to the world, and by the time they did, it was too late. He had set himself for a day of reckoning that would make him Australia's worst mass murderer until Martin Bryant and Port Arthur.

On a hot Tuesday afternoon in 1987 the failed law student walked into a Queen Street office block in Melbourne's central business district to settle a score that existed only in his head. He was bent on killing an old school friend, then taking as many lives as he could before taking his own.

It was a tragedy that he killed eight people, one more than the pathetic Julian Knight had at Hoddle Street a few months earlier. It was a miracle he didn't kill many more.

A thousand people worked on the eighteen floors at 191 Queen Street. In the brown bag Vitkovic carried into the building, he had a sawn-off military carbine and ten magazines loaded with enough high-powered ammunition to shoot scores of them.

Afterwards, investigators were to find forty-one empty shells and 184 live ones, proof that the pudgy loner with a gun and a grudge had been prepared to keep shooting until police arrived. But chance, although it dealt death to eight and wounded five others, ruled otherwise.

By some twisted blessing, Vitkovic had been cheated when he bought the .30 calibre M1 carbine at a West Melbourne gunshop a few weeks before.

As a firearms expert was to explain in the coroner's court much later, the semi-automatic's trigger spring was faulty. Instead of springing back into position after each shot, the trigger had to be manually jiggled back into position before being squeezed again.

It meant that instead of spitting out a stream of bullets as it was designed to do, the rifle was effectively reduced to a 'bolt action'.

Security film footage of the first minutes of Vitkovic's rampage shows him repeatedly looking down at the weapon as he clumsily fiddled with it. This was to give a lot of people a chance to flee and hide before he could shoot them. It also might have given a brave man the opening he needed to tackle Vitkovic and disarm him. But that was later ...

NO-ONE knows when Frank Vitkovic felt the first twinges of alienation that festered like a boil in his brain and burst into the atrocity of 8 December, 1987. He was to leave behind a note that said he felt 'the seeds of doom' as young as eight years old. But if anyone noticed that the boy was disturbed, they didn't talk about it then and haven't since, at least publicly.

Vitkovic was born on 7 September, 1965, two years after his only sister, Liliana. Like hundreds of thousands of young Australians of his generation, he had migrant parents. But, unlike most, his parents came from different countries and had married across different cultures. His father, Drago, was a Yugoslav, and his mother, Antoinetta, was Italian.

Drago Vitkovic was a self-employed painter until he hurt his back in a car accident and became unemployed, circumstances Frank later hinted might have led to tensions in the family. Antoinetta Vitkovic worked as a domestic in hospitals. They lived in a neat house in May Street, West Preston, in Melbourne's northern suburbs, where they nursed ambitions for their children.

Frank and his sister worked hard to live up to the migrant dream of forging a better life in a new country. Liliana became a legal secretary. Frank was renowned among his contemporaries at local Catholic schools for the prodigious amount of homework he did, often studying more than four hours a night.

At secondary school, there was little outward sign of inner turmoil. But, in 1983, when he was seventeen, he was caught lying on the floor at Northland shopping centre, looking up a woman's dress.

Police called his mother and referred him to a psychiatrist, who reported that it was an 'adolescent adjustment'. Vitkovic was mortified and remorseful, and claimed he had done it as a dare to impress his friends. It wasn't the last time he was referred for counselling. But, to those who knew him casually, he kept up a mask that covered deepening depression and anger.

Later, his sister was to give evidence that painted him as a normal young man. He was witty, intelligent and good company. He cracked jokes, did impersonations of politicians and teachers, could twist his mouth a funny way and make a sound like a tennis ball being hit. He was a passionate Collingwood supporter and liked pizza and McDonald's fast food. He also loved classic horror films like *King Kong* and *The Creature From The Black Lagoon*. But, then again, a lot of people do.

There was another, more intense, side to Vitkovic. Unlike most young males in that time and place, he had a social conscience, and did charity work for the Australian Birthright Movement. He felt for the underprivileged, and agonised about the sufferings of people in Ethiopia. He sometimes said that if he had a lot of money, he would give it to the hungry. He was awkward with girls, and subtly cut off from his male schoolmates by his self-imposed discipline.

Friends marvelled at his freakish ability to recall facts and figures – especially football statistics. Sometimes they called him 'the stats man'. They also called him 'Viko' and 'Vik the Dick'. Like most nicknames, it had a double edge. There was the faint inference that some of his friends laughed at him behind his back.

Vitkovic was ambitious and, as he grew older, his ambition had an increasingly obsessive edge. By the time he studied HSC, he was a perfectionist who hated to lose, and this fuelled his relentless study and practice at tennis and snooker. He scored outstanding marks – three As and two Bs – and won a place in the Melbourne University law course in 1984.

It's tempting to speculate, in light of later events, that Vitkovic was the victim of his own supercharged, over-reaching ambition. If he had failed or done poorly, he would have been bitterly disappointed and ashamed at letting his family down. But, ironically, by doing so well, he got into a tough course in which he may well have felt constantly under pressure and, maybe, subtly out of place.

Fellow law students were to recall him turning up at university on the first day with his father, wearing a collar and tie. They also remember that, in first year, he studied long and hard. And that he displayed a fierce will to win in the two games he excelled at, snooker and tennis.

ONE friend remembers finding him at Lindrum's pool rooms in Flinders Street, practising alone. Others recall that he trained as if he hoped to play professional tennis. If he lost at either, which wasn't often, he would become strangely quiet. It was, looking back, verging on odd behavior.

He occasionally chatted to Mary Cooke, the kindly head receptionist who fielded inquiries in the university union house.

Once, she remarked to him that he 'must have come from a Catholic college'. Vitkovic said he was and asked how she knew. She told him that 'all the quiet ones came from Catholic colleges'.

Vitkovic passed first-year law well. But, towards the end of the year, a small thing happened that was to assume huge proportions in his mind. He hurt his right knee while running, an injury he later aggravated at tennis.

At first, doctors could find nothing obviously wrong with the knee. But they weren't so sure about the patient's mind. Ben Davie, who referred him to another orthopaedic surgeon, Ian Jones, wrote a letter describing Vitkovic as 'a most peculiar young man'.

Surgery found the cause of the knee problem – a damaged cartilage

Alphonse John Gangitano ... charismatic, impulsive, violent ... and dead.

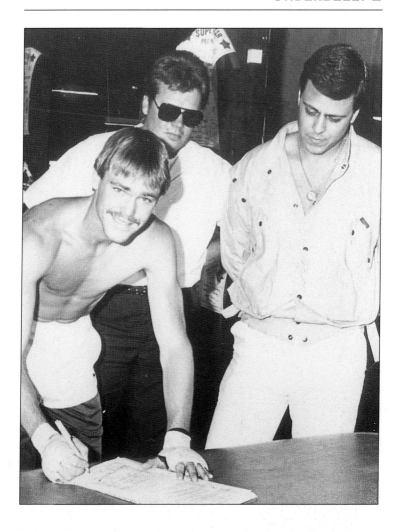

LEFT: Alphonse Gangitano with his arm around a visiting boxer. He loved the fight game.

ABOVE: Here (right) with world champion Lester Ellis. At least he saw who signed this contract.

Alphonse's best form … Form Four Gold at Marcellin College, 1972.

The Premier and the pen thief ... Lindsay Thompson (far left) when he was a teacher, and the young Peter Lawless (bottom right).

Alphonse pictured on his own home security video days before he died.

Senior Constable Rod Miller ... a former soldier and new father who was shot dead in a routine car check with Gary Silk.

Gary Silk … an old-school detective who was shot dead during a
surveillance operation.

An impression of one of the two men wanted for the shooting of policemen Gary Silk and Rod Miller.

Bandidos president Michael Kulakowski (left) … a former soldier and rodeo rider who drove a Mercedes. Shot dead at a Sydney nightclub.

'God forgives, Bandidos don't.'

Something to look up to … sons of Bandidos members with their
fathers and friends.

A Harley Davidson
bought by
undercover police
from the Bandidos
for $17,000. 'We
were ripped off.'

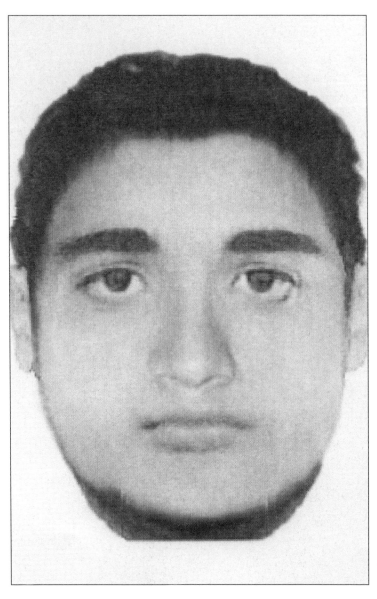

Hot Chocolate Rapist … drugged his 'victims'.

The Beaumont children … the great Australian mystery.

Mersina walked this path before she was killed.

Mersina Halvagis (right) with her sister Dimitria. Mersina was tending her grandmother's grave (right) when she was stabbed to death.

Mersina Halvagis … stabbed to death at her grandmother's grave.

– but failed to fix it. At least, Vitkovic kept complaining of pain. The injury depressed him. He couldn't play tennis, which made him unhappy and unfit. He even found it hard to play snooker.

The clean-cut first-year law student changed in second year. He began to put on weight, grew his hair longer, often went unshaven and saw less of his friends. Significantly, he began to lose interest in studying so hard.

The various effects of the knee injury were enough to fracture his already fragile self-esteem. He became introspective and brooding. He was teetering on the edge of a precipice only he could see.

The crunch came in the second term of 1986, when he deferred his law studies. He told everyone it was the knee injury that had forced him to leave. He was suspended from the law faculty at the end of that year, and switched to arts. This followed a bizarre essay he handed in after a contract law examination.

The essay was a rambling diatribe advocating capital punishment for civil libertarians, and had no relevance to the question set. It read in part: 'The reforms I would make to the present laws are to reintroduce capital punishment for all civil libertarians. The present criminal laws are a farce. One person has lost all his civil rights (i.e. has been murdered) whilst the son of a bitch who killed him is entitled, according to 'civil libertarian philosophy', to have his future considered, his reform considered, his state of mind considered, the stress he was under, the so-called provocation of the deceased … the fact that he only meant to scare the deceased, the gun just "went off" … '

There was much more in this vein, broken up with a strange cross-heading that read 'Warning: prophetic – St Paul'. Vitkovic was referred to the university counselling service by the sub-dean of the Law Faculty. The first appointment was on 5 December, 1986.

The counsellor, a psychologist called Malcolm Morgan, noted that Vitkovic had 'many problems' and was 'distressed by violent fantasies which focused on damage to himself and others'. His knee injury meant he 'felt that since he could no longer play any sport his life was virtually meaningless'.

Vitkovic claimed that his father was a 'bit crazy and violent'. He said he would kill anyone who tried to burgle his family's home, and said there were plenty of guns there. He complained that his friends were deserting him. The second appointment was four days later. This time Vitkovic guiltily recanted his previous complaints about his family. He was guarded, and said he was 'unworthy'. He agreed to a third appointment on 16 December. But on the morning of that day, he telephoned to cancel it.

Meanwhile, the psychologist discussed Vitkovic at a case conference, and agreed that a psychiatric assessment, medication and even hospitalisation might be in order. But when Vitkovic broke the appointment, he did not insist on referring him to a psychiatrist. He thought it would be a breach of ethics. It was a voluntary counselling service, after all, and patients had a right to decline treatment. In the circumstances there wasn't a lot the psychologist could do. He didn't have a crystal ball, and neither did anyone else.

Vitkovic often dropped into the university in 1987, but he didn't take up the offered arts course. He sometimes stopped to chat to Mary Cooke. He worked at occasional part-time jobs, but spent most of his time at home.

His mental condition was eroding. He was now far heavier than he had been when playing tennis. In October, he was treated for mild hypertension, and was given tranquillisers. He complained of tension headaches, and took a CAT scan, which revealed nothing physically wrong.

The same month, he saw another doctor and told him he was under stress at university and had split up with his girlfriend. He was not studying, and had never had a regular girlfriend, but he got the drugs.

Other things happened that month. He took a 'personality test' carried out by the Church of Scientology. The volunteer who took the test was not a trained psychologist, but her assessment was no less useful than those of the professionals who had treated Vitkovic. She said later he was extremely depressed.

Here, brooding alone, was a perfectionist who had failed to meet his own high standards. A favored only son, and baby of the family, of whom much had been made but much expected. A spoiled and guilt-ridden child inside a man's body, angry with himself and with the world, and with only one fantasy left. Someone was going to pay.

The last time Michael O'Riordan spoke to his old schoolfriend Frank Vitkovic was at the twenty-first birthday party of a mutual friend, David Fennessy, in November, 1986. They had known each other since primary school. At first Vitkovic seemed happy, but he became more depressed, telling O'Riordan that his knee injury had ruined his tennis, and that he couldn't study any more.

'Frank told me he had nothing to live for. I think he thought he was a failure in his dad's eyes. I don't think he had much contact with females,' he was to tell the coroner's court later.

One thing stuck in O'Riordan's mind. 'He made the comment, 'you know, sometimes I could get a gun and end it'.

'When Frank mentioned ending it all, I replied jokingly, "Oh, come on, it can't be all that bad." Frank replied again to the effect that life was pretty bad.'

O'Riordan didn't see him again until late the following year. 'I saw him walking down Gilbert Road whilst (I was) driving. He was walking in a funny bobbing motion and he was talking to himself. I had never seen him do that before.'

Another friend, Con Margelis, had met Frank Vitkovic in fourth form at Reddan College. Others described them as best friends. They played tennis and snooker together, and had been out to discos occasionally with other friends after leaving school.

When Vitkovic went to university, Margelis had taken a job as a credit officer with the Telecom Credit Union. At first they kept in touch, but saw less of each other as time went on.

In 1987, Vitkovic channelled his swelling anger into a towering hatred of Margelis. In October, Margelis telephoned his old friend to see how he was going. Vitkovic said to leave him alone. It was a warning of what lay ahead.

On 8 October Vitkovic applied for a shooter's permit, which would allow him to buy and use any firearm except pistols or machine guns. He wrote on the application form that he had 'a desire to go hunting'. On 16 October he paid a deposit on an M1 carbine at Precision Guns and Ammunition, in Victoria Street, West Melbourne. He returned on 21 October to pay the balance of the $250 purchase price. He also bought ten rifle magazines and 250 rounds of ammunition.

No-one in his family knew about the weapon, which he hid in his room. He'd shown no previous interest in guns, although had gone once to the university rifle range with a fellow law student, Eric Tesarch, who was to recall how clumsy he had been with the single-shot .22 target rifles.

IT was hot, and there was a train strike. About 2.30pm on 8 December 1987 when Mary Cooke looked up from her desk at the university. The student she called 'Viko' was there. She had seen him the previous week, when he had become angry with her assistant. This time he looked sad. She noted he was untidy, was wearing his glasses, and hadn't shaved. She asked him if anything was wrong.

He told her he had failed three subjects, which wasn't true. He was no longer enrolled. She sympathised, and he replied: 'Don't worry, I'll go to see the bureaucrats.' She offered to get him a counsellor, but he said, 'I don't think so'.

He told her he had 'a job at the post office to do'. Then he added: 'You're always a lovely lady to me,' and grabbed her hands, adding 'but I hate your assistant'.

She noticed he kept looking down at a brown bag he was carrying, as if he was worried about something in it.

No-one knows what Vitkovic did for the next hour and a half, but at some time before 4.15pm he entered the Australia Post building at 191 Queen Street. Con Margelis worked in the credit union on the fifth floor. At 4.17 Vitkovic walked in and asked to see him. Then, without warning, he pulled the sawn-off carbine from under his jacket, pointed it at his friend and pulled the trigger.

Nothing happened. He hadn't cocked it properly. Margelis ran back into the office and warned other staff. Vitkovic climbed over the counter and started shooting wildly. Margelis escaped and hid in the toilets. Judith Morris, 19, and newly engaged, wasn't so lucky. She was shot dead. The security alarm started at 4.17 and thirty seconds.

After firing more shots, Vitkovic went to the twelfth floor. It was a random choice. He knew no-one in the entire office block except Margelis.

John Dyrac helpfully opened the security door to let Vitkovic into the Philatelic Bureau. He was shot, but survived. Staff cowered behind desks and doors as he stalked up and down, shooting. Dead: Julie McBean, 20; Nancy Avignone, 18; Warren Spencer, 30.

He walked down the stairs to the eleventh floor. Michael McGuire met him at the door and was shot dead. Terrified staff scrambled for cover as he sprayed the room with bullets. Marianne Van Ewk, 38, and Catherine Dowling 28, were shot dead hiding under their desks. Rodney Brown, 32, died soon after. Five others were wounded. One of them was Frank Carmody, who took a bullet in the back and suffered four other wounds. He watched as the gunman turned his back on a fellow worker, Tony Gioia.

Gioia, a quiet father of four, and much smaller than the gunman, took his chance. He jumped on Vitkovic from behind, pinning his arms. Carmody ignored his wounds and jumped up to help. He wrestled the rifle from Vitkovic and handed it to a female worker, who hid it in a refrigerator.

Disarmed, but not overpowered, Vitkovic lunged at a window, already broken by gunfire. Gioia hung on to his legs as long as he could. Then Vitkovic kicked clear, and fell to his death on the footpath below, as armed police stared up at his plunging body.

Until that afternoon, when circumstances brought them together, no-one knew Frank Vitkovic or Tony had it in them. One a crazed killer. The other an unassuming hero. It's the quiet ones you have to watch.

# Society has no defence: coroner

By PETER GREGORY

Society could never eliminate the risk of an illogical force like the Queen Street gunman Frank Vitkovic, the coroner, Mr Hal Hallenstein, said in delivering his findings on the shootings yesterday.

Mr Hallenstein found that Vitkovic, 22, was insane when he killed eight people in a Queen Street building last 8 December, before jumping to his death from the 11th floor.

Mr Hallenstein said in delivering his findings on the deaths that the multiple shootings at the Australia Post building were reminders that society's freedoms and assumptions were fragile and could not survive an irrational, irresponsible and illogical force.

All the community could do was try to understand why such horrors occurred, and try to reduce the risks.

The coroner found that Vitkovic caused the deaths of Judith Morris, 19, Julie Faye McBean, 20, Warren David Spencer, 29, Annunziata (Nancy) Avignone, 18, Michael Francis McGuire, 33, Catherine Mary Dowling, 28, Marianne Jacoba van Ewyk, 29, and Rodney Gerard Brown, 30. Vitkovic also caused his own death, Mr Hallenstein found. Vitkovic died as a result of multiple injuries, his victims from gunshot wounds.

Mr Hallenstein defended the actions of police and ambulance officers who were criticised during the month-long inquest. However, he said that many police at the scene were without hand-held radios or bullet-proof vests.

The coroner also found:

● That similarities were noted

*Vitkovic: insane at time of killings.*

considered to assist the referral to psychiatrists of those needing psychiatric help.

● That, in general, recent amendments to the Firearms Act would not screen out someone like Vitkovic. But, with his secretive nature, Vitkovic might have had problems in obtaining the M1 semi-automatic rifle he used.

● That security akin to a state of siege would be needed to deal with events similar to those of 8 December.

Mr Hallenstein said it was clear that Vitkovic enjoyed, owned and watched video films with violent subject matter, and made references in his diaries to Rambo.

Psychiatrists had said it was not uncommon for a disturbed person like Vitkovic to model his thoughts on violent activities in movie scenes. Violent films did not adversely affect a balanced adult, but disturbed the disturbed, Mr Hallenstein said.

bizarre and inappropriate essay about punishment and death in a law exam, had been assessed as being severely disturbed, with deep psychological and pre-psychotic problems.

However, Vitkovic had spurned a counsellor's suggestion that he see a psychiatrist, and had not attended a third appointment with the counsellor, a trained psychologist. For ethical reasons of confidentiality, the counsellor had not told anyone about Vitkovic, and had not pursued the matter.

Mr Hallenstein said a mechanism for helping the referral to psychiatrists of people needing help could be considered in the drafting of regulations in the yet-to-be proclaimed Psychologists Registration Act 1987.

He said requirements could include that anyone administering or interpreting psychological tests who had the opinion that a patient was likely to be a danger to himself or herself should take all steps to ensure that the patient had institutional or private psychiatric care.

Mr Hallenstein said tougher gun laws introduced since the incident did as much as any laws could do to stop a man like Vitkovic. "If a psychotic decides not to disclose information, then he will not disclose it. We live in a complex society; our society is one of freedom and based on the assumption that people are logical and rational and will deal with dangerous activities and dangerous objects accordingly,' he said.

"A case like the Queen Street shootings simply reminds us that our own freedoms, on which society is based, are extremely fragile and can be challenged by an irrational and illogical person. In the

174

# CHAPTER 18

# Liar, liar

## How a goose cooked himself

*You'd rather confess to a murder you
didn't commit than to a fling?*

IT was the sort of crime to whet the interest of any self-respecting homicide detective. It had everything ... the secret confession, contrition, the cover-up, a weak link in the chain and a desperate hunt for an unidentified corpse.

It began with the mysterious death of a woman in October, 1997, which turned out not to be suspicious, but which led to another, stranger scenario.

Police were about to close the original case in February, 1998, when an informer contacted them with a name. The killer, he boldly declared, was a Melbourne man in his twenties, heavily involved in the movie world. The man had allegedly confessed to his family that he had killed someone in October.

Detectives made checks. They found out that the suggested killer had his van stolen at that time but, oddly, had not reported the theft until the vehicle was recovered by police.

It was only one unexplained fact, but enough to warrant a chat with the movie man's wife.

The homicide detectives knocked on the door with no great hope of a breakthrough. Just a few questions, they told her. 'Purely routine.' To their surprise, the woman burst into tears. 'I've been waiting for you to come. He's told me he killed a man.' Suddenly, the bored detectives were all ears. This sounded serious.

She told the police she had been worried about her husband's strange behaviour and his absence from the family home, so she asked him if he had any problems. 'I've killed a man. He was at the back door and I killed him,' he confessed.

Days after the revelation the wife called a crisis meeting of the extended family and Mr Movie again confessed to being a cold-blooded killer. He said he had taken the dead man in his van to the Mornington Peninsula, where he dumped the body. Checks by police found that the van had been found in scrub at the Peninsula, in a perfect place to dump a corpse.

While his parents went into damage control to protect their son, the wife could not bear the thought of sleeping with a killer. It made her blood run cold. She kicked him out.

For months the man urged his family to remain silent. To keep his awful secret. But he knew the police were closing in. Again and again they interviewed friends and family. They looked for enemies. Was this quiet, ordinary suburban man Melbourne's Hannibal Lecter?

They impounded his van for scientific tests. Take it to forensic, Senior. But, through it all, Mr Movie was curiously confident they wouldn't find anything. After all, he told his parents, he'd spent three days cleaning the van.

Police examined his house. *'Take all the prints you find, photograph everything,'* Constable.

The suspect remained cool. They wouldn't lay a glove on him, he predicted.

The detectives were up against it. No body, no hard evidence. Their case was on the nose. After interviewing more than twenty people, they risked playing their ace. They grabbed Mr Movie for a taped interview. *'Let's grill him, chief, give him the third degree.'* But after taking advice from his solicitor, he refused to comment.

The ace wasn't a winner. The cops then played the joker. We know you've got a sheila on the side. *'Now tell us the truth, you goombah, or we'll charge your whole family with conspiracy.'*

It worked like magic. The man began to sob. Yes, he would tell the truth. No, he hadn't killed anyone. He had made the story up because he didn't want his wife to know he'd had a dirty weekend down at the beach.

The police were incredulous. *'You'd rather confess to a murder you didn't commit than to a fling, you idiot?'* He nodded sheepishly. Even though he'd been banished from the marital home in December he continued to pretend he was a killer.

He was allowed to leave. The police bill for the investigation stands at around $40,000.

The man has not been allowed to return home. He lost his job after police found some irregularities in the books of the movie business. His girlfriend has also lost interest. And he is unlikely to be invited to the next police ball.

# CHAPTER 19

# No Idea
## The betrayal of Debra Byrne

*'You look to the police to trust them,
and then this happens.'*

WHEN troubled singer and celebrity, Debra Byrne, came home to find her house burgled in September, 1997, she thought things couldn't get worse.

She was wrong.

Stolen from her inner suburban home was the usual berley for burglars – video player, television, computer and cordless phone. But also missing was a private video of Byrne taken with her then lover, a little-known Melbourne musician called Chris Bekker.

For days she worried, knowing that if the adult video fell into the wrong hands, her career, already damaged by her well-documented bouts of ill-health and depression, could be further tarnished.

After more then twenty years in the business she knew the combination of sex and stardom would make the video hot property should anybody be unscrupulous enough to copy and sell it.

But while most burglary victims never see their goods again, the singer was one of the 'lucky' ones. Within three days she received a call from police that the burglar had been caught and her possessions recovered. Her relief turned to suspicion as police promptly returned all items except the video tape. For five days she repeatedly rang the police asking for her property. 'They said they wanted fingerprints from it but that surprised me because the burglar was pleading guilty,' she said.

It turned out she had been burgled by a so-called friend, a fellow patient she had met while undergoing treatment at the Heatherton Clinic.

Byrne, the mother of two teenage girls, knew the sexually explicit video had the potential not just to embarrass herself and her family – but to re-ignite showbusiness rumours that she was out of control.

Her worries slowly began to dissipate when police finally returned the tape. But, almost eight months later, she received a call from her then manager, Steve Copeland. He had heard rumours that she had appeared in a pornographic video being privately pirated. 'It took me three days to get my head out the door. I shed a few tears back then,' Ms Byrne was to recall of that moment.

'This was a private video. It was not to be made public. I haven't broken any laws and I haven't hurt anyone, but I've become the victim.'

She complained, and the police Ethical Standards Department began investigating whether police had copied the video when they had possession of the stolen property.

Regardless of the formal investigation, it had been an open secret in police circles the tape had been copied. At first only a few police had seen the one pirated copy. The plan was that it was to remain in a 'safe circle' and kept for a laugh, but eventually another copy was made, and then another.

Within months it became freely available and had been seen by large numbers of detectives. Then it moved out of police hands, and the group 'in the know' became larger still. Copies ended up with members of AFL football clubs, fire brigade officers and several high-profile media identities of the sort known by their first names.

Football commentators on one radio station began to make thinly-veiled references to the tape and to the singer. One of the biggest stars in television, a man easily stung by intrusions into his own dubious private life, breathlessly described the tape as 'broadcast quality' and one radio identity asked any listeners who had seen the tape to drop a copy off at the station. Ethical standards investigators found two copies of the tape, proving it had been pirated. Soon after the investigation began the message went out on the remarkably efficient police bush telegraph system: 'dump the tape.'

The official line was that there was no proof police had copied the tape, but privately they admitted it could have been no-one else.

Ethical Standards Department investigators told the singer it was unlikely they would ever find the police officer who originally copied the tape. This didn't mean they were not trying and that there was a cover-up; it meant they couldn't get the proof to find the culprit.

The tape had been in a busy station where more than fifty police could have had access to it. Without a confession this investigation was heading nowhere. And a voluntary confession was considered about as likely as finding the $3000 of charity money stolen from the Prahran police station safe in late 1998, but that's another story.

Byrne faced the humiliating truth that there could be hundreds of copies made of the tape. 'You look to the police to trust them and then this happens,' she said.

The performer whose personal problems have always attracted keen public interest had to face yet another hurdle: how to deal with people who may have sat at home and watched her in her most intimate moments, courtesy of an illegally copied video.

Understandably, she feels betrayed by police who distributed the tape, and nervous about the effects on how she is perceived.

'When I am out somewhere like the bank and I see someone looking at me I wonder whether they are staring because I am well known, or because they have seen the video.'

Byrne, who is in her early forties, was forced to tell her daughters, aged eighteen and sixteen, that their mother was in a private video that was gaining unwelcomed public notoriety. 'I was very proud of them. They said "you've done nothing wrong; it's the people who copied it who should be ashamed".'

Word of the tape's existence inevitably leaked to the mainstream media. One published story said there was an internal investigation into police pirating a tape involving a celebrity. The paparazzi started to circle, wanting to 'out' the star.

Soon, *New Idea,* once a middle-of-the-road magazine that had developed the sex and celebrity edge to compete in the increasingly cut-throat women's magazine market, was at her door, offering $20,000 for the exclusive.

According to the singer the magazine included the promise that 'as women we will treat this sympathetically.' It was well known that she was short of money, so to *New Idea* $20,000 must have seemed a fair price for national shame and humiliation.

'I have financial problems, but I wouldn't stoop to that,' she was to say. 'They told me they would be sympathetic but all they want to do is sell copies with this sort of trash.'

Having refused to do an interview she gave the magazine the name of the ethical standards policeman handling the case. For about two weeks there was silence. More in hope than expectation, she thought the story might die.

She tried to kid herself the people with the tape would get bored and if she just got on with life everything would go back to being as normal as it ever gets for a celebrity.

But when she went to perform at a charity function for the Royal Children's Hospital and a *New Idea* journalist and photographer turned up she said she realised they were going to 'do her over'.

Days later she rang her former boyfriend – the man in the tape, Chris Bekker – to break the terrible news that they could be about to be exposed. She felt terrible that a man with no independent celebrity status could be embarrassed because of his relationship with her.

But Bekker, apparently, had no such concerns. Having been knocked back by the 'star' *New Idea* went to the next best source – the support act.

When he told her he'd sold the story for $10,000 she felt so ill she could hardly breathe. She said he showed her a transcript of the story that would be on news-stands around Australia within days.

The day before the magazine appeared, *New Idea* took out newspaper advertisements trumpeting 'STAR IN STOLEN LOVE VIDEO OUTRAGE.' Alongside a picture of Byrne it said 'The full story of Debra Byrne's heartache, exclusive to *New Idea*.'

The story was cunningly crafted to appear as if she was telling the story. Quotes were placed over pictures of Byrne although they were from the Bekker. Pictures of nonentities don't move magazines, even if they are prepared to betray friends to sell tawdry stories. The article spoke of the 'outrage' of the tape being made public. Nowhere did it say that the woman on whose behalf they were so outraged had actually knocked back $20,000 to tell her story.

'I don't want to be known as the bloke in the Debra Byrne video,' Bekker told *New Idea*. 'The fact that people are making money out of this is disgusting,' he said, apparently without a hint of irony.

'It's just another tragic event in her life,' he said.

Byrne spoke to *The Age* newspaper in Melbourne days before *New Idea* hit the streets. If the story was to come out, she reasoned, she wanted it on her terms. She wanted to expose the invasion of privacy and to stop the magazine profiting by touting an 'exclusive' story on her private life.

'*New Idea* will make a big story out of this and then move on, leaving me to pick up the pieces,' she said bitterly.

For an entertainer struggling to regain momentum in her career, the pirating of the video was another body-blow.

'It's been the worst year of my life, but I think its toughened me up. I feel like I could handle anything. The next few weeks are going to be hard but I'm not going to hide away.

'This is not a real story about an entertainer but they'll run it even though they must know it could damage my family.

'I've been betrayed three times. By the person who burgled me when I tried to help them, by the police, and by the man who sold his story.'

She said the only way to stop magazines intruding into people's private lives and causing distress was for decent people to stop buying them.

'They're filled with rubbish. We'd all be better off without them.'

On the Monday *New Idea* was published, radio 3AW's top-rating breakfast announcers, Dean Banks and Ross Stevenson, spoke to the magazine's editorial director, who rejoices in the name Bunty Avieson.

AVIESON: 'Chris Bekker, Debra Byrne's boyfriend, or ex-boyfriend, the man who appears in the video with Debra, chose to speak out on behalf of them both. After we printed the situation changed and Debra decided that she did want to speak.'

BANKS: 'Did you originally offer her money?'

AVIESON: 'Those things we try to keep private despite what we see in *The Age* this morning.'

BANKS: '*The Age* says *New Idea* offered her $20,000 to tell all.'

AVIESON: 'We were talking to her lawyers and Debra spoke to us, but she decided not to go and do the full story at the time. But she has since changed her mind.'

BANKS: 'Presumably Mr Bekker then put his hand up and said "look, I'll tell the story, give me a cheque".'

AVIESON: 'Well, Mr Bekker has been having phone calls from all across Australia saying, "I believe you're in a video I've just seen" from friends. He's read about it in newspapers and heard about it on radio. He felt that the way he wanted to approach it was to come out and say 'stop all watching it, stop all talking about it.' There's peculiar stories about what's in the video and from what I understand and from what he says it's not that peculiar. But he wanted to come out and speak about it to say it was done out of love and it is not something either of them are ashamed about and they feel quite betrayed and they are keen for the police investigation to pursue the matter'

STEVENSON: 'Did you pay him $10,000 for the story?'

AVIESON: 'That's something I wouldn't go into.'

STEVENSON: 'Did you pay him for the story?'

AVIESON: 'Yes.'

STEVENSON: 'Do you have any idea as to whether he is intending to give half to Debra Byrne?'

AVIESON: 'I have no idea what their relationship between them is.'

DEBRA Byrne was to receive letters and phone calls from strangers supporting her and some readers contacted *New Idea* to express their disgust. But it has often been said that you can't go broke under-estimating the public's taste. Even while the police internal inquiry was continuing, the vice squad raided a series of Melbourne sex shops and seized about twenty pirated copies of the tape. They were selling for $40 a pop.

# CHAPTER 20

# After the smoking gun

## The other side of police shootings

*'The fear never goes away. It is there all the time. You fear for your own safety and you fear you may have to shoot someone else.'*

TRISH Carl's ten-year love affair with policing died the night she shot dead a disturbed, drunken woman armed with two knives.

What began as just another mundane nightshift in the provincial border city of Wodonga ended with a fatal confrontation that made headlines in two countries, and ultimately cost Senior Constable Carl her job, her house and her sense of well-being.

Carl and her police partner, Barry Randall, were called to a noisy party at 2.55 am on 12 November, 1995, a Sunday morning. They were confronted at the front door of a modest defence forces house by Helen Merkle, who was drunk, irrational and ready to fight anyone in her path. She had already assaulted her husband, a quiet Australian soldier, before police arrived. Merkle charged screaming from the house and attempted to attack the policewoman. Senior Constable Carl ran backwards down the drive and yelled at the woman to drop the knives before firing three shots, the last from a distance of one metre.

The third shot hit the berserk woman in the heart, killing her instantly.

The Merkle killing was the second since the safety-first police retraining program, Project Beacon, and the twenty-fifth since 1988. To add to the controversy Helen Merkle was a Papua New Guinean national with strong political connections.

She was the niece of the PNG Foreign Affairs Secretary, Gabriel Dusava, which led to extraordinary political fallout after the shooting. No less than the PNG Prime Minister, Sir Julius Chan, and his High Commissioner to Australia, Sir Frederick Reiher, disputed that Mrs Merkle was armed when she was shot, even though her husband, Mark Merkle, confirmed the police version of events.

A PNG paper was even less subtle, and carried the inflammatory headline: 'It was murder.'

Even the Australian Foreign Affairs Minister of the day, Gareth Evans, seemed to be infected by the rush to prejudge the incident without knowledge of the facts. Evans was quoted as saying: 'It just staggers the imagination that something has not gone fundamentally wrong in the way in which the police are administering themselves.' It was politician-speak for joining in the chorus of accusations aimed at Trish Carl.

For eleven months Senior Constable Carl could not defend herself from public attacks. She was finally vindicated by coroner, Jacinta Heffey, who found the shooting justified and described Helen Merkle as 'a walking time bomb ready to explode and kill someone'.

The day after Carl was cleared by the coroner her six-year-old daughter went outside to play and found daubed in paint on the lawn and front fence of their Albury home the words: 'COON KILLER.'

Senior Constable Carl continued to work and tried act if nothing had changed. But she felt that something had been stolen from her and that she was the real victim.

She was short with her two young children and was apprehensive when working. She was frightened that her husband, Andrew, also a policeman, could be shot on duty. But she told friends and family she was getting better and time would heal her problems. The answer, she thought, was to throw herself back into policing to regain her enthusiasm.

But she found she was living a lie.

'I was putting on a brave face, trying to keep going.' The shooting was always at the back of her mind, and on duty she would think of it constantly. She had that numbing emotion that can paralyse – and that police rarely talk about – fear.

'I lost it. The fear never goes away. It is there all the time. You fear for your own safety and you fear you may have to shoot someone else,' she said.

'I lost confidence, even when we had to pull over a car. The feeling was there every time I put on the uniform.'

She said she resented the woman she shot. 'Her stupid actions changed my life for the worse. It has turned my life upside down. I could only react to her actions.'

She told people her enthusiasm was returning but in July, 1997, she was called to a routine disturbance. It turned out to be a mentally disturbed woman with a knife.

Trish Carl persuaded the woman to drop the knife and drove her to a hospital, where she was committed. 'She didn't want to hurt us, but she would have killed her husband if he had been there.'

The incident took her back to the Merkle shooting. 'It was the eyes. She had the same scary look as Helen – the eyes of death.'

Carl was diagnosed with post-traumatic stress and was placed on sick leave. By November, 1997, she knew her career was finished. Her husband Andrew also quit the force and, a few weeks later, they sold their house (at a loss) and moved to Queensland.

They both felt the family needed to move from the Albury-Wodonga area to leave the shooting behind. In Queensland Carl feels she is no longer the policewoman who killed, but just another parent trying to bring up a couple of kids. 'No-one here knows. I think we are slowly getting it behind us and want to get on with our lives.

'I wasn't sleeping well and I was really cranky with the kids. We had to try and start again.' But while her state of mind has improved, small things can still trigger flashbacks.

If she sees even low-level violence on television she dreams about the shooting. And she still simmers with anger at the media and politicians who, she believes, condemned her before the inquest.

News of shootings involving police brings back her resentment at the system that she believes let her down. 'Do people really think police think, "Oh, it's a bit boring today, I might go and shoot somebody,"?

'They try to crucify the poor coppers who are just trying to protect people.'

Carl is acutely aware that often when police are involved in a shooting self-appointed community watchdog groups are contacted by the media and offered the chance to pass judgment, even before the police involved in the incident, and any eye witnesses, have been interviewed.

That pattern was followed after the shooting of a man in the Melbourne suburb of Bentleigh on Good Friday, 1998. Two police on the afternoon shift in a divisional van on routine patrol were sent to check a report that two men were trying to break into an automatic teller machine.

In the divvy van was a constable, with about nine months experience, and a more experienced senior constable. When they drove down Centre Road they were flagged down by the man who had made the original report.

He said the one of the two men had actually been interfering with a telephone box, and not an ATM.

The police drove slowly towards the men, who had left the telephone box. The two suspects split and walked in opposite directions, and the police approached one of them, John Stewart McConnell, 34.

According to the police, when McConnell saw the police vehicle he changed directions and headed back towards his friend.

The constable said he left the car, walked towards McConnell and asked him to stop. He said the man started to jog away from him, despite being asked not to run.

The police version of events is that the suspect turned right into a small shopping mall and the police followed. According to police, the constable, who was directly behind McConnell, turned the corner, drew his extendable baton with his right hand, but did not open it to its full length. The senior constable, who was standing off to the side then yelled, 'Drop the hammer.'

McConnell then turned around and moved towards the constable, who dropped his baton and pulled out his police issue .38 Smith and Wesson revolver. The senior constable also pulled out his handgun. Both were to claim they repeatedly yelled on McConnell to halt.

Police say he had the hammer above his head and screamed 'Shoot me, shoot me' as he gathered pace.

The constable backed away on to Centre Road, but said his escape was blocked by passing traffic. Police said McConnell continued to run towards the policeman, who then fired two shots – hitting him in the chest and killing him instantly.

After every police shooting two homicide crews, comprising a total of up to fourteen detectives, are called to investigate.

Interviews with police involved in the shooting are conducted only by senior members of the homicide squad and each interview is observed by investigators from the ethical standards department. The coroner also attends.

Police psychologists are called to counsel police involved, who are also routinely advised by police association lawyers not to participate in any filmed re-enactment.

Homicide squad detectives are acutely aware of the need to be thorough. They remember that Detective Sergeant John Hill was charged with being an accessory to murder in relation to his 1988 investigation of the police shooting of the armed robber Graeme Jensen. Devastated, Hill committed suicide two months after he was charged.

FORMER policeman Cliff Lockwood has moved interstate and changes his telephone number regularly to avoid the crank calls he still occasionally gets. It's just one of the prices he pays for shooting and killing a suspect in a Carlton flat in 1989.

It was a famous case, a tragic footnote to the Walsh Street shootings in which two young uniformed police were gunned down in a South Yarra street, apparently in reprisal for the Graeme Jensen shooting by detectives a day earlier.

Lockwood's sudden fall from grace happened after he shot Gary Abdallah, aged twenty four, while he and another detective searched the flat. Police said Abdallah was armed with a replica handgun. He died forty days later. Lockwood was charged with murder and later acquitted by a Supreme Court jury.

In 1994 Lockwood left the police force after twelve years service because he believed he could never live down his involvement in the shooting. He believed he would always be seen as Gary Abdallah's killer and resented the groups that continued to condemn him over the shooting, although he was cleared of any wrongdoing both at the Coroner's and Supreme Court. 'People still bring it up and it was ten years ago,' he says.

But in 1998 he began to have second thoughts. He missed policing and began to talk of going back to the job that had once been his life. 'I went as far as getting the (application) papers sent out to me. But I just couldn't do it. I just couldn't go back to driving the van and dealing with the public.'

He said that when his thoughts drifted back to the shooting he would consciously block them from his mind. 'I just get really angry so I try and set them aside.'

Lockwood said he rarely talked about his feelings over the Abdallah shooting. 'I don't want people to think of me as a bloody great sook.'

He said when there was a police shooting he would not watch television news or buy papers. 'I get really angry at the way it always seems to be the fault of the coppers.'

He has tried several businesses after leaving the force, but five years on he remains unsettled. 'If it wasn't for what happened over the shooting I would still be a policeman.'

Like Trish Carl, Cliff Lockwood craves anonymity and wants to leave the shooting in the past. His business now often take him to Bali. 'I love it there. No-one no-one knows you and no-one cares about your past. You can just disappear into the wilderness.'

Distance from Melbourne helps. That is one reason why he has toyed with joining the Northern Territory police force. It might be one way of being a policeman again, and yet to leave the Abdallah controversy behind. He hopes that in the 'Top End' no-one would remind him of the Carlton shooting.

Police involved in shootings often want outside reassurance that they have done the right thing. One policeman who killed a man he believed was armed with a gun was shattered when he learned he was mistaken. It was only when a senior policeman went to him at the scene and said 'Son, you've done nothing wrong,' that he regained his composure. The senior policeman was criticised at a later inquest for being less than objective.

THERE was no controversy when Constable Wayne Sherwell shot dead Ian William Turner near St Arnaud in June, 1988. The country traffic cop, whose daily routine was to book speeding drivers, simply waved in a car to issue a ticket when he was confronted by Turner, who was armed with two guns.

After a terrifying hand-to-hand struggle, Turner, who was later found to be an armed robber, was shot dead. Wayne Sherwell won the police Valour Award for bravery. He was a hero whose name appears on the Honour Board at the Victoria Police Centre.

But, seven years after the shooting, Wayne Sherwell feared he was cracking up. He took six months off on sick leave and considered resigning. 'I had reached rock bottom,' he was to confide.

'Taking a human life is the most serious thing you could do.' He said that for years he thought about the shooting every day and even now thought about it every second or third day. 'I have to remind myself that Turner was the architect of his own demise.'

He thought about every split-second action he took when struggling with Turner. 'If I had belted him over the head with the gun it may have been different. If I'd been a bit nastier he would be alive.'

Wayne Sherwell was counselled days after the shooting but, still filled with adrenalin, he felt on top of the situation. 'I didn't feel bad at all. I felt bad about not feeling bad.' He had a cup of coffee and a chat with the counsellor and then went home. But in the days, months and years that followed, his mental state deteriorated.

Promoted to senior constable, Sherwell was unable to leave the shooting in the past. 'I was consumed by it. I thought I was going around the twist.' He said he suffered from broken sleep and became moody for years. It was only when he read a newspaper report that quoted a Victorian policeman involved in another shooting that he realised his feelings were natural. 'I thought "that's exactly what I'm going through, I'm not going nutty after all".'

He believes that only police involved in shootings truly understand the trauma and is a strong supporter of peer group counselling. In 1998 when police shot dead a man armed with a rifle at Maryborough he rang the station and left a message. 'If you want to talk, talk to me.'

He said that he now tried to force the shooting out of his mind. 'I'm dealing with it differently.' But he can never pull over a car without thinking of Turner. The police force has to confront conflicting demands when there has been a police shooting. The police involved may need immediate counselling, but the investigators into the actual incident must be given priority. They must not only do their job professionally, but be seen to be doing so. It is no easy thing.

Senior police psychologist, Gary Thomson, says counsellors are available immediately after shootings but they make sure they don't intrude on the investigation.

He said police involved in the shootings usually went into shock but, while some suffered emotional problems for years, others remained relatively unaffected.

'Some people can become fixated and it can be a turning point for the worse in their lives'. He said counsellors tried to 'be supportive without being judgemental.'

US law enforcement studies showed that most police shot in the line of duty remained psychologically scarred for up to fifteen years.

A study at the Los Angeles police department found that seventy six per cent of police involved in shootings retained vivid memories of the incidents for years.

About seventy five per cent suffered from crying depressions and eighty five per cent suffered from sensory distortion, where they felt incidents were happening in slow motion.

Some of the main symptoms included depression, crying for no reason, withdrawal, paranoia, irritability, flashbacks, and fear of going insane.

An example. Two Massachusetts policemen were ambushed in the street by two burglars. One of the police officers was shot dead and the second fired four shots, wounding one of the burglars. But one of his bullets accidentally killed a six-year-old boy, playing in a nearby yard.

The policeman who fired the shot was shattered. Although he suffered no physical injuries one hand became paralysed. It was the hand that held the gun that killed the child.

# CHAPTER 21

# Death in Brunswick

## Savage end to a life of quiet decency

*She was a mother, a grandmother and a
great-grandmother. She could have been yours.*

YOU expect the very old to die, but never this way. Not at the hands
of someone who breaks into a nursing home late at night, goes to a
bedroom and stabs a ninety-five-year-old woman in the neck. A
woman who has suffered two strokes and is so frail she uses a walking
frame and has trouble speaking.

But that is how Kathleen Downes was killed in a quiet residential
street some time before dawn the last day of 1997.

Mrs Downes would have turned ninety-six a month later, on 29
January, and many of her far-flung family would have gathered for the
birthday. Instead, they gathered for her funeral.

And the service, instead of being the peaceful passing they would
have expected, was overshadowed by the brutality of a crime that has
had police puzzled for a year.

The facts, as known, are few.

Mrs Downes was one of twenty-one residents at Brunswick Lodge,
a nursing home in Loyola Avenue, Brunswick, an old working class
suburb just north of Melbourne's inner city area that is steadily
becoming gentrified, like its near neighbor, Carlton.

Loyola Avenue is a quiet cul-de-sac of mostly 1920s red brick and tile-roofed houses, lined with palms and plane trees, a block from Lygon Street, one of the main thoroughfares and shopping strips.

Brunswick Lodge is a cheerful, modern place where Mrs Downes had spent eight happy years. She had the front room, overlooking the street, and was popular with other residents, staff and the owners.

The last member of her family to see her alive was her granddaughter Jenny Irwin, who visited her a few days after spending Christmas with her parents at Anglesea, a seaside town of holiday houses and retirees on Victoria's scenic west coast.

'I didn't see her on Christmas Day, so I wanted to see her before I went back to Deniliquin,' Jenny was to recall a few days after her grandmother's death, when she was still red-eyed with grief and fatigue. 'She was excellent. She was giving me cheek. She liked a bit of a laugh and a joke.

'I got there about 11.30 in the morning. I stayed about twenty minutes or half-an-hour, then walked her down to lunch.'

On 30 December, Mrs Downes went to bed between 8pm and 9pm, leaving her bedroom door open into a hallway, as she usually did. It might have cost her her life.

About 12.30am, when staff made a routine check, she was sleeping peacefully. At 6.30am, a staff member found her body on the floor beside her bed.

At first it looked as if she had suffered a heart attack, but ambulance officers who arrived a few minutes later found she was lying in a pool of blood from a wound in her neck. Detectives later found a window had been forced. They can only guess that a would-be burglar attacked Mrs Downes. No-one saw or heard anything.

It was a savage end to a life of quiet decency. Kathleen Downes, a great-grandmother, was born in 1902 at Fryerstown, near Castlemaine, central Victoria. She was the youngest of four children of a gold miner, David Fraser, and his wife, Phoebe.

Kathleen often told her children she didn't meet her father until she was nine because he had gone to the Western Australia goldfields after the Victorian mines petered out. He sent money to support his family for eight years until he returned about 1910.

The Fraser family shifted to a house in Ascot Vale before the First

World War. There, as a teenager, Kathleen met Lionel Downes, who was three years older.

Like many other patriotic young men with an itch for adventure, Lionel put his age up to get into the army and was sent to France. He survived the trenches of the Somme and returned to Melbourne to court Kathleen.

The couple married in the late 1920s, just in time for the Great Depression. Lionel built a weatherboard house in Hillsyde Parade, Strathmore, where they were to raise three children and live the rest of their married lives.

The young bride was proud of her home. It was one of the first 'all-electric' houses in Melbourne, and included an early model Hecla electric range that Mrs Downes was to use until she left 60 years later.

The house had two bedrooms, and Lionel, who could turn his hand to most things, added a 'sleep-out' on the veranda as the family grew.

Unlike many in the Depression, he held a secure job – as head of a section in the ordnance factory at Maribyrnong.

But money was scarce. To make ends meet he and his sons melted down scrap lead to make fishing sinkers for sale, and Kathleen bottled fruit from her trees.

Their eldest child, Patricia Lack, a grandmother, flew from her home in Brisbane on New Year's Day to join her brothers, Bill and Geoff Downes, in mourning for their mother.

She was, says Patricia, 'a bright and caring lady who spoke her own mind' and worked hard to help her family and other people.

As a young woman, she nursed her older sister, Doris, who was dying of tuberculosis. Later, she was to nurse her own mother through a long illness.

She was awarded the long service medal from the Glenroy branch of the Queen Victoria Hospital Auxiliary for her charity work.

During the Second World War, she and her husband took in service-men on leave.

'I don't know how she fed them, because everything was rationed, but she did,' recalls Geoff Downes. 'Dad would play the piano and sing songs. They were kind and public-spirited people.'

Like many of her generation, Mrs Downes outlived her husband by many years. He died of a heart attack in February, 1963, at the age of sixty four. She stayed in the family home until suffering her first stroke after a heart operation ten years ago. After eight months with her son Bill and his wife Yvonne, she moved to Brunswick Lodge.

Her family visited her often and she was happy. On Christmas Day, Geoff and his wife, Phyll, drove over from their home in Templestowe and took her to the house of his daughter, Melinda, at Diamond Creek.

There, with three of her grand-daughters, the grand old woman the family called 'Nan' had her last Christmas dinner, a traditional meal with all the trimmings. 'She had a fantastic appetite,' recalls Geoff. 'She ate more than I did.'

After chatting all afternoon, and a 'bite of tea', she packed up the presents the family had given her and Geoff drove her home. He didn't see her again.

Homicide detectives know little more than they did the morning the murder was discovered. They have no motive, no suspects and no strong leads.

The only thing in their favor, they believe, is that the crime is so cowardly that someone who suspects they know who might have done it will make an anonymous telephone call.

The head of the homicide squad, Detective Chief Inspector Rod Collins, sees it as an offence that crosses the boundary between criminals and police. 'This is a crime not only unacceptable to the community but to the criminal element. We're waiting for that call.'

Kathleen Downes was a mother, a grandmother and a great-grandmother. She could have been yours.

# CHAPTER 22

# Taking the Mickey

## Beware the date rape drug

*It is a prosecutor's nightmare — a star witness with amnesia.*

AN attractive young woman wakes up in her bed with a throbbing hangover. Partially dressed, she can only vaguely remember getting a lift home with the pleasant man she met in a Melbourne nightclub several hours earlier.

She may have been a little tipsy, but certainly not rolling drunk, when she finished clubbing about 4am and stepped into the young man's pale blue Falcon sedan. Yet her last memory was of sipping an overly sweet cup of hot chocolate the good samaritan had kindly bought her at a twenty-four-hour convenience store on the way home.

Within fifteen minutes she was woozy, drifting in and out of consciousness, helpless in the hands of a man who had carefully plotted her fate. She was drugged — and later raped in her own bed — by the friendly stranger in what police believe may be an example of a crime that goes largely unreported throughout Australia.

The head of the Victoria Police Rape Squad, Detective Senior Sergeant Chris O'Connor, says police know women are being drugged and assaulted. He frankly admits, 'We don't know how big the problem is.'

Police in Melbourne know of cases where girls have been given an unidentified drug that has left them semi-conscious for more than eight hours and with no memory of what happened.

'We certainly have one offender on our books and there may be more,' Detective Senior Sergeant O'Connor said.

Detectives have targeted one man, dubbed 'The Hot Chocolate Rapist' who has drugged, or tried to drug, at least twenty-two Melbourne women, and probably more, since 1995.

The Hot Chocolate Rapist's style is consistent. He picks up girls at, or near, nightclubs and offers them a lift home. He stops at a convenience store where he offers to buy his potential victims a coffee, hot chocolate or soft drink. If the girl accepts the drink, within fifteen minutes she feels the effects of being drugged.

According to police the drugging of women for sex could be a major unreported crime as the victims can't remember details of the assault. Most can't be sure whether they drank more than they thought or had been slipped a mind-altering drug.

They can't give police detailed statements of the crime. It is a prosecutor's nightmare — a star witness with amnesia.

Detective Sergeant Jim Macdonald from the rape squad says victims of the Hot Chocolate Rapist reported struggling for control after having the adulterated drink. 'Some of the girls reported becoming really groggy and trying to fight off the effects of the drug.

'Others have woken up in their own beds with no idea how they got there and no recollection of what happened after they had the drink.'

Police know that of twelve women who have accepted lifts with the man in 1997, four have felt drugged but have remained conscious, six have woken up in their own beds, and two have been offered drinks but refused.

Detective Sergeant Macdonald said some of the women reported that when they woke up they felt as if they had been given an anaesthetic or heavy sedative and often fell asleep again for several hours.

'This man is a very cunning predator who presents well to the women he approaches,' he said. In three cases he has offered two women a lift and another occasion he has struck twice in the one evening.

While police cannot be sure of the drug the rapist is using, the case is remarkably similar to that of a Qantas steward who drugged and raped colleagues using Rohypnol, a powerful prescription sedative.

In 1996 a former Qantas flight attendant, John Travers Robertson, was sentenced to six years jail after he was found guilty of using Rohypnol to drug female crew members for sex.

One victim said she was given an 'incredibly sweet' hot chocolate in Cairns. Police believe Robertson drugged and attacked fourteen crew members using Rohypnol. He was eventually caught and successfully prosecuted only because police found the photographs he took of his naked, unconscious victims.

Melbourne rapist and killer, Daryl Suckling, who is serving a life sentence for the murder of Jodie Larcombe, 21, bragged that he used Royhpnol to drug his victims.

In the United States and United Kingdom the use of drugs to spike drinks at nightclubs and parties has become a big concern to law enforcement and health authorities. In both countries law enforcement bodies can test possible rape victims for traces of Rohypnol.

Rohypnol is ten times more powerful than Valium and is used to treat sleep disorders and heroin addiction. Doctors say it can cause short-term amnesia and decreased inhibitions when used in conjunction with alcohol.

US law enforcement authorities have been particularly critical of the drug, which cannot legally be sold in America.

In the US it has been called the 'date rape drug' and has been blamed for hundreds of alleged sexual assaults. In 1996 the US Drug Enforcement Administration described Rohypnol as the nation's fastest growing drug problem. Cases of abuse have been reported in thirty-two states by mid-1996.

The London Metropolitan Police have set up a group to look at the abuse of Rohypnol in rape cases. UK authorities have described the consequences of the use of Rohypnol as a doping agent as 'horrific' with rape victims being unable to testify to details of their crime.

A senior drug enforcement officer, Terrance Woodworth, told a US sub-committee 'untold numbers of unsuspecting young women' were having their drinks spiked with Rohypnol and then being sexually abused.

One law enforcement agent went as far to suggest women should accept only unopened drinks in nightclubs.

One of the problems facing police is the difficulty of establishing whether a woman has been drugged with Rohypnol or simply drunk too much, as the effects are similar: staggering, slurred speech, memory loss and hang-overs.

Even forensic tests can be unsatisfactory. Blood tests screening for Rohypnol must be done within thirty-six hours and urine tests within seventy-two hours and experts say the drug must be present in large doses to be identified.

Police say some woman might suspect they were drugged to try to explain why they behaved in an uncharacteristic manner. Others may conclude they just drank too much, unaware they were drugged by a someone planning to manipulate them.

Chemists say the drug has legitimate uses as a sedative and to control the withdrawal symptoms of drug addicts, but that it is waning in popularity because it is such a powerful drug with potential side effects. Police worldwide are concerned it is gaining popularity as an illicit club drug.

Roche say more than a million people in eighty countries are prescribed Rohypnol every year. According to Federal Health department figures the number of prescriptions filled for the drug Flunitrazepan (including Rohypnol) has fallen from 336,062 in 1990 to 223,888 in 1996.

Its effects can include amnesia. It is colourless, odourless and dissolves easily and has been described as 'the perfect crime in a pill.'

Its effects are magnified when used with alcohol. US authorities have said the drug has been smuggled through Mexico and is now abused by many college students in Florida.

The Drug Enforcement Agency says the drug is popular with Texas high school students and and is considered Floridas's biggest growing drug problem. US authorities claim some students mix the drug with alcohol to boost the effect.

Known as 'ropies', 'roofies' and 'roughies', a combination of alcohol and Rohypnol can result in blackouts that last up to twenty-four hours. Medical reports in the US say it is used as an alcohol extender to exaggerate the effects of a few drinks to that of a bender.

US authorities say another drug, known by the acronym GHB, is also being used to spike girls' drinks at clubs. It has been given the nickname of 'Easy Lay'.

Police fear some people may drop drugs in people's drinks at nightclubs as a misguided prank — an extension of spiking the punch at the high school social — but police say it can result in death.

Detective Senior Sergeant O'Connor said: 'It is highly irresponsible. The offender could not know what reaction the drugs would have on the victim.

'It should be made clear that giving someone drugs without their knowledge in order to have sex is a rape offence with a maximum penalty of twenty-five years.'

The head of the drug squad, Detective Chief Inspector John McKoy, said heroin addicts sometimes used drugs such as Rohypnol when they could not get their drug of choice.

'We are finding more and more deaths involve people who are found to have several types of drugs in their system including heroin, tranquilisers and alcohol,' he said.

He said it was available for about $10 a tablet on the street.

Prison officers said that about nine inmates involved in riots at the Victorian private jail, Port Phillip Prison, tested positive to Rohypnol.

The makers of Royphnol, Roche, are well aware of the drug's dark reputation in date rapes. The company has developed a new formula so the drug dissolves slowly and turns any drink blue. It plans to introduce the improved version in Australia.

Meanwhile, the Hot Chocolate Rapist was unlikely to stop before he was caught, according to a rape squad policeman. 'He may change his methods slightly but he will keep going as there are women he can dope.'

# Rohypnol

## U.S. Customs Seizures

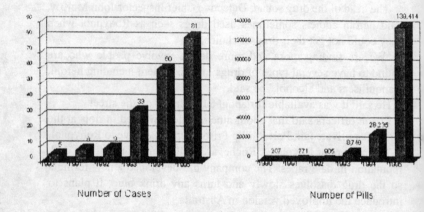

Number of Cases                    Number of Pills

A world-wide problem … figures from the US show a huge jump in
the amount of Rohypnol coming into the country.

# A routine shift

## Dying in the line of duty

*It always seems unlikely anything
will happen. But it did.*

THERE was just enough late Saturday-night traffic to remind them of what they were missing.

Sergeant Gary Silk and Senior Constable Rod Miller were in an unmarked Commodore, sitting off the Silky Emperor Chinese restaurant in Warrigal Road, Moorabbin, with odds of 200-to-one against anything happening.

Miller had a wife and a seven-week-old son at home. Silk was single and treated his colleagues at St Kilda as his extended family. Both were popular and respected officers in the Victoria Police. Both could think of better things to do on a Saturday night. Silk would have preferred to sit with his mates, downing a few ouzos and coke, while watching his beloved Hawthorn Football Club beat the Brisbane Lions that night. Those who know say he probably listened to the game on the radio while sitting in the car looking for crooks.

For Rod Miller, leaving home was difficult since his wife, Carmel, and son, James, had come home from hospital. It was his first child and it seemed likely he would rather spend a Saturday night at home with the baby and his wife than sitting in a police car listening to a footy game. But on Friday, and again on Saturday, up to sixty police were doing the same thing, from Frankston to Brighton, and across to Nunawading and Box Hill. This was Operation Hamada.

Armed robberies on so-called 'soft targets', such as takeaway food stores, restaurants and convenience shops, soared by twenty-six per cent in 1997-98. Police knew there was nothing 'soft' about suburban armed robberies from the victims' viewpoint. When a gun is stuck in someone's face they can remain traumatised for years.

That's why, in July, 1998, senior police launched a rolling strike-force of police, moving from district to district to deter armed robberies.

But the August operation was bigger than a well-publicised police show of force to deter armed robbers; this was designed to nail a gang that may have been active as far back as 1992. In the two years up to 1994 bandits robbed twenty-eight restaurants and shops in the eastern suburbs. They were never caught. In 1998, there have been eleven similar robberies — five of them on Chinese restaurants — leading police to believe the same offenders may be involved.

For months, the armed robbery squad has been trying to identify the robbers who commonly raid Chinese restaurants around closing time on weekends, when the takings are greatest. They tie up staff and patrons, often robbing the customers. Sometimes they would wear novelty rubber masks — the scariest being 'Bob Hawke' faces — as disguises. Senior police authorised an operation to sit off as many likely targets as possible in the hope of grabbing the robbers at the scene.

In each police district where the bandits had been active police chose four to six likely targets. It was based on logic and a little guesswork.

For officers with a watching brief it seems unlikely anything will happen. This time, it did.

As restaurants go, the Silky Emperor is isolated, sharing Warrigal Road with car yards and warehouses. Behind it is a sprawling industrial estate of panel-beaters, car wreckers and small factories. It was remote and had a main roadway at its front door for a fast exit. That made the Silky Emperor vulnerable, a soft target.

It was on a list of about six Moorabbin targets to be watched by police in unmarked cars. Similar lists were drawn up for Frankston, Dandenong and Nunawading. Common among the targets were that they were medium-sized, with few staff and in isolated locations.

The Silky Emperor was a typical target, but Silk, 34, and Miller, 35, were not supposed to be there. They had been assigned to sit off another restaurant in Moorabbin district, but that had closed without incident.

They were both known as dedicated officers who loved the job. And so it seems, because they drove to the Silky Emperor as back-up for another car from the Moorabbin Regional Support Group that had been stationed there.

It is understood that before midnight, Sergeant Silk saw something that alerted his suspicions. A car, since described as small, dark-coloured and of Asian manufacture, moved slowly by the restaurant and stopped briefly. About twenty minutes after midnight, it reappeared.

The two officers in the back-up unit decided to intercept it. Silk and Miller followed the car into Cochranes Road. As they did, one of them placed the portable blue light on the roof of the Commodore and switched it on. They did not switch on the siren because it still appeared to be a routine intercept.

The dark car pulled up in Cochranes Road and the police vehicle stopped behind it.

Having seen the move, the second police car followed the Commodore's path into Cochranes Road. As they drove past the scene, its officers noticed nothing untoward. By then, Silk and Miller were out of the unmarked Commodore and talking to the driver of the dark car. The body language indicated all was under control; it was just another routine check during a boring shift.

The unknown driver was wearing a blue-checked shirt, jeans and runners. He was about 182 centimetres tall. The three were standing in front of the police car.

The second police car continued down Cochranes Road about 200 metres where it made a U-turn and parked to observe from a distance.

Seconds later there was gunfire. The police in the second car saw the sharp flashes from the gun muzzles. They grabbed their bulky ballistic vests from the car boot and put them on. They didn't know whether it was police or suspects doing the shooting, nor how many gunmen there might be.

They were faced with a life and death dilemma. Do they chase the suspects, (police now know there were two) or look after their mates? The two police decided to go to the aid of their colleagues. The killers' car sped out of the district while the police attempted first aid.

Sergeant Silk died almost instantly from a gunshot wound to the head. He was also shot in he stomach and hip. One of the first police at the scene knew him and although he could see he was dead, he was filled with the desire to put a pillow under his head, to make him comfortable. He knew he couldn't. Years of police training told him not to touch the crime scene.

Constable Miller was shot in the abdomen but was able to return fire. As a former SAS soldier he was a good marksman. Police believe the killer's car may have been struck and could bear gunshot damage.

At 12.27, an emergency call went in to Moorabbin ambulance station, and two ambulances, including an intensive care vehicle, were dispatched a minute later. Ambulance officers were at the scene within ten minutes. They realised they could not help Sergeant Silk, and were directed to Constable Miller, who had struggled back to Warrigal Road, where he had collapsed.

There are three possibilities: He ran from the gunman who chased him to finish him off. He chased the gunman while wounded, then collapsed. Or, knowing he was seriously injured and bleeding profusely, he ran back towards the restaurant for help.

If so, he didn't make it.

When he was put in the back of the ambulance he pulled off his oxygen mask and told a colleague he was dying. 'I'm fucked,' he said.

Constable Miller was transferred to the intensive care ambulance and driven to the Monash Medical Centre, but he died hours later.

Sergeant Silk had been in the job thirteen years. He had wanted to be a policeman as long as anyone could remember. In year eight he had been asked to write an autobiographical essay for school. In it, he said he wanted to join the force.

He had worked at Port Melbourne, the prison squad and St Kilda, in uniform and as a detective. He had cradled the head of a colleague shot during a drug raid in Hawthorn and had learned the need to be careful and well-prepared when on the street. In an occupation where people can be judged harshly, no-one had a bad word for a man seen as a hard-working investigator who loved the job and was one of the most popular characters at the St Kilda station.

Rod Miller had seven years experience after joining the police in his late twenties. He was stationed at Prahran and colleagues said his main interest apart from work was his wife Carmel and baby son, James.

Only weeks earlier he had sat and told his wife what sort of father he intended to be. His own father had died when he was a toddler and he told Carmel he intended to be there for his own son. He vowed not be a part- time dad and take his son for granted. Through his own background and loss he knew that every day was precious and how important a father was to a boy.

All James Miller will have is other people's memories of his father and yellowing newspaper clippings of how he was killed on duty.

When the Operation Hamada surveillance teams were briefed, they were warned of the possible dangers and told not to tackle the armed offenders, but to observe and call for back-up.

Some top-ranking police had expressed concern over the operation because of the possibility of armed confrontation. Under Project Beacon, the force's safety-first program 'The safety of police, the public and offenders and suspects is paramount.'

Police considered allowing detectives to continue to try to identify gang members, or placing officers in every possible restaurant. After an internal briefing it was decided to proceed with a blanket operation.

Asked if the officers should have been wearing protective vests, Assistant Commissioner George Davis said: 'It's easy to be wise in hindsight. The bullet-proof vests we have are cumbersome and are impossible to wear for the whole duration of an operation like this.'

Operation Hamada has been cancelled.

A team led by Detective Chief Inspector Rod Collins, the head of the homicide squad, was set up to investigate the murders.

Hundreds of police were used to chase down snippets of information provided through thousands of tips from the public. Police volunteered to work on days off. Others wanted to cancel holidays.

It was a crime the force and the community needed to solve.

VICTORIA POLICE

## Gary SILK
### Detective Senior Constable

St. Kilda C.I.B.
90-92 Chapel Street,
St. Kilda, 3182.

Phone 536 2626.
Fax. 537 1196.

# CHAPTER 24

# A mate's farewell

## Show of force for one of its own

*The line of blue uniforms and white hats
stretched for more than a kilometre.*

IT was the morning for a funeral. Fog shrouded the bell tower of the police academy as completely as the Australian flag covered the casket in the chapel below. Cold seeped from the damp ground through the soles of a thousand highly-polished shoes into the souls of those who had come to say goodbye.

They started to arrive an hour before the service was to begin at eleven. They crowded the lobby in front of the chapel, spilling into the wide halls, faces set and voices low. They queued for two hundred metres to sign the condolence book. They stood in knots outside, talking quietly.

The chapel can seat 480 people, but 600 crowded in. The marquee set up in the grounds the day before was made for 350 people; twice that number stood in it. The rest — more than 2000 of them — stood silently on the manicured lawns of the former Corpus Christi college at Glen Waverley. Inside, pews were reserved for family, friends and colleagues of Gary Silk, the sergeant shot dead with Senior Constable Rodney Miller in the early hours of a winter's Sunday morning a week before.

At the front sat the chief commissioner, his command officers and politicians: the deputy premier, the police minister, opposition leader and police shadow spokesman.

There was also a couple for whom the week's events brought back terrible memories — Wendy and Kevin Tynan, parents of Steven — the young policeman who, with Damian Eyre, was shot dead in Walsh Street, South Yarra, almost exactly ten years earlier. Damian's father, retired policeman Frank, was there too.

There was much pomp and pageantry — and yet ordinary touches that revealed the man as well as the force he served.

Across the coffin, underneath the formal wreath of bright yellow flowers, in front of Gary Silk's police hat, was the Hawthorn football scarf he wore in the outer.

To the right of the altar is a space that is the spiritual heart of the Victoria Police. This is the Memorial Chapel, and in it burns a blue flame that is never extinguished.

On the chapel walls are two sets of plaques. One set holds a full complement of twenty names of police 'feloniously slain' on duty since 1856.

The other also holds twenty plaques — but only seven have names inscribed on them. The last two are Tynan and Eyre. Soon there would be two more beside them. That will leave eleven blank spaces. The unspoken message to all operational police is that any of their names could one day be there.

The huge brick building on the hill at Glen Waverley has been Victoria's police academy since 1972, and has dominated the local landscape far longer than that. It loomed large in Gary Silk's short life.

As a boy, he could see the tower from the family's Mount Waverley home — and from the grounds of the local primary and high schools he attended.

Like many a schoolboy, young Gary had wanted to be a policeman. Unlike most, he didn't grow out of it. When he graduated from the academy in 1985 it was the beginning of not just a job, but the rest of his life. Gary Michael Silk was the youngest of three boys. The eldest, Ian, faced one of the toughest tasks of his life at the funeral, delivering a eulogy that moved not just friends and relatives, but strangers.

Ian's steady voice cracked, not for the first time in half an hour, when he told how a station mate had described his little brother. 'Gary loved the job, and the job loved Gary,' was the way the policeman had put it.

Ian sketched a picture of his brother as an old-style policeman in a modern force. A man who worked hard and played hard. One who received commendations for his diligence on the job — and who is to have a bar at a St Kilda hotel named after him because of his fondness for a drink after work 'talking nonsense about Hawthorn.'

Ian Silk said that a cornerstone of democracy was respect for the law, and that the murders of his brother and of Rodney Miller had to be solved to preserve it.

'We must never become blase about this — must never accept that the lives of police are expendable in the pursuit of general community security,' he said.

'It's not that a policeman's life is more valuable than anyone else's but (when police are killed) the fabric of the community is weakened.

'The so-called police brotherhood gets a bad press from time to time ... but police officers are unique. Members of no other profession run the risks that they do in the service of the community.'

He paused for emphasis. 'I want to make a plea to the members of the police force: please pursue this matter with thoroughness, dedication and professionalism — so that these criminals ... these bastards ... are detected, convicted and imprisoned.'

In the hush after the eulogy some sniffed and reached for handkerchiefs. In the crowd outside, a bullet-headed detective wearing a grey suit and a dark squad tie fished out a mangled pink tissue and pretended to blow his nose.

A uniformed constable broke down. Three others, one weeping, guided him to sit on the steps at the side of the chapel.

A policewoman in tears asked three male colleagues for a handkerchief. They couldn't help. They were using theirs. A female hand came from behind and gave her a tissue.

A woman arrived in a wheelchair, pushed by her husband. She was a former detective who had discharged herself hours earlier from hospital against medical advice. Her last nightshift on patrol had been with Gary.

A group of detectives and Special Operations Group police who had worked through the night raiding the homes of known amphetamines manufacturers, came straight from the office. Puffy eyed from lack of sleep and collective grief they stood, heads bowed, on the manicured academy lawns.

The only group that couldn't make it were the men and women assigned to investigate the double killing. The first few days of a complex murder investigation are the most important and they knew the clock was ticking.

There were police from every rank and of every type. From police heroes — valor award winners — to one on bail facing serious criminal charges. From the chief commissioner and his command team to the twenty-three recruits training at the academy.

A few even came from overseas. One policeman cut short a year's leave overseas to fly back from Turkey. He was one of the pallbearers.

Most of the 4000 people at the funeral were police. Some were friends who had worked with Gary Silk. Others didn't know him, but were equally moved. The mates were the ones who laughed at the jokes and murmured in recognition at the anecdotes in the eulogy. The colleagues remained solemn; they were there as an act of solidarity. It was also a show of strength, as if to prove by their presence that the killers of Gary Silk and Rod Miller will be pursued by thousands of blue uniforms.

A lone piper led the pallbearers from the chapel.

Outside, four police horses waited. The police band played softly as the pallbearers — one crying silently — lowered the coffin into the waiting hearse. A distraught woman slipped over on the bitumen. Family members wept and held each other as the minutes passed.

The delay was for a good reason: thousands of police were silently moving to form a guard of honor in the street outside. They lined both sides of View Mount Road, at some points six deep. The line of blue uniforms and white hats stretched for more than a kilometre. It was joined by dignitaries, members of the public and the Silk family.

Just before the order to march was given, the chief commissioner, Neil Comrie, and the former chief, Mick Miller, moved from the grounds to the head of the honor guard. They stood shoulder to shoulder. Miller has rarely been seen at police functions since his retirement more than a decade ago, but this was different.

The horses — two greys and two chestnuts — wheeled and led off the march. The band leader followed, and the band fell in behind him. The escort of twenty-four uniformed police — sixteen of them the newest constables in the force — slow-marched ahead of the hearse to the beat of a muffled drum. By then the mist began to clear. It was 12.45.

The chief commissioner was first to salute as Gary Silk passed. Then they all did. Thousands of them, making a long, slow ripple as the hearse inched past. They stood silent, and at attention, until the hearse cleared the guard of honor. It took twenty-five minutes.

The next day it all happened again, when Rod Miller took his final ride.

*Gary Michael Silk*
*Testimonial Luncheon*
*Friday 23rd October 1998*

# CHAPTER 25

# A month later

## Eliminating suspects, one by one

*'We go to bed at night and wonder if the
doors are going to come off in a raid.'*

WITHIN days of the murders of Gary Silk and Rod Miller, police had
a short list of possible suspects, but there was only one in bold — the
name of armed robber and escaper Peter Gibb.

Gibb was one of the few criminals in Australia to end up having a
movie made about him, or more correctly, about his love life.

His twenty years as a violent criminal had not excited great public
interest, but when he blasted his way out of the Melbourne Remand
Centre in March, 1993, with the help of his lover, a prison officer and
married mother of two called Heather Parker, he was headline
material.

He was on the run for six days with Parker and fellow escaper,
Archie Butterly, but it was long enough to make Gibb a national
name.

Butterly, a tough career criminal, was destined to be a bit player in
the film. He was shot dead at the recapture in circumstances that have
never been adequately explained. Parker and Gibb were caught during
a shoot-out near Jamieson in north-eastern Victoria. Butterly was
found dead with a bullet in the head. The State Coroner, Graeme

Johnstone, was unable to conclude if Parker, Gibb or Butterly himself fired the fatal shot.

During their escape a policeman who tried to apprehend them, Senior Constable Warren Treloar, was shot in the chest and shoulder. Butterly shot Treloar and Gibb and took the injured policeman's gun, emptying all but one bullet from the chamber.

He then gave the gun to his fellow escaper. It was that bullet that killed Butterly.

In the early 1980s another associate of Gibb's, Stephen Kenneth Haines, was murdered. He was allegedly killed because Gibb believed he was given bail after informing to police.

Detectives from Operation Lorimer, the task force investigating the police murders, were given Gibb's name as a possible suspect within two days of the killings. He was violent, had used guns and had been involved in an escape where a policeman had been shot.

Even more intriguing was the fact that one of the key investigators into the Gibb escape was Gary Silk, then with the prison squad. Perhaps Gibb was one of the bandits who had been robbing the Chinese restaurants? Maybe when Silk stopped the car the two recognised each other and Gibb knew he would never be able to bluff his way out, so he opened fire.

It was only a theory, but one that had to be checked by the Operation Lorimer detectives.

Police began to look at Gibb. While he was known to be a cool criminal he showed no signs of behaving as a man who had just killed two police. He was seen going to work and living a seemingly straight forward life.

By the middle of September Gibb knew he was 'tropical' and under investigation. He accurately predicted he was likely to be questioned over the killings.

He spoke to *Woman's Day* to announce his engagement to Ms Parker, in an article clearly inspired by Mills and Boon, and said he was aware of police interest. He said he knew his name had been mentioned in connection with the police murders.

'We go to bed at night and wonder if the doors are going to come off in a raid,' he said.

It was around this time police decided to move. It was time to pull in Gibb, and his associates, to see if they were involved, to interview them and get their statements.

If they were not involved then it would be in everybody's interest to eliminate then from the investigation. He didn't need to wonder for long. On 16 September, one month after the murders, Gibb was arrested as he left his Bayswater home about 6.30 am. He was not surprised. In fact, he had been waiting for it.

But since Gibb was named as a suspect into the double police killings, intense police investigations have failed to turn gossip into fact.

The former tough criminal has behaved normally and may have even developed a social conscience. He was seen at the Jabiluka protest outside the North Limited building earlier this month. He may have just been heading to a building site nearby where he works, not far from the St Kilda Road police building that houses Operation Lorimer taskforce on the sixteenth floor.

Police decided to question Gibb and associates to either strengthen the case against them, or eliminate them from inquiries so resources would not be wasted on wild theories.

But Gibb's arrest became public knowledge only after attempts to grab an associate did not go exactly to plan.

The Special Operations Group was called in to control the arrest. While Gibb and his crew were drifting as likely suspects the SOG had to work on the belief the men they were going to grab were armed and prepared to shoot police.

They did their homework and planned to pull over one of the targets, Ian Burtoft, near his home in a quiet St Albans street. But they had to wait for the right moment, and that moment came on the Western Ring Road in early peak hour traffic.

Motorists with mobile phones rang the media within seconds and most of Melbourne was informed over breakfast that detectives from Operation Lorimer had made arrests.

Detective Chief Inspector Rod Collins was quick to hose down expectations. He said this was not a major breakthrough, just one line of inquiry. It is believed Gibb spoke to police and provided an alibi. He is no longer seen as a prime suspect.

The SOG conducted at least twenty level-three raids (where armed offenders may be present) over the police murders in the first month. Safe breakers, amphetamine dealers, armed robbers and criminals who deal in guns have been interviewed. 'It is a process of elimination at this stage,' a senior policeman said at the time.

Some have been charged with offences unrelated to the murders. Heather Parker was interviewed at the Knox police station on the day Gibb was arrested. While she was apparently unable to assist the Lorimer investigation, police were happy to chat to her about other matters. She was charged with handling stolen property and unlawful possession of a windsurfer.

Many of those questioned by police can prove where they were at the time of the killing. One had to admit he was in bed with another criminal's wife. The red-faced woman confirmed his whereabouts.

Many names have been thrown up in the investigation, including a convicted murderer who has breached parole, a veteran armed robber and murderer, as well as a series of drug-addicted offenders with violent criminal offenders.

'There are a lot of criminals in society who will be asked where they were on the night. We would prefer they came to us before we had to come looking for them,' Detective Chief Inspector Collins said.

'If they can justify their movements on the night then we will get out of their lives.'

More than 30 police were working on Operation Lorimer backed by forensic experts, divisional detectives and the serious crime squads.

They are looking at several theories of who killed Gary Silk and Rod Miller.

An armed robbery squad team is looking to find the bandits who robbed at least eleven restaurants and convenience stores in the eastern suburbs as part of Operation Hamada. Silk and Miller were killed near the Silky Emperor restaurant in Warrigal Road while on surveillance duty.

Police intelligence indicates the bandits who robbed the restaurants may be the same two responsible for about twenty eight unsolved raids from 1992 to 1994.

At the time police launched an investigation, code-named Operation Pigout, to find the men who robbed pizza shops and restaurants from Seaford to Nunawading. The methods were always the same. They wore masks, entered through the back door and used tape to tie up staff and customers.

At a Blackrock restaurant in Melbourne's southern bayside area on 1 November, 1992, one of the bandits shot two victims when he accidentally fired his gun. During another robbery on 4 April, 1994, the robbers threatened to shoot staff and patrons who tried to follow them.

Police who know Gibb say he would not be involved in a series of small-time armed robberies which each net less than $2000. He was also in jail during Operation Pigout.

But police also have to consider the possibility that the killers of Silk and Miller were not the bandits they were after, but two other armed criminals who happened to be stopped by the police just after midnight on 16 August.

Detectives have been told to keep open minds and not to discount any possibility.

They have checked files looking for known violent criminals with access to guns, but they also know the killers could be 'cleanskins' — offenders with no criminal records.

It has happened before. The offenders responsible for the Russell Street bombing in March, 1986, were not known as heavy criminals and were discovered only after an investigation into stolen cars.

Two of the most prolific robbers of the 1970s were unknown to police. They were twin brothers, known as the After Dark Bandits, and they robbed more than twenty TAB agencies and banks before they were caught when one shot a policeman.

Lorimer investigators had to deal with nearly 2000 intelligence reports containing all the leads that came in the month after the killings.

The information was collated on a specially-designed computer program so analysts could provide all data on any element of the inquiry immediately and cross-check intelligence reports.

But each intelligence report has to be checked and each piece of information can take weeks to verify or discard.

A fortnight into the investigation 250 police were given information from Operation Lorimer to check in order to clear the backlog. With such massive amount of information already on file detectives have to be sure every lead is checked thoroughly. It is easy for the right clues to slip through the net.

A taskforce in the US investigating a triple murder failed to solve the case for more than six months because one vital tip from a member of public was mislaid and not checked immediately. Detective Chief Inspector Collins has said publicly that this will be a long investigation.

A month into it, detectives had a list of names to work with.

But they didn't know if the killers' were on it.

# CHAPTER 26

# Last roll of the dice

## The death of Mersina Halvagis

*One phone call could provide
the breakthrough*

IT was more than a year since her grandmother had died, but still she travelled across town each fortnight to visit the grave and leave fresh flowers. That's the sort of girl she was.

This time, it was the Saturday before the 1997 Melbourne Cup. She got to Fawkner Cemetery, in Melbourne's northern suburbs, around 3.45 pm. Her plan was to tend the grave, make the long trip home to Mentone to change, then drive back to her fiance's house in Mill Park so they could go out to dinner together.

As usual, she stopped at the cemetery's florists to buy some flowers and a drink. She chose some pretty, long stemmed blue and white statice blooms before driving on.

She travelled slowly along Seventh Avenue in the Memorial Park, past the rose bushes and the Methodist area, to the neatly-kept Greek section, pulling up in the small carpark to her left.

The mourner passed a small, weathered picnic table and thirty two graves on her left as she walked along the gravel path before she got to the dark grey headstone on the grave of her grandmother, Mersina, who'd died on 14 May, 1996, aged eighty six.

On other visits she had often put flowers on graves that looked neglected. She hated the thought of anyone, even strangers who died years earlier, being forgotten. That was the sort of girl she was.

She was about to put water in the matching stone urns on the grave ready for the flowers when she was stabbed to death.

Her name was Mersina Halvagis. She was twenty five.

DIMITRIA Halvagis had been to the movies at Crown Casino with four friends. She was surprised when she arrived home early Sunday morning to find the lights on and her parents awake. They said her sister, older by two years, had been missing for hours.

Her younger brother, Bill, took one car to look for the missing woman and Dimitria, too, headed off to search. She knew Mersina had left her fiance Angelo Gorgievski's home at Mill Park, intending to drive to the cemetery.

Dimitria drove past relatives' homes, looking for Angelo's red Telstra, which Mersina had been driving. Because her sister was so reliable and predictable, Dimitria was frightened. She knew only an accident, or worse, could have kept her from coming home on time.

Although she feared the news would be bad, she could not imagine it would be the worst.

Angelo and his father were also looking for Mersina. They could see his car in the cemetery carpark and after a brief, fruitless search they called the police. It was about 4 am.

When Dimitria arrived at the Sydney Road entrance of the cemetery she saw a police car parked out the front. She went down Box Forest Road, to within fifty metres of the Greek section, and could see the several more police cars and the area ribboned with crime scene tape. 'I thought "Goodness me, what's going on"?'

Her mobile phone rang. It was the Broadmeadows police. They wanted her to come to the station to talk. She refused. 'The police are here, you come here,' she told them.

They persuaded her to come to the station. Dimitria and Bill were kept in separate interview rooms until 11 am.

In a case of a suspicious death homicide detectives have priority. Solving the case is the most important thing. Counselling and support for relatives comes later. In the beginning, everyone has to be treated as a suspect. Investigators like to break the news to family and close friends to watch their reaction.

Nick and Dimitria were told in the Broadmeadows police station and their responses could not have been more varied. Bill, instantly filled with shock and grief, began to vomit. Dimitria hardly reacted. 'All I can remember was seeing a policewoman crying. I wasn't. I was wondering why,' she was to recall.

She was asked whether she could drive home. She responded, 'Of course I can. I've got a licence.'

When she arrived home relatives tried to grab her for a compassionate hug and she pushed them away. 'I pushed them away because I thought there was nothing wrong.

'I couldn't believe Mersina was gone.'

ON the first weekend of November, Crew One of the homicide squad was on call. This meant the detectives on that crew would be first called to any suspicious deaths in Victoria from 3pm on Saturday to 9am on Monday.

The head of the crew, Senior Sergeant Greg Hough, was doing an internal course. His team was being run by veteran homicide squad investigator, Senior Sergeant Roland Legg, when the beeper went off in the early hours of Sunday to say there'd been a stabbing.

Legg rang three members of the squad and told them to head to Fawkner Cemetery immediately. The other three members were allowed to sleep on for several hours. It was not a matter of kindness. They would be needed in the morning. The crew would run nearly two days around the clock trying to break the back of the case.

In murder cases the first seventy two hours are the most important. If police have no suspects after three days it can mean settling in for a long and difficult case.

Greg Hough returned to head the investigation after a week. He knew then it was going to be 'a hard slog,' as he put it.

Police looked into the background of the victim. Did she have enemies? Had she done anything that could enrage someone enough to kill her?

But Mersina Halvagis wasn't the sort of person who made people angry. They couldn't find anybody who would say a bad word about her. Workmates, friends and family said the same things. She was was warm and kind, loving and compassionate. She worked voluntarily with the underprivileged.

Secret love interests also drew a blank. Mersina had only had one boyfriend, Angelo, whom she had known five years and planned to marry within twelve months.

The detectives began to sift through a wider range of possible motives. Perhaps there was someone obsessed by her, who followed her to the cemetery, where she was known to go on most weekends. It would not be the first time a young woman was stalked without her knowledge. In 1984 a woman walked into a shop in Hawthorn followed by a man, a vague associate, who was besotted by her. He noticed a new engagement ring on her hand, flew into a rage and stabbed her to death.

Had Mersina surprised a thief? There had been a series of minor thefts from cars in the cemetery. Certainly, while she was obviously ambushed, it seemed unlikely an attacker could have sneaked up without her sensing their presence. The gravel paths made it almost impossible to approach silently.

She may have assumed the person walking towards her was just another mourner and, by the time she sensed danger, it would have been too late. 'She may have initially been surprised and then struggled with the offender,' Detective Senior Sergeant Hough speculated.

The killer would have been splattered with blood, but he would only have to walk or run forty metres to the car park or about fifty metres in the opposite direction to a small, tree-lined creek bed that led out of the cemetery.

Perhaps some mentally-disturbed person was in the cemetery that day and attacked Mersina, at random, because she was the only person there. But if that were the case, why hasn't he struck again?

Some police suggest a psychotic offender may have stopped taking medication and committed the murder; then, once back on his drugs, has no recollection of the crime.

The crew worked full time on the case for more than three months. The seven investigators, aged from twenty-nine to forty, chased down four hundred leads and interviewed 1500 people. They organised police to walk shoulder to shoulder around the murder scene, trying to check under every bush and every blade of grass along the creek bed.

Detectives worked eighteen hours a day on the investigation as the weeks blurred into months. They compared the case with similar murders around Australia and sent all their material to the FBI crime-profiling centre for review. It came back with nothing new. The government then offered a $50,000 reward, a sure sign the trail was going cold. A year later, the reward was doubled.

'We have looked at every scenario. We throw up every possibility to see if we missed anything,' Hough says.

But the truth is that they are no closer to catching the killer than when they were on the night of the murder.

For homicide investigators it is not so much life, as death, that goes on. By February the crew was back on call and in the next eight months they had another thirteen jobs.

While they continued to investigate the Halvagis case, the detectives had other obligations. Not only new cases, but internal courses to attend, autopsies to observe, suspects to interview, prosecution briefs of evidence to complete and sworn evidence to give at magistrates, coroners and supreme courts.

Five of the seven detectives are married and three have children of their own. Solving murders is their job, but they are also entitled to holidays and private lives.

The six big blue binders that contain the Halvagis file sit on the desk of one of the detectives in Crew One and is constantly updated and reviewed. 'There is still work to be done. This investigation will not be complete until we get a result,' says Hough.

But police concede it will probably not be brilliant detective work that will provide the breakthrough. They remain convinced that someone in Melbourne has a nagging feeling that a person they know killed Mersina Halvagis. The killer must be someone's brother, someone's husband or someone's son.

One phone call could provide the breakthrough.

GEORGE and Christina Halvagis are an Australian success story. Separated from his family in post-war Greece, the young George Halvagis joined the Greek merchant navy with the aim of one day being a ship's captain. But his ambitions changed in the first few days of 1956, when his ship was moored at Station Pier.

He jumped ship.

He had no money, no contacts, a smattering of French but no English, and a burning desire to succeed.

For the next seven years he was on the road, seeing more of Australia than do most people who are born here. No job was too hard. 'Work never really worried me.' He cut cane in Queensland, learning how to do it the right way while watching fellow workers' hands turn to bloodied pulps, hacking away for days amongst the snakes, rats and dust. He picked pears in Shepparton, grapes at Murray, built railways and bridges and cleared scrub from Hamilton to Edenhope. He drove taxis in Melbourne and taught himself English, listening to his fellow workers.

While many itinerant workers gave their wages back to publicans, two-up schools and brothels, George saved. He was a man with a plan.

He believed that to make it in Australia, to have real financial security, you must be the boss. Less than three years after he jumped ship he went to the authorities with his work record. Nearly thirty men who arrived as illegal immigrants were interviewed. He was the only one allowed to stay.

Christina had seven brothers in Greece. She was told that as a girl her duty was to care for the males of the household. She resented being taken out of school. People couldn't understand why the young girl wanted an education when her future was to look after her family until she married and started her own.

But Christina wanted more. She emigrated to Australia in 1964. She met George in 1967 and they married the next year.

By 1969 they had a big-enough stake to buy their first business, a modest milkbar in Warracknabeal. After the first week they began to doubt what they'd done. Their takings from that first seven days were $45. Christina burst into tears and wondered if they would be ruined, but they decided to just work harder.

'We had to do it, we had no alternative,' George recalls.

Eight years later the small milk bar was a restaurant, mixed business, greengrocers, a takeaway and bakery. George drove to Melbourne once a week to buy fresh produce.

Their takings had risen to $7000 a week. 'We worked seven days and twenty hours a day,' Christina says. They had four children over seven years.

The family was happy in country Victoria. In their rare spare time, they went yabbying and fishing in the bush together, but both parents were driven by the need to give their children what they themselves had lacked – formal education. They moved to Melbourne where they bought and sold businesses. They retired in their late fifties, close to the beach in the southern bayside suburb of Mentone.

The wanted a house big enough for their children and grand-children, and they got it. The walls are decorated with photos of family members in happier days and the garden is filled with flowers and fruit trees.

It is a home built for a large family, and ideal for entertaining. But the family doesn't use the formal dining room any more. It has been turned into a shrine for Mersina. Photographs, teddy-bears, a condolence book, the cross from her coffin and paintings of Christ sit on the table as a daily reminder of the tragedy. Upstairs, Mersina's bedroom has been almost untouched since she was killed. Fluffy toys sit on the bed and bookshelves, a sewing machine on her small desk. Her parents say she taught herself to sew to make linen for when she was married.

Dimitria points to the bookshelves filled with children's books. Mersina began to collect them when she was studying child develop-ment at university, then continued to buy them for the children she planned to have with Angelo.

Outside the bedroom is a polished wooden glory box, carefully packed with items Mersina selected for married life.

George, a strong, self-sufficient man, stands in the middle of the room, tears silently rolling down his cheeks, arms moving in little gestures of helplessness.

He points to a dark backpack that was delivered by police. It was found in the car at the Fawkner Cemetery. 'We have never opened it. We don't know what is in it,' he says.

On the desk a candle flutters. It is kept alight all day, every day.

Christina opens the wardrobe, filled with pretty party dresses, all carefully covered in dry-cleaning plastic. She grabs them, buries her face in her daughter's clothes and begins to sob: 'The bastard, the bastard.' She then asks the question they have asked thousands of times since November 1997. 'Why? Why us? What did we ever do to deserve this?'

You look at the floor, and out the window into the darkness, searching for words of comfort.

There are none.

MERSINA Halvagis was not the sort of young woman who would take risks. While many of her friends were out clubbing she was more likely to be home, studying or sewing.

In years eleven and twelve at school she was determined to excel. 'She would lock herself in her room every night to study,' says Dimitria. 'We would tease her because she didn't know what shows were on TV or what were the latest songs on the radio.'

Her efforts were worth it. She was accepted into an early child development course at Melbourne University and later worked in child care.

But after a few years Mersina decided on a career change and moved into banking, starting as a teller before being promoted into a responsible position in the International Tax Department of the ANZ bank while studying accountancy at Monash at night.

Christina and George Halvagis are proud of their kids. In a time of drug abuse, crime and unemployment all their children moved into adulthood without great problems.

But of the two boys and two girls, Mersina was the one who was the least likely to get into mischief or be caught up in the wrong crowd. 'She was never the sort to put herself in danger; she didn't go out like me,' Dimitria said.

The Halvagis girls were close as sisters but like many siblings, had differing personalities. Dimitria could be fiery, determined, stubborn and outgoing. Mersina was quiet, compassionate and caring.

'I wanted to be more like her, to be patient and have time for people,' Dimitria said.

Weeks before she was murdered Mersina was sick for a few days and Dimitria gave her a get well card. It read: 'Just remember, every time you feel a bit down, think about how much I love you and you and all should be OK!' She was later to learn that Mersina had told friends she wished she was more like her sister – prepared to ruffle feathers to get what she wanted.

Everyone says that Mersina was that last person likely to upset anyone or place herself where she could be a victim of crime.

But somebody killed her.

HOMICIDE squad detectives who stare into the faces of grief with depressing regularity have never seen a family so shattered by a death. 'It is eating them up,' says one.

The family swings from disbelief to mourning and then to anger – set on an emotional loop that appears never ending. Their life was built on the unshakeable belief that if you work hard you can reap the rewards of your efforts.

Then how can this happen?

Family members contacted police and asked if they could do anything to help. George wanted to mortgage the family home, to spend all their savings to put out a reward for information. He wrote letters, spoke to the media and demanded meetings with politicians.

He got sympathy when he wanted answers.

Dimitria had been a travel agent for three and a half years when Mersina was murdered. She tried to go back to work to get on with her life, but she was still in shock.

'People save for years for a holiday and it is one of the most important things in their lives. I like to share their excitement, but after Mersina nothing else seemed important.'

She found herself excusing herself from clients, who were bubbling with anticipation as they scanned glossy brochures of their planned destinations. She would slip outside the office and burst into tears.

In April, 1998, she quit. 'I slept for three weeks. I was exhausted.'

She then decided that she would not sit at home and wait for news from police. She wanted to get involved. She had more than a thousand posters printed urging anyone with information on the murder to contact police.

She saturated the suburbs around Fawkner, including Broadmeadows, Thomastown and Brunswick. She put posters in banks, post offices and convenience stores, looking to spark people's memories before it was too late. She remains bitter that some people she approached would not believe the attack was random. It is as if some want to demonise the victim because if they accept the killer struck without reason then they must face the fact he could strike again and anyone, including their own families, could be at risk. It is much easier to 'blame' the person who was attacked as if it is somehow their fault.

Dimitria refuses to accept the killer may never be found. She constantly thinks of ways to keep the case alive. Anything to get people thinking.

'I know that nothing is going to change what happened and even if we find who did this it will not bring Mersina back,' she said. 'But I can't accept that in a community like Melbourne we have someone like this on the streets.

'I'm doing everything to be a good person. And he's out there, unpunished, buying his dinner at the supermarket and going to the movies.

'I'm not going to give up. I'm running out of options, I don't know what else to do.

'People can get on with their lives. They can't understand what this does to a family like ours.'

# POLICE NEED YOUR HELP

**Mersina HALVAGIS** murdered at the **Fawkner Cemetery**,
approx 4.30pm (Greek Orthodox section)
on the **1st November, 1997**, All Saints Day.

## DO YOU KNOW THE KILLER?

Do you know someone who was acting out of character on or just
after the 1st November, 1997?

After the murder the person responsible may have washed their own
clothing for the first time or simply disposed of them.

This person may have taken any opportunity available to not attend
work or school in the days after the murder.

This person may have shown an increased interest in the news
following the murder.

If you have any information please contact

# CRIMESTOPPERS 1800 333 000

*(Information can be reported anonymously and details which lead to a
conviction will be cash rewarded).*

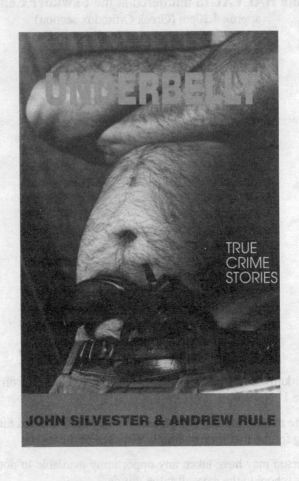

The original *Underbelly* is available
at all good book stores.